Dear Jim House Fellow

Thank you for today.

Ninter Miller
Sept 15, '77

IF THE PATIENT IS YOU

IS YOU

(OR SOMEONE YOU LOVE)

IF
THE PATIENT
IS YOU

(OR SOMEONE YOU LOVE)

PSYCHIATRY INSIDE-OUT

Milton H. Miller, M.D.

CHARLES SCRIBNER'S SONS / NEW YORK

Copyright © 1977 Milton H. Miller

Library of Congress Cataloging in Publication Data

Miller, Milton H   1927–
    If the patient is you (or someone you love)
    Includes index.
    1. Psychology, Pathological. I. Title.
RC454.M49515   616.8'9   76–45472
ISBN 0–684–14823–4

1 3 5 7 9 11 13 15 17 19 H/C 20 18 16 14 12 10 8 6 4 2

Printed in the United States of America

Hermann Hesse, *Siddhartha,* translated by Hilda Rosner.
Copyright 1951 by New Directions Publishing Corporation.
Reprinted by permission of New Directions Publishing Corporation.

Jean-Paul Sartre, *Nausea,* translated by Lloyd Alexander.
Copyright © 1964 by New Directions Publishing Corporation.
All Rights Reserved. Reprinted by permission of New Directions
Publishing Corporation.

To
Helen L. and William B. Miller
of Indianapolis, Indiana
THE INDELIBLE LINES
and
Harriet Sanders Miller
THE WONDROUS FREE SPACE

ACKNOWLEDGMENTS

This is not a long book, but it took a long time to write. Earlier versions were typed by Vickie and Lynn Gessler of Madison, Wisconsin, and critically read by Miss Mary White at the University of Wisconsin, Department of Psychiatry. The final edition was prepared by my faithful secretary, Mrs. Ilona Lee, "Lee Taitai," at Vancouver, Canada. Mrs. Esmee Graham, my English secretary and English tutor, did her best to eliminate the "hokey" parts. Don't blame her.

Those nearest and dearest suffer most. Our three grown-up kids, Bruce, Jeff and Marcie, and my long-time colleagues, Norm and Will, Sy and Helen; Carl and Eng-Kung, Carl and Erv and Leigh, Aris and Nancy and Marg, Fikre and Gwo and Sherwyn, Peter the Dean and Phyllis, Lois and Harry and Ethyl, John and Bill and Katherine and Vancouver Harry, Rob, Tsung-Yi and Mei-Chen are all part of the head space of this small volume.

Special thanks indeed to Miss Elizabeth Otis, literary agent, who kept saying yes to me and who suggested a chapter unashamedly advisory. My editor at Scribners, Patricia Cristol, brought good judgment and meticulous concern to the manuscript.

And my appreciation to those remarkable and patient people who were my patients should be on every page.

CONTENTS

PREFACE   *xi*

PART 1. *An Existential Approach in Psychiatry*

   Introduction   *3*

     Prologue. If the Patient Is You (or Someone You Love)   *7*

     1. Beginning at the Beginning: The People Who Count   *20*

     2. Health and Illness: An Existential Point of View   *37*

PART 2. *The Three Generations: Love, Responsibility and Property*

     3. Once Upon a Time, Old People Didn't Like Young

       People: A Legend   *62*

     4. No More Grandmothers, No More Grandfathers:

       Learning from Peers   *73*

     5. Living as an Older Person   *87*

PART 3. *People Who Fail, Trouble and Disappoint*

     6. Violence and Weakness, Rebellion and Surrender   *105*

     7. Alcohol and Drugs: "Making the World Disappear"   *123*

     8. Life in a Prison: Doing Time   *133*

Contents

PART 4. Neurotic and Psychotic Patterns of Living

   9. Obsessive and Compulsive Living   *151*

  10. Hysterical Living   *160*

  11. Depressive Living, Mania and Suicide   *172*

  12. Alanda's Autobiography—An Introduction

       to Schizophrenia   *187*

  13. Schizophrenic Living   *196*

PART 5. Conclusion

  14. Helping   *219*

     Epilogue   *241*

     NOTES   *245*

     APPENDIX   *251*

     INDEX   *263*

PREFACE

Sometimes I have trouble remembering the psychiatry of twenty-five years ago. So much has changed. Yet, it was then that I began my career as a student in the Menninger School of Psychiatry in Topeka, Kansas. In those days, most of our patients were so very sick that they lived out long periods of their lives in wards of mental hospitals. And the hospitals —like the patients they housed—were neglected, forgotten, abysmal and without hope. They were sad places where broken lives were stored. In those early days, happy outcomes were painfully won. Joyous outcomes were rare.

My teachers were visionaries. Karl Menninger talked of hope and love. Even more incredibly, William Menninger patiently worked to win over the leaders of the community, the mayor, the businessmen, the newspaper people and the ministers. He told them they were desperately needed as advocates for people who had been put aside and forgotten. My first teachers of an existential approach to psychiatry were John Chotlos, a philosopher-psychologist, and George L. Harrington, an extraordinary clinician-psychiatrist who could reach into the most hidden, remote or violent person: "Hey, fellow, c'mon back, I gotta talk to you." Harrington and Chotlos told me to worry less about the symbolic meaning of symptoms and to worry more about all the life that wasn't happening for my patients. They helped me to understand that, above all, the doctor and the patient alike are caught up in the same tricky, uncertain, often sad venture called "doing the best we can."

During the seventeen years between 1955 and 1972, I had the great good fortune to work as teacher, clinician and, for ten of those years, head of psychiatry at the University of Wisconsin. During the last five years, with equal luck, I have been the head of psychiatry at the University of British Columbia in Vancouver, Canada. These more than twenty years have seen the balance shift, and the psychiatric visionaries have become prophets. Hundreds of thousands of our patients have left the hospitals and returned to their families. Many times that number were successfully treated in such a way that they never knew that only a few years earlier their "problems" would have interrupted and sabotaged their lives in a profound manner. Instead, they had trouble, they went for help, they worked it out and went on with the rest of their lives.

The new drugs that were beginning to emerge from the research laboratories in the early 1950s were a major cause of the greatly improved outlook. There were other reasons as well. Most importantly, by the 1950s the severely mentally ill had acquired enough friends and advocates to make a difference. Mental illness, and then mental health, had become public matters. And in that process, it became clear that these problem areas were not separate and discrete. Instead, they were intimately a part of the life of the people, of the prevailing value systems, of the traditions that picked only some for success. The cliché which claimed that mental illness was a luxury disease, one that only rich people could afford, proved 100 percent wrong. As usual, when there is suffering to be done the poor, the uneducated and those without family suffer more than all the others. Public reclamation of the field also served to enlighten and broaden the perspectives of many psychiatrists and other mental health professionals. In retrospect, many of our earlier theoretical formulations seem painfully limited. Beyond the Freudian "primal scene" and "Oedipus Complex," we now discover a panorama of concerns about social status, poverty, broken homes, premature births, racial conflict, population mobility, sexism, ecology, city deterioration, war and violence on television. Simultaneously, research findings of scientific groups from all parts of the world have greatly increased understanding of the structure and neurochemical processes which underlie the activity of the brain. Assembling that information has been akin to solving a thousand-piece monochromatic picture puzzle. Until recent years, progress was slow. However, hundreds of individual pieces are now intricately linked and the connections between brain activity, genetic endowment, early life experiences and life stress to behavior and illness are taking form. We are closer to precise explanations of why some mental illnesses recur in the same family through successive generations, why various tranquilizers and antidepression medications work well (or fail) and what a person with a vulnerability to emotional difficulties should undertake to speed recovery or minimize the risk of recurrences.

In the midst of the many changes and the constant bombardment of consciousness-expanding events of the last decades, the patients have come in a steady stream. Eight million North Americans consult psychiatrists every year and many consult other health professionals about their personal concerns. Millions of people who might profit from similar consultation carefully keep their distance. For me, it has not been easy to achieve a sustaining and dependable perspective. Each of the people who come is different. And yet we are all so much the same.

Many authors have written ably about one or another side of psychiatric practice. Ordinarily, a single therapeutic technique is highlighted and its impact upon a particular problem in living is detailed. However valuable and interesting that approach may be, it fails to reflect the extraordinary diversity and complexity encountered in a single day of clinical practice. The first of twenty patients may present problems that require simultaneous and skillful interventions from biological, psychological and social fields. To be helpful to the next patient, however, you may need to forget you are a psychiatrist and remember that you are only another human being.

I hope to share with the reader some of my own perspectives and ways of discerning meaning from the complex mixture of facts, hopes and fears disclosed in the dialogue and relationship of clinician and patient. Even more, I hope to convey what it's like when another person's struggle becomes yours . . . and you both win.

IF THE PATIENT IS YOU

IS YOU

(OR SOMEONE YOU LOVE)

Part 1

AN EXISTENTIAL APPROACH IN PSYCHIATRY

Introduction

For a psychiatrist, there is too much to know, too many areas to cover, too many things to manage all at once. There are serious illnesses produced by subtle, often unmeasurable abnormalities in the chemical reactions within the brain; there are individuals who suffer intense interpersonal conflicts rooted in lifelong insecurities and deeply held prejudices; there are others who receive so much reward for functioning badly that they skillfully resist any effort to enhance their skills; there is the increasingly complex personal task of retaining perspective about what is good and bad, sensible and absurd, of value or outdated in a time of never ending, rarely slowing, upside-down, worldwide change.

All this is obviously much too much to encompass in any profession. But, there seems to be no easy remedy. People's lives are not divisible into compact, separate and tidy compartments. Everything in life connects to and is influenced by everything else.

Nor is it easy to explain what has happened when things go wrong. And pat theories rarely help. Quite the opposite. Commitment to one point of view as to what causes unhappy and unsuccessful human behavior is an arbitrary stance by the clinician with results that are often excruciating for the patient. Some people claim that there are no mental illnesses, only people spinning myths or playing games; perhaps they are right about some people, but more often—much more often—the illness is all too real. Sometimes an analysis of madness demonstrates that madness makes a lot of sense; usually, however, madness translates as a bitter sequence of dead-end, bridge-burning, expensive, confused and painful events.

Uncertainty is also a reality when one tries to find the right remedy. You simply can't know in advance what will work. There are times when talking something over helps or cures; however, very often, prolonged dialogue is a total waste of time and even the most eloquent script proves irrelevant to changing the life situation of the patient. Sometimes, almost like a miracle, a one-week trial of the right medication in sufficient dosage interrupts suffering that has continued for a decade. Yet for many patients, any and all drugs distort thinking and make things worse.

Another complicating circumstance, though a good one, is the last decade's proliferation of therapies, each with records of success where other remedies had failed. There are various individual, couple, family and group psychotherapies, and a wide range of relaxation and deconditioning therapies. Or, perhaps a dozen possible combinations of drug approaches may be utilized to control specific symptoms. There are still some very few patients who respond best (or only) to electrical shock treatments. Many others find satisfaction, direction and relief from symptoms when they turn from their therapy and use their energy and passion to contribute to one of the major social or humanitarian movements of our time.

In the midst of so much uncertainty and faced with so many possible choices, where, then, does one begin?

I think of myself as an existential psychiatrist because in my work, as in this book, it is the "lived life experience" of the person called "patient" which is the starting place. What is it like to *be* that person whose way of living is called schizophrenic, or neurotic, or perverse, or normal? What happens in that life? And equally, what doesn't happen? Where are the hopes of the years that were good? Who are the people who counted? When the troubling complaint goes away, what will take its place?

An existential approach is one that can never take for granted the wonder and uncertainty that surrounds our being here at all. It makes the problem life itself. How does one live it? How do most people live their lives? Has it always been the same? This point of view makes the person more or less synonymous with what his life is like and this in turn relates closely to the nature of the experiential world in which a person does his living. Thus, two central issues in an existential approach are, first, the wonder of the fact that there is life, and second, the unity through experiencing which makes the person himself very much the same as the world that is experienced.

To the first point, the wonder and mystery of life, Pascal and Kierkegaard, Hesse, Buber, Tillich, Castaneda, Becker and many others have written so eloquently that further elaborations seem pale. The miracle of one's being here at all and the almost impossible to fathom certainty of one's not being here at some future point are matters of such overriding importance that one could continuously contemplate them for a lifetime. Or, as is more often the case, the individual may, through a kind of relentless denial, fill up a lifetime not thinking about such concerns.

A second issue central to existential thought pertains to the nature of experiencing itself, beginning with the realization that one did not discover the world and the things in it on a basis of "Once, I had nothing to do on a Saturday so I discovered my world." Instead, one's very beginning *is* experiencing, is experiencing something, that is, experiencing world. Martin Heidegger, a German existential philosopher, expressed this indivisibility of person and what that person experiences, and the further indivisibility of what a person experiences and the world (of or for that person) in the concept of "being-in-the-world." There is, in Heidegger's definition, no "being" who is "being in" some kind of "in the world." All parts of the definition need all other parts to make any sense. "Being in the world" is the irreducible minimum.

More explicitly, then, we are what we see and how we see it. And, in a fairly consistent way, one tends to see (and thus be) what one saw before. With regard to those things we have seen a lot of, we resist seeing them differently. In a way, this is certainly how it should be. If every time one saw something it was as though for the first time, one would have no history, no "experience." Part of any therapeutic effort involves "seeing" more and thus making a discovery. At times the seeing is a bringing into focus of something that was actually seen but only dimly perceived—for example, in the way one sees objects that are off to the side of one's vision and about which one has no interest or plans. And of course, sometimes, that which is "there but not seen" is a variety of "bad news" that the individual doesn't want to really recognize. One is thus selectively inattentive. All of us have parts of our worlds that are like that. One's cheeks are flushed, one's hands are clenched, one's jaw is set, one's voice quivers. Any and all who are witnesses can see. But the individual is surprised when someone suggests, "You had a lot of feeling about that matter, didn't you?"

A person provides information about how he "sees" his world in many ways other than through the words that are spoken. Often one's dreams tell a good deal. And there can hardly be a more eloquent statement of how one person feels about another than in that embarrassing moment when one's shift of body position provokes a startled response or a pulling away by the other.

An existential approach in psychiatry begins with, and emphasizes, general human concerns, and in the process called therapy one discovers over and over again that the person called patient is you and I as well and not simply some stranger, as one might have hoped or pretended. Rather than someone else in a remote asylum or the alcoholic man or woman in every third or fourth family, instead of one of however many disappointed, poor and complaining black, brown, red, yellow and white people, or criminals, addicts or lonely old people, on closer examination the person with the problem is us. And the problem is life. How does one live it? Nurse, doctor, patient, family, teacher, friend, minister, stranger, we share so much with one another that the questions "What's wrong with him?" "Why doesn't he behave like me?" and "Why am I like I am?" cannot be separated.

Here we are, mysteriously, coexperiencers of life. We each have a measure of time and space, greater or lesser capacity to care, possibilities of turning toward or turning away. What and who we choose to care about, how we invest our time, the spaces we choose to occupy and avoid, whether we elect to consider at all or ignore (with determination) the mystery and wonder of our being here—these are the matters of overriding importance in an existential approach in psychiatry.

> I am interested in how you spend your time and intrigued by the choices you have made. I am curious as to what will come next for you and moved by your uncertainty and pain. I will be your doctor.

It will be no surprise to the reader that in the course of coming to know about another person through hearing (and *hearing*), one learns a good deal about oneself. What may be unexpected, however, is that most of what is suddenly learned one knew all the time.

6

Prologue:
If the Patient Is You
(or Someone You Love)

Since the "patient" is—or could be—you or someone you love, this prologue is personal and direct, written for you, your family and friends. It begins with the advice "Have hope and keep trying."

Many times, "sickness" is that moment just before life becomes deeper, richer and more satisfying.

> What is called neurotic or psychotic anxiety is very often the "growing edge" of the person, that part which hungers for a deeper life and won't settle for a conventional, pretending, "me too" in the way most people live their lives. Sickness of this kind turns out to be a signal that a real person is about to spring forward.
>
> —Carl Whitaker, M.D.[1]

> Some patients have a mental illness and then they get well and then they get weller! I mean they get better than they ever were. This is an extraordinary and little realized truth!
>
> —Karl Menninger, M.D.[2]

People, with encouragement, often prove very adaptive. Their wish to get well and then "weller" is the central ingredient in every truly successful helping relationship. The "helper" works to mobilize and free a potential for improvement which is already there. In the treatment process, the patient discovers or rediscovers excitement and satisfaction in being the one-of-a-kind, unique and special being that he or she is. In

7

truly successful therapy, not only do troubling symptoms recede or disappear, but a discovery of previously overlooked potentialities takes place as well. The helper assists the patient in the therapeutic task of unlocking chains, untying hands, removing blindfolds, commuting "life sentences," smashing trick mirrors and turning off a searing blowtorch of guilt and shame that has been in hot and relentless pursuit.

> Free at last! Free at last! Thank God Almighty.
> Free at last!
> —Martin Luther King, Jr.

Free to be me!

IF THE PATIENT IS YOU

Don't settle for a "half-recovered," "half-incapacitated" outcome. Keep trying. The late Vince Lombardi, football coach extraordinary of the Green Bay Packers, taught his teams that it was impossible for them to lose any game—though sometimes the clock ran out before they had a chance to win. In particular, don't abandon a belief and trust in your own abilities and your own capacity to make things right for yourself. When turned upside down, there is an inborn righting process which often takes over and places people back on their own two feet. You are the contemporary product of a hundred million years of mammalian evolution and there is a good deal of survival built into you and into all of us.

To my own patients or as consultant to the patients of my colleagues, I almost always say: "Trust your guts. If you can be honest with yourself, you'll be right about you more than anyone else will be"; and as to accepting or continuing as "patient" of a particular therapist: "Trust yourself. You'll know very soon whether he or she can help you. If you feel 'no,' look elsewhere." It happens in a rather predictable way that when the patient doesn't like the doctor, the feeling is usually mutual and in the end the therapy doesn't work. Perhaps the most important line in myth, rhyme or prose is the one which explains,

> Why does the lamb love Mary so?
> Well, Mary loves the lamb, you know.

Prologue

No matter what the system of treatment, whether psychotherapy, group therapy, drug therapy, hospitalization, deconditioning, relaxing programs or any combination of these, the quality of relationship between your therapist and you is very important. Almost without exception, regard for one's therapist as a person, developing early and extending throughout the relationship, proves so important that its absence is a clear signal to seek help elsewhere.

The pace of recovery is another matter for concern. There are always ups and downs and the process takes time. Even in the most successful therapy, there are inevitably moments when "holding one's own," "keeping going," "hanging on" and "not making things worse" are the best *anyone* can do. In retrospect, such days and weeks seem to have been necessary as periods of accommodation, solidification and stabilization before lasting improvement takes place. All therapies take time. If medications that modify mood are used, a number of days must pass before sustaining relief is likely to come. If the treatment undertaken is a form of individual, family or group psychotherapy, persistence and patience may be particularly necessary. Learning to be honest about one's feelings often proves to be a more difficult process than one might think. It too takes time. Carl Jung's words are a good summary of the inevitable discomfort experienced by all people as they become "aware":

> Most men go to their graves as children . . . [for] there is no coming to individual consciousness without pain. The critical survey of himself and his fate permits a man to recognize his individuality. But this knowledge does not come to him easily. It is gained only through the severest shocks.[3]

The role of patient provides an unusual opportunity to explore the validity and here-and-now relevance of assumptions concerning the obligations, commitments and possibilities of one's life. Usually, the fact that "it's up to me to make it the kind of life I want" comes more into focus. In that process, many of the attitudes that secretly rule (and quietly ruin) one's life come under examination. Pried loose and brought out into the open, they dogmatically assert:

> "You must, of course . . . !"
> "The right kind of people all feel . . . !"
> "I have no choice but to . . . !"

9

Once examined, these secretly held, imperative commands lose their exclamation point! They become, instead, questions about self:

> "Who says I must?"
> "How do *I* really feel?"
> "Who can speak for me other than me?"
> "Dare I experiment?"

This important change makes it possible to undertake either of the two great risks in life. They are, first, to be personally responsible for one's decisions by choosing rather than letting it happen; and second, to be looking for what is true in life rather than to live to avoid appearing foolish to others. When these risks are assumed, major life change is often the result. Still, more often than not, long-held relationships with family and friends and one's values and traditions are strengthened and deepened by an honest, personal questioning. When the treatment ends, you will find you are still you.

I usually tell my patients that major life changes are best not made in the first days and weeks of therapy. People who are under great stress are inclined to want to change everything in their lives all at once, only to discover later, "There was an awful lot of me in all those things I gave up." Change of job or marital status, moving to a new community, undertaking major financial commitments and similar matters are best postponed for a short time. Often, the relief of anxiety or the lifting of depressive symptoms becomes an important new factor in whatever is to be decided. And clarification as to "whose life it really is" usually leads to better choices.

However, undergoing treatment is a poor reason for postponing important personal decisions and a poor substitute, a dreadful substitute, for getting married, going to school, advancing in work or traveling around the world. One of my personal regrets is that in the early years of my practice I failed to recognize that intense and prolonged commitment to therapy with me made it difficult for several of my patients to live the other parts of their lives. They gave so much of their energy, love and hope to therapy that there wasn't enough left over for the other people who counted on them. There was too much postponement, too little choosing. One patient's discovery that "he is the one after all" took place only after he had grown tired of waiting and had left. People too often find excuses as to why *now* is not the moment. "Treatment" may offer a moratorium of a few days, weeks or one or two months, but only rarely longer. Therapy should serve to heighten one's understanding that by not choosing, one chooses.

While family and friends are no substitute for a needed therapist, it is also true that, over time, a therapist is no substitute for mate, family or friends. If your therapy excludes your spouse (which it shouldn't), keep in mind that no person is so totally secure and confident as to be unthreatened by a relationship between their mate and a stranger (therapist). He or she is likely to feel a sense of failure and guilt that the love in the marriage did not solve the problems. No matter how loud the accusation "You had trouble long before I met you," there is almost always the secret self-accusation "Perhaps it *is* my fault!" The same applies to parents, children and close friends. Most clinicians now choose to include other family members from the very beginning of treatment and this is always the case in my own practice. While protecting individual privacy is very important, I find that the exclusion of family members from a role in treatment is a mistake that in time proves a hardship for all parties. And, beyond the pain such exclusion produces, there are many times when great potential therapeutic gain is sacrificed in the name of privacy. When possible, I urge my patients to let their families share in this important time in their life. There are occasional exceptions, but not many. Actually, the exceptions in my practice are fewer each year.

If the patient is you, try to accept what will be repeatedly emphasized in all the chapters of this book, that is, the empirical, trial-and-error nature of psychotherapy, drug therapy and all the other forms of treatment for emotional problems. While it is often possible for an experienced clinician to predict accurately which therapeutic approach will be most useful, there is no advance certainty. This is disheartening news to anyone who feels bad. But absolute precision is not possible when modifying human events. It is definitely not possible in either general medicine or psychiatry. This means at times an experimenting approach to find the treatment or treatments that will prove most helpful. The relationship between you and your therapist needs to be a kind of partnership in which both parties have a responsibility to evaluate the progress of treatment and to share their assessment with the other. In my own clinical work, neither two decades of practice nor my most conscientious

11

efforts guarantee the right choice the first time. My first judgments are often inaccurate and at times a second, a third, a fourth or more changes in the initial treatment plan are necessary. I feel a great sense of gratitude to those patients, not few in number, who were willing to continue to work with me despite disappointing changes in their treatment. Their trust, understanding and patience are among my most moving life experiences.

For some, the optimistic words of this chapter will not match your own experience. If you are one of those who have tried without success to obtain help with your problems, it is not easy to know what to say to you. Perhaps whatever interferes with your life has been going on for a long time; perhaps you have been cared for in a "good" hospital, have tried medicines, have spent hundreds of hours and thousands of dollars in the hope of receiving help which has not materialized. Unhappily, there are many of my own patients whom these words describe. If that patient who has failed to respond to treatment is you, there are at least two steps you may consider. You can seek further psychiatric or psychological therapy. Or you may choose to turn for a time to other ways of working toward your personal goals. If you elect to discontinue treatment and choose to work on your problems in another way, you won't be the first. "Not making it" as a patient is not to be equated with "not making it." There have been many others who not only succeeded in independently overcoming the problems for which they had unsuccessfully consulted a psychiatrist, but achieved success in every area of their personal and professional lives as well. Actually, all "successful" therapy ends with the discovery that therapy is not the real and full answer. One continues to look for that throughout life.

If your therapeutic efforts to date have been unsuccessful, you might well focus on two matters:

1. In each of the last ten years, a number of new therapeutic techniques have been developed. Have you had an *adequate trial of each treatment program* that might offer assistance?
2. If the answer to the first question is yes (which is not usually the case) and there is no present prospect of immediate help, you may consider an annual reevaluation of your condition to see if something newly developed will provide the help you need.

In this process, it is not always easy to decide whether to return to someone with whom you have worked or to consult a new clinician. Should you decide to seek a new consultant, your former therapist may be the very best source of referral. It takes courage to say to a therapist with whom one has worked, "I'd like to talk with someone else who uses a different approach. Will you think about who that should be and help me to give him any information he should have?" But if you can do that, it is a kind of tribute to the relationship you and your therapist have established. Otherwise, one of the many hundreds of newly established mental health care clinics could be a good starting place. Or you may, with the assistance of your family doctor, seek consultation at one of the major university clinics or hospitals in your state or province. Listed in the Appendix of this book are the addresses of the commissioners of mental health in each state and the ministers of health in the provinces of Canada. Listed also are the names and addresses of various public and private organizations to whom you might write for suggestions as to where to turn for help. If you contact someone who is not familiar with you, a brief one-page listing of the therapies which you have received should be helpful to whomever you consult. Include in this listing the dates and length of prior hospitalization, the medicines taken and, if you can, the dosage and the total period of time the medicine was used, the extent of psychotherapy programs including a description of how often other family members were included, and so forth. One important goal in seeking advice, even advice from individuals who are far away, is to find the best source of help close to your own home.

It is terribly discouraging to work in therapy for relief which seems never to be forthcoming. Yet each year, more of those who could not be assisted earlier now find help in mental health programs. If all else has failed, I urge that in precisely one year you again seek consultation. In that time, it may have become possible to offer help to you which, till now, has been denied.

IF THE PATIENT IS SOMEONE YOU LOVE

Have hope! And give hope! For, as will be emphasized in several chapters of this book:

> Over a period of time, a highly troubled, disorganized or depressed individual whose circle of relationships includes people genuinely and lovingly committed to him may fare much better than a seemingly less troubled person who is without close friends or mate.
>
> And very often, the best "therapist" is . . . someone who admires, approves of, understands and loves the person who is also a patient. One of the most important goals in any therapy is that of helping those who care for the patient make their caring count.

In particular, your belief in the ultimate success of his efforts to improve his life, and thus yours, is very important. *The maintenance of hopes, of high expectation and of faith in the recuperative and restorative powers of the patient by those who love him or her are of almost incalculable value.*

In this respect, I think very often of Martha and of Lenore, women who are strangers to each other but who shared an unquestioning, persistent and ultimately correct faith in the recovery of their supposedly "hopeless" husbands. I respect and admire them greatly.

Martha's husband, Ned, was unable to work at all from his fifty-fifth year until the middle of his fifty-ninth year. He suffered a severe depression which drained him of hope, strength and sanity. He was constantly self-depreciating and attempted several times to kill himself. Increasingly, as those years passed, he withdrew into himself. But Martha's loyalty, persistence and optimism were astonishingly sustaining. She never conceded during those difficult days, weeks and months that extended into years that Ned would not someday be well. And, in the end, she was right! The same was true of Lenore whose husband Arthur was not only severely depressed but also was said to be "incurable" because of a neurologist's diagnosis of "early brain atrophy secondary to chronic alcoholism." Arthur, also a man in his fifties, was extremely agitated and unhappy. He reversed days and nights, was unable to work or to communicate in any effective manner. And, when left to himself, he would slip off and buy a bottle of wine.

But both men recovered! And they recovered fully! The faith, persistence and support provided by each spouse helped save both husbands' lives. As a matter of fact, that faith and hope sustained not only their husbands, it sustained me, their doctor. It caused me to keep thinking about them, looking for an answer, trying each new treatment that offered any hope. Their quiet insistence, "Please keep trying!" kept me

14

a full and participating partner with husband and wife in working out what ultimately was a complete recovery for both men. For one, talking plus medicines plus the passage of time seemed to help. For the other, a combination of antidepressant medications in high dosage produced a rapid improvement. Recommendations in the second instance came from my psychiatric colleague, Dr. Heinz Lehman, of Montreal, who was good enough to see my patient in consultation.

To you who love the patient, I say with sincerity born of many years of working in this field, "Stay hopeful, keep trying, and ask your doctor to do the same!"

There is perhaps only a fine line at times between "stay hopeful" and the refusal to "face reality." But reality changes. Both in the practice of general medicine and the mental health professions, hope has come often to the hopeless. The possibilities that one clinician could not recognize, a second or a third was able to envision and help bring to actuality. And even more often, what cannot be accomplished at one interval in time becomes possible at a later point. Optimally, the patient and family need not travel from coast to coast in a perpetual search for such assistance. A single clinician who retains hope about his patient, who seeks periodic consultation and continues to read and study, offers as much as the painful, constant migration between health centers.

As with the patient himself, these are times when the best that family and friends can do is "hang on," "don't make things worse," "stay alive" and just *survive.* During such periods, a deeply held hope, a sense of humor and perhaps a silent prayer may be all the encouragement available to you. Controlling your own guilt feelings is very important in such periods. When the patient is someone you love his unhappiness is, of course, your unhappiness. But guilt is a much more complicated emotion. Unhappiness and sickness in the life of someone close always raise the questions, "What have I done?" "What have I failed to do?" and most importantly, "What can I do now?" To care about someone is simultaneously to be at risk when things go badly for them. But this is an insufficient explanation for the enormous sense of guilt which so many feel.

Many family members fall victim to the prejudices to "explain" mental illness that have grown. Whenever there is no adequate explanation for what is happening and people are experiencing a painful and uncertain time, a search for an evil event or a harmful person is likely to begin.

15

When things go badly, patients, doctors and family members, like all people, look for someone else to blame. Persons "nearest and dearest" are likely targets on what are at times no more than geographic grounds (physical proximity). If the problem goes on for a while, all who care about the patient and are nearby may seem suspect.

Or, your sentence of guilt may be self-imposed, the result of your long-standing personal insecurity and lack of confidence. Perhaps that insecurity causes you to fear that anyone who is associated with you will fare badly. Or worse, you may be one who feels, "I must take responsibility for everything that happens to everyone." Whatever the basis, guilt is such a destructive emotion that you must search for help to become free of it. While there are times in a clinician's office, in the movies, on the radio, in the comics and elsewhere when it was clear to someone that "X made Y sick," this probably has *little or no relevance to you.* * One needs always to consider Y himself or herself, his personality, his biological constitution, his own life choices, the social circumstances and values of the peer group and the many other people and events in his or her life from which you are excluded. Mental health clinicians are frequently accused of having named (indicted) some person or persons as the X who made Y sick. This is always unfortunate. Actually, moments when the therapist accuses the family probably occur much less frequently than reported. The willingness of some families to hear that they are guilty and the tendency of some patients to blame someone else is sufficient to create the search for a family villain without much outside suggestion.

If the patient is someone you love and if you feel great personal guilt about what is happening in his life, by all means tell him how you feel, express your sorrow and then, as best you can, *put it aside.* Guilt removes the spontaneous, clouds the sincere and makes easy and spontaneous loving too risky to chance.

To describe the good things that can come into the life of a family as the result of one family member's symptoms of mental illness is to risk sounding like a Pollyanna or a fool. But, just as symptoms quite frequently represent a "growing edge" in the individual, it can work that way for the family as well. If the patient is someone you love, openness on your part as to what he or she is working toward may be very valuable.

---

*And, in truth, it may have little factual relevance to X or to Y.

16

Prologue

It is tempting to think only of getting him "back on the right track," "as good as new," "back to his old self" and thereby to discount the part of his struggle which can become a thrust *toward* a more meaningful life. However, for many couples and families, the illness of one member has served as a turning point leading to greater honesty, appreciation of the feelings of all family members and a more open sharing of tenderness and affection.

It is also true that one of the most difficult and painful circumstances that can befall any family is the presence of a family member who is incapable of protecting and caring for himself. It is particularly difficult when someone is too confused, anxious or angry to recognize his need for outside help and also shuns or fights the efforts of family members and others in his or her behalf. In such dreadful moments, it is almost always a good idea to attempt to assemble *all* immediate family members (preferably with the patient present) to discuss the problems which are presented by the patient's behavior and needs. Of course, families that are experienced in talking together in an open and mutually respectful fashion are much more likely to be effective in this effort. And conversely, a family that is unaccustomed to talking together to work out ordinary family decisions may find it almost impossible to face confusion, depression or anger in a family member. Still, it is worth a serious try for two reasons: first, shared family responsibility from the very beginning prevents later misunderstandings, and second, assigning the responsibility to one person is usually unfair to that person and unwise for the family group.

Because these are such painful matters, people often resort to guile or deception. The patient is lied to and tricked in order to place him or her in a hospital. Perhaps, but only rarely, there is no other reasonable choice. In the overwhelming majority of instances, honesty is the better policy and this is the case irrespective of the patient's age. Honesty and a direct and full disclosure of what the family members are planning help prevent a later guilt compounded by the need to explain, "Why did you lie to me?" No matter how disturbed the patient may seem to be, no matter how confused, angry or deluded, there is almost always within him an "island of reason and rationality" which should be addressed. Directing one's efforts toward that unseen area of rational and reasonable thought is frequently effective, though not always immediately. Persis-

17

tent, honest, sustaining and gentle efforts to communicate, continued for as long as is necessary, often lead to cooperation that would have been difficult to anticipate. The sequence is often, "NO NO NO NO NO NO —YES."

Fortunately, there are growing numbers of knowledgeable others to whom the family can turn for assistance in protecting and caring for loved ones in this moment. The family physician, the minister, the family lawyer or another trusted friend may join family members in addressing themselves to the "islands of rationality" within the patient. Suicide prevention centers, "Recovery Incorporated," "Alcoholics Anonymous," departments of mental hygiene, the local medical society, the judge of family court and lastly, but often far from least, the local police are also potential resource persons and agencies. Persistence is important. So is patience. Beyond family and friends, every large community and many rural counties have a mental health center and/or a mental health association. Very often, such agencies are extremely helpful in offering advice or direct professional assistance. Many will arrange home consultation to help families come together to think about, discuss and plan for the future well-being of the family member (and the family as well). This outside assistance may be of particular value when the family member in question is an older person no longer able to care for himself at home. Often in such moments the family is divided by guilt. Old disputes and financial concerns arise. The group fails to agree on a unified plan and one person assumes responsibility and the others "wash their hands" of the matter. The family feud begins. The young cousins never get to know each other.

A good part of the history of progress in mental health care has been written by individuals who started out as a patient's relative or friend. Those most influential in reclaiming the closed-off and abysmal chronic mental hospitals of the 1940s were more often than not people whose initial commitment had been to a single individual. Similarly, those seeking to enhance the opportunities for the retarded, for the alcoholic, for the troubled adolescent and the forgotten prisoner are often led and given spirit by individuals whose capacity to care began with, but went beyond, a family member. When the patient is someone you love, being witness to their growth and sharing in their recovery is a very moving experience. For most of us, there is nothing quite like it. When it happens, there is a debt accrued which makes the well-being of others one's personal responsibility.

CHAPTER 1

Beginning at the Beginning:
The People Who Count

Underlying much of what happens in life is the fact that people are both uniquely individual and yet powerfully affected by each other. Each of us is the one-and-only, never-before, likely-never-again variety of our special self. And more poignantly, each moment that we live is its one-and-only, never-to-recur point in time. Yet, our individuality notwithstanding, we know each other and are mutually involved in the most basic sense. Life is "life with others" even when one is temporarily alone. And the most significant moments are likely to be those with, because of, en route to or away from some significant other person. Human anguish and human exultation are largely dependent upon what some other person said, what he or she did or failed to do. Human nature is powerfully modified depending upon which other person is around. To some degree, most people could say of themselves, "What person I am depends upon which human being I am with. I can go from being the best of men to the worst simply by changing my companion."

Just how important people are to each other and the complex ways that they seek for, grieve for and turn from each other is something ever present in a psychiatrist's office. Some of the people who come for help are simply not willing or not able to accept and overlook what isn't happening in their lives. They aren't good sports about what they aren't getting. And for some, there is simply too much unfinished business for them to go on in search of the "what could be" in their future. One such person who felt she couldn't go on till she had gone back was a young nurse hopelessly divided in the here and then.

20

Case Study 1: *A Nurse in Search of Her True Parents*

Annette Wrigley, a thirty-one-year-old registered nurse, unmarried, working regularly and effectively as a general duty surgical nurse, agreed reluctantly to a single psychiatric interview because of the urging of a surgeon friend. She had confided to this professional friend her conviction that her mother and father were not her true biological parents and she had devoted most of her free time to seeking proof for this belief. Specifically, she felt that she was the child of an aging minister in her family's church and that her mother had most likely been a paternal aunt who had died some thirty-one years earlier. She had held fast to this conviction for more than six years despite angry and continuous denials by her parents, her parents' friends and the minister she felt was her biological father. She not only believed her theory, she believed it with a desperate hope. She felt that she could not go on to other parts of her life until "the true facts are known." And to the search for the "true facts" she had committed a considerable part of her life.

She remembered her childhood as miserable and bereft of hope. Her parents always seemed indifferent to her but consumed with hatred for each other. They fought continuously and blamed Annette for having to sustain the marriage. That they were still together ten years after Annette left home was quite incomprehensible to her.

After a lonely and unhappy childhood, Annette graduated from high school with the expectation that she would go on to college. But her father said he couldn't support the schooling and so she went to work until she had earned enough to begin nurses' training. It took her four years. At twenty-three, she began a nurses' training program and finished at twenty-six.

Some two months after graduation, Annette Wrigley became very depressed and for a period of almost one month was unable to work. This followed her decision not to marry a young suitor. She had felt herself to be in too much personal turmoil. Her depression was severe. She stayed in her apartment, cried a great deal, brooded

21

about her life. She went a time or two to tell her folks how bad she felt but felt worse after each visit. She decided to talk with a minister whose church she had twice visited during the preceding year. He received her kindly, patiently, listened to her as she had never been listened to in her entire life. Through her own tears she saw tears in his eyes and she felt a union, communion, friendship and peace almost unknown to her. About a week later she returned and again was deeply touched by his concern. As she was crying, he reached and put his hand on hers and said, "Don't cry, my dear." It was the most important moment in her life. She suddenly felt a total exhilaration and awe at the discovery which needed no other proof—"This is my father."

The weeks, months, then years that were to follow were, understandably, complex. There was pain, embarrassment, self-doubt, rejection, bitter denunciation by her mother and Annette's sad decision that she should stop contacting the minister who, though kind, had become uncomfortable with her. Yet through it all, extending to the moment of psychiatric consultation six years later, she never gave up the conviction that she had found her biological father, her true father. During the first of the days that followed her decision that the minister was her true father, she also suddenly remembered a family story about an aunt, her other father's older sister, who had taken her own life after an unhappy love affair. This had taken place, she had been told, before her birth. At first, she was incredulous as to what she was thinking, but the coincidence of timing and various other discoveries taken from her memory seemed to build too strong a case to deny that this aunt was her true mother, that she was born of a union of this woman with the minister, her father, and that the people who had reared her were her uncle and the uncle's wife. That would explain everything!

She pursued her quest in many ways. She followed many clues. She read old newspapers in the libraries, sought various public and church records, would await a key moment in casual conversation and then mention the name of her dead aunt and the minister in close succession and intently watch for reactions. She made frequent visits to the town where her aunt had lived, tried to find people who had known her, then would produce a blown-up and retouched photo of the minister (made to look thirty years younger) and ask if he too was remembered. Some weren't sure, but maybe . . .

And here she was sitting with me, talking seriously, intently, a woman who was intelligent, kind, polite but wanting just one thing from me— encouragement to continue her lonely search. I asked her if she would tell me a dream and she said that on the night before our appointment she had this remarkable dream: "I was standing in a garden, a beautiful garden; I had never seen it before. There were yellow and red and purple flowers and rich, green grass and lovely spreading trees. But I was standing there crying, fiercely crying. At the same time, I was turning back the layers of some kind of bulb, like an onion, layer after layer, and crying and crying." It was a beautiful dream that said so much about her own life. The bulb was her life, the seed of the flower she was meant to be. But she sought that flower through the ritual of examination. She dared not entrust herself to the soil of her life.

THE NATURE OF HEALING

Healers, religious leaders and the rulers of society share a common history. Other people turn to them in search of meaning in their lives, to seek relief from pain and danger and to establish a basis for hope. That person or coalition of persons who could influence others would be called upon, or would feel called upon by their own needs, to become the healers; and frequently, the healers became the rulers. Faith was always important in healing because the patient's belief in the healer made the cure more likely. And conversely, as the cure worked, the patient and his family and friends came to believe in the healer and in whatever medical, theological and/or political system gave birth to the recovery.

This process which interweaves healing, believing and governing is not simply of historical interest. It is a very contemporary reality in every part of the world. Faith healers, folk healers and plain board-certified healers (whether they practice in the bush, on television or in carpeted offices) owe their success to a combination of their knowledge, the belief that people have in them, the endorsement of the most influential (governing or religious) agency. Interestingly, in some parts of the world where people have a choice of Western medicine (doctors, nurses, hospitals, prescription drugs) or native healers (magic, spells, religious rituals, animal sacrifice, singing, dancing), many try the folk healers first. In Singapore and Malaya in the late 1960s, 90 percent of the people in Western hospitals had first gone to the folk healers.[1] Of course, one need not travel to other continents to witness the linking of healing to magic, power and faith. For, the emergence of the various helping professions is not simply a logical development coming from some new science or special therapeutic skill. Healing derives from the hope and trust that people have in each other.

I have visited, observed and at times traveled with folk healers in many parts of the world. The people who await them do so anxiously, the concern and hope they bring are the same as one finds in clinics and emergency rooms all over the Western world. I remember traveling in Sarawak, Borneo, with a rather sophisticated native healer and watching as he placed a chicken's beak into the belly button of a colicky, crying baby. As the chicken was sucking out the poison, the man's thumbs were tightening around the chicken's neck and when all the poison had been removed, the baby lay quietly and the poisoned chicken was dead. All present were watching and subsequent patients needed no further animal sacrifice. The healer's credibility was established with all present and this was important. It cannot be the patient and therapist alone who believe in what they are doing. Important others must believe in and add credence and validity to the therapeutic effort, be it a night-long ritual dance or a well-considered referral to a board-certified specialist. Therapist and patient do not come together by accident. Many assumptions surround and allow their meeting, and much of what will transpire is prewritten.

The initial meetings are also important since it is in the beginning that agreement is reached as to what, if anything, is wrong and what must be done if improvement is to take place. Under what auspices is that decision made? Who decides that a particular therapist has the needed capacity to heal? Who selects the persons who are to be included in the healing process? How is it decided that the individuals involved are important enough to warrant all the effort? And, titles and endorsements aside, how does one person help others? These and related questions will be taken up in some detail in the consideration of love, charisma and empathy.

LOVE

If one is to talk of what is important to people, it is well to begin with love. In loving relationships, people intuit, discover or build their meanings. Martin Buber, an existential philosopher, summed it up in these words: "Feelings one has; love occurs. Feelings dwell in man, but man dwells in his love."[2]

Without meaning to disparage any of the helping professionals, we all know (and often forget) that the most important and helpful relationships are not ordinarily offered by a doctor, nurse, social worker, psychologist, rehabilitation worker or religious counselor. The best helper in most situations is someone who admires, approves of, understands and loves the person even if that person is also someone else's patient. There are many moments in life when the thing that keeps you going is the fact that someone loves you no matter what you do. Long after other kinds of therapists have come and gone, the loving relationship is likely to persist in serving, enriching and restoring the former patient. Among the most crucial determinants as to whether a patient will recover and stay recovered are answers to the questions "Who loves this person?" and "How well can my patient receive, enjoy and grow in the soil provided by a loving relationship?"

Over a period of time, a highly troubled, disorganized or depressed individual whose circle of relationships includes people genuinely and lovingly committed to him will fare better than a seemingly less troubled person who is without close friends or mate. This is not to deny that there are times when loving relationships are confusing, overconfining or contaminated with unloving emotions. Neither is it to suggest that a person who is loved won't get sick or that once sick, love alone is always sufficient to effect the cure. Nevertheless, loving interpersonal relationships are an important deterrent to the development of the pain called mental illness, a restorative during the period of healing and an antidote to its long-term consequences.

Overshadowing all prose (however majestic) is the personal experience of an intense, loving relationship. Few will fail to understand why loss of or serious threat to such relationships is quite regularly the chief cause of the anxiety, withdrawal from or distortion of life which underlies much mental illness. Objectively speaking, the Bard was right about the advantages of loving and losing (over never loving). But the collapse of this love is often very hard on the participants. Suicide, the chief cause of death among young adults, is more often than not provoked by the turmoil of a dissolving love relationship, and the same is often true of suicidal threat and gesture in adults and older people.

By contrast, the warm climate and rich psychological soil of loving relationships provide the source and site in which normal growth and most healing occur. And, trite though it seems, asking an individual, "Whom do you love?" often reveals a great deal about his life. Nor should one overlook "acute" love in mature and older people. That intense and focused state of awareness which makes other matters inconsequential is an extraordinary event in any person's life at just about any age. A good many career and life changes have to do with experiencing (again) "being in love." And without question, a good many of the most dramatic therapeutic "cures," as contrasted with "improvements," center around the discovery or the rekindling of an intense, alive, here-and-now personal loving relationship.

Carl Rogers, a distinguished American psychologist who was my colleague at Wisconsin for seven years, has demonstrated during his many years of study of the process of psychotherapy that therapists best serve patients and their families when they are personally respectful and accepting, when they demonstrate their concern and in that process help the patient learn to receive and enjoy those persons in his own life who love and admire him.[3] Successful psychotherapy very often succeeds because it lets loved ones be loved. One of my patients, a forty-four-year-old business man who entered treatment because of problems he was having with associates in his work, found that he was talking mostly about relationships within his own family. Discussion seemed to help both areas of his life. He summarized his feelings as follows:

> I think the most important thing I got out of all this talking was to understand that I could trust my wife all the way. It seems silly to say it about somebody you've been with for nineteen years but I needed help to find out that she is really, actually on my side. In a way, the same sort of thing was going on with our daughter. Looking back at it now, I guess I was afraid she was going to make a fool of me by getting pregnant and then if

26

my folks ever found out, I'd have been ashamed. And so, here I've been juggling the three generations instead of seeing what really fine women live with me.

This man, like some contemporary parents—and almost all who were parents in the days when the three generations lived in close contact— had trouble being good son, good mate and good parent. He felt caught in the middle. And the defensiveness that was rather intense in his dealings with his often critical parents carried over and interfered with his ability to recognize the personal qualities in his very gentle wife and daughter. Also, he saw himself as the person responsible for making the activities of the second and third generations acceptable and pleasing to the oldest generation. His therapy helped him to excuse himself (partly) from responsibility to his parents for making their world appear to be what it wasn't. Freed of some of that burden, he was more able to come openly and without agenda into other family relationships. When last seen he was trying, with difficulty, to resign from the role of messenger boy. The magical words were "Tell her yourself."

Some therapists make no bones about wanting to facilitate an individual's opportunities to experience and determination to seek love. If there are problems within a family, they work on those. If there is no family, they work on that.

> Dr. Richard Stuart, behavior therapist: "Well, you're a pretty alive person, Mrs. D., how about another man all the way in your life!"
>
> Mrs. D., four years a widow, fifty-three, a fine musician, drinking too much, depressed, "alone" despite a circle of social friends: "Well, not just anyone, you know."
>
> Dr. Stuart: "I'm already married."
>
> Mrs. D.: "I didn't mean that. I meant I couldn't love just anybody. If I ever get involved again, it couldn't be, well, how do you say, just a 'roll in the hay.'"
>
> Dr. Stuart: "People I know are happiest if there's somebody they love all the way in their life."
>
> Mrs. D.: "Well, sure, I would be too, but there aren't all that many like that. I mean, I'm fifty-three and you don't meet too many people you could respect and who would respect you. And, well, it's just not easy at my age."

27

Dr. Stuart: "So, you've been trying hard and have discovered it's not easy? And anyway, you could start with one and maybe you wouldn't need all that many."

Mrs. D.: "Well, no, I haven't tried *that* hard. And I'd settle for one good one."

Dr. Stuart: "So, good, we're agreed. It's important to you and you should try harder."

Mrs. D. was my patient and we had seemed to be on a kind of therapeutic plateau after three months. I invited Dr. Stuart to join us as a consultant to us both. Mrs. D. took that consultation seriously, appreciated Stuart's candor, didn't get mad at him (or me) and took his advice fairly literally. She made her plans, established a kind of contract with herself and followed it. It helped her a good deal, seemed to strengthen her determination to stand up for herself, helped her to say yes when she meant yes and no when she meant no instead of maybe when she meant either no or yes. Also, the challenge to put on paper what she wanted and what she would change in order to achieve it gave her the courage to risk the most feared of all human situations, that is, appearing foolish. The Stuart exercise has made her more direct with me, with others and finally with herself.[4]

Another very remarkable therapist who is not vague at all about love and loved ones is Dr. Carl Whitaker, a psychiatrist who teaches and practices family therapy at the University of Wisconsin. Whitaker talks a good deal about the "temperature" in a marriage and he insists that both members of a marriage have their hands on the "thermostat" and that it takes an explicit agreement between the two to raise the temperature. This would explain the paradox of a marriage too cold to keep tropical fish even though both partners can cite many examples of their individual efforts to warm things up. Whitaker says they have a secret deal with each other to take turns turning the heat up, then down. That way, both can make some effort but not really do all the work required to keep a marriage (and life) alive.

Another Whitaker idea is that "an affair" is usually a secret agreement between a couple to "bring in an amateur psychotherapist to warm things up for the two of you." Then he usually adds, "You'd be better off to stick with a professional. It's usually cheaper in the long run." He thinks that every couple should have a chance to turn their exclusive and unhurried attention to their relationship at least once every year or so:

> No, not sick couples, just couples. I'm proposing a center for couples, normal, everyday crazy couples like us and our spouses. A place to put it on the line again, to get reacquainted, to practice listening again, to exchange complaints and brag about what's good with other married people, to remember again where it is we want to be going . . . pardon me, to remember why you chose each other in the first place. I think most people choose with a wisdom that's smarter than they are.
>
> No, not sick couples, all couples, every year. Put it back up front where it belongs.[5]

In earlier years, many therapists tended to overlook the importance of contemporary family relationships and chose instead to focus their attention upon the intrapsychic problems of the individual designated as the "patient." But that approach has many problems. Often, the patient proved to be the healthiest person in the family. Sometimes, the patient seemed to be the one who said "ouch" for a whole group of people who were doing badly. And, all too often, ignoring family members during a prolonged individual therapy program was very threatening to those others, to the very persons closest and most important to the patient. In my own work therapy almost always includes working with loved ones and a fairly definitive effort to keep a clear focus on what they are all working on together.

In this respect I've changed. Early in my career I preferred to work almost exclusively as therapist to a single person. And that system has some merit. It's quite a wonderful thing when therapist and patient admire, respect and work well together. But I think it's much better when a therapist can help people who are already deeply involved with each other to learn to help each other and make their lives more openly, unashamedly, reciprocally loving. Once established, or reestablished, the process can continue and extend without outside help.

The subjects of love, loving and intimacy will be considered in a number of places in this book. They seem to thread through almost everything.

Call it what you will, helping people to acknowledge, to cultivate and/or to repair their loving relationships is a major part of most contemporary therapies no matter what the formal orientation of the therapist may be.

CHARISMA

The charismatic person is defined in the dictionary as one who "restores emotion, awe and magic to the conduct of affairs and would appear to himself and/or to others to be endowed with authority analogous to that of the original theological meaning of the word." A charismatic healer—and the charisma in all healers—is the heir of the sorcerer, the witch doctor, the hypnotist, the miracle cure and the religious shrine. In our contemporary world, the heart replacement, the fertilized ovum transplant and the promise of life synthesis all add to the drama and elevated image of the healer. Now as always, most heroes are created and maintained by consensus of the many. People hunger for heroic figures and make their own lives more exciting by identifying with these inspiring, powerful individuals. Those who hunt and would kill a president express their awe and hungering in a mean, blunted and perverse way. But for most of us, our heroes are treasured. Intimacy with President John Kennedy or Premier Pierre Trudeau (made possible by television, radio and newspaper), the memory of Martin Luther King walking up an Alabama highway, the moving words of Winston Churchill instructing the English people about the last stand against the nazis they never had to make—all these are not only historical matters, they are personal legacies granted to us by the times in which we live. No less, the opportunity for the architect to have been a student of Frank Lloyd Wright or Mies van der Rohe, for the artist to have worked with Hans Hofmann, Willem DeKooning or Henry Moore, for the philosopher to have shared dialogue with Alfred North Whitehead or Suzanne Langer, such contacts both direct and vicarious have been important in the personal development of countless men and women. Why is this so? Why does it happen that each field has its great and legendary people and that their importance extends to so many? What is a hero?

"Living heroically" is a topic of consuming importance in the 1974 Pulitzer Prize book, *The Denial of Death*. It was written by the late Ernest Becker, a distinguished sociologist at Simon Fraser University in Vancouver. Becker's inquiry turns to the question of how anyone could live well, live optimistically, sustaining a sense that his is a worthwhile life in the face of the absurd extremes of everyone's life. We are poet and maker of dreams. Yet we are simultaneously an animal body committed to consuming as much other animal flesh as is needed. In his analysis Becker emphasizes the importance of those who live life with style, with certainty, with such conviction that it would seem that there is no problem about the meaning of life. There is nothing to be concerned about! The answer is clear! It is (God, work, science, love, making money, sex, the welfare of the children, writing music, building a pension) whatever you declare it to be! Once declared, you stop asking if it really is the answer. He titles this meaning "causa sui," that which is its own cause and thus needs no explanation. It is an Aristotelian concept. Average people can take courage and hope from those who live with genius and/or style. Identification with the great and the near great men and women who seem to perform as if life itself was not an issue offers comfort and hope to those aren't sure.[6]

Much in the tradition of medicine and the helping professions fits into the charismatic style. Whether symbolized by a mask, a painted body or a wailing siren carrying a white-coated medic to an automobile accident, the message is the same: "He has come. A very powerful person is here! No need to question the meaning of life." Harvey Cushing, Charles Mayo, Karl Menninger, Sigmund Freud—every doctor has stories to tell about these men or their students or even their students' students. This writer firmly believes a story told about his professor of pediatrics, a man so commanding in demeanor that whenever he walked into the newborn's nursery, all of the crying infants fell silent.

It is when people are sick, discouraged or endangered that heroic figures in reassuring stances are particularly welcome. In such circumstances even half-heroic figures can be blown up to full size. Not without importance, when the crisis is medical, the clinician receives the patient in a medical office or clinic, surrounded by books, journals and other tools of the trade. There are white coats, nurses obeying instructions, disinfectant smells and other patients who are convinced. On the wall hang licenses which permit almost anything since they are written in Latin. Power to those ordained! One chooses to forget how many patients and how many doctors are no longer with us.

Sometimes, when the wish to see the doctor as powerful and omnipo-

31

tent is thwarted by the unpredictable outcome of real-life ventures, the patient's disappointment reaches extreme levels. Some patients feel they have been cruelly betrayed. Every medical complaints committee receives many reports like the following:

> The doctor gave me pills to take and after I had taken three of them, I began to feel much worse. The next day I had a rash that covered my whole body. I called him on the phone and a telephone answering service said he wasn't available and gave the telephone number of someone I had never seen before. I couldn't believe it! How could he give me a dangerous drug and go off on a vacation? What kind of man is he?

One of the harsh realities of a therapist in any of the medical or other helping professions is that some people, 2, 3 or 4 percent of those who come with hope and admiration, become disappointed, angry and sometimes physically or litigiously vengeful. In such moments, it's not easy to be the one who has proven disappointing, especially since, as often as not, the therapist feels as much victim in the situation as do the angry patient and his angry family. This is one of the reasons most experienced workers are slow to criticize colleagues and are themselves shy of criticism. Sometimes it comes in torrents.

Charisma in any form provides a transient antidote to the anxiety inherent in the life of mortal beings. The charismatic life is one that seems to proclaim, "Look no further. The answer is here." Such proclamations are scornfully heard and categorically challenged by existential writers like Jean-Paul Sartre, Albert Camus, Martin Heidegger, R. D. Laing and Carlos Castaneda.

Sartre is merciless in his repudiation of any and all who claim by word or deed to know how other men should live. "The doctor" gets special attention in his writings. In *Nausea,* his classic first novel, Sartre traces the elements of a charismatic medical stance and notes the relief felt by all when the doctor comes to "set things straight." But, as with all heroes in this illusionless view of life, in the end there is little to cheer about.

> M. Achille is joyful; he would like to catch the doctor's eye. But he swings his legs and shifts about on the bench in vain, he is so thin that he makes no noise.
> The waitress brings the calvados. With a nod of her head she points

out the little man to the doctor. Doctor Roge slowly turns: he can't move his neck.

"So it's you, you old swine," he shouts, "aren't you dead yet?"

He addresses the waitress:

"You let people like that in here?"

He stares at the little man ferociously. A direct look which puts everything in place. He explains:

"He's crazy as a loon, that's that."

He doesn't even take the trouble to let on that he's joking. He knows that the loony won't be angry, that he's going to smile. And there it is: the man smiles with humility. A crazy loon: he relaxes, he feels protected again himself: nothing will happen to him today. I am reassured too. A crazy old loon: so that was it, so that was all.

The fine wrinkles; he has all of them: horizontal ones running across his forehead, crow's feet, bitter lines at each corner of the mouth, without counting the yellow cords depending from his chin. There's a lucky man: as soon as you perceive him, you can tell he must have suffered, that he is someone who has lived. He deserves his face for he has never, for one instant, lost an occasion of utilizing his past to the best of his ability: he has stuffed it full, used his experience on women and children, exploited them.

M. Achille is probably happier than he has ever been. He is agape with admiration; he drinks his Byrrh in small mouthfuls and swells his cheeks out with it. The doctor knew how to take him! The doctor wasn't the one to let himself be hypnotized by an old madman on the verge of having his fit; one good blow, a few rough, lashing words, that's what they need. The doctor has experience. He is a professional in experience: doctors, priests, magistrates and army officers know men through and through as if they had made them.

A little while ago M. Achille felt queer, he felt lonely: now he knows that there are others like him, many others: Doctor Roge has met them, he could tell M. Achille the case history of each one of them and tell him how they ended up. M. Achille is simply a case and lets himself be brought back easily to the accepted ideas.

How I would like to tell him he's being deceived, that he is the butt of the important. Experienced professionals? They have dragged out their life in stupor and semi-sleep, they have married hastily, out of impatience, they have made children at random. They have met other men in cafes, at weddings and funerals. Sometimes, caught in the tide, they have struggled against it without understanding what was happening to them. All that has happened around them has eluded them; long, obscure shapes, events from afar, brushed by them rapidly and when they turned to look all had vanished. And then, around forty, they christen their small obstinacies and a few proverbs with the name of experience, they begin to simulate slot machines: put a coin in the left hand slot and you get tales wrapped in silver paper, put a coin in the slot on the right and you get precious bits of advice that stick to your teeth like caramels.

Doctor Roge has finished his calvados. His great body relaxes and his eyelids droop heavily. For the first time I see his face without the eyes: like a cardboard mask, the kind they're selling in the shops today. His cheeks have a horrid pink colour. . . . The truth stares me in the face: this man is going to die soon. He surely knows; he needs only look in the glass: each day he looks a little more like the corpse he will become. That's what their experience leads to, that's why I tell myself so often that they smell of death: it is their last defense.[7]

EMPATHY

In the example of charismatic healing, the patient may say, "This powerful person with special knowledge and training has the capacity to change my very life." The patient is the one acted upon and the power and responsibility reside outside, that is, in another person. A contrasting interpersonal pattern has been called the "empathic relationship," and in this situation there is more reciprocity. Empathy arises in a meeting of equals as a kind of intimacy and understanding shared between people "in the same boat." The dictionary says, "Empathy is the ability to know how another person thinks or feels." We have no direct knowledge of the state of mind of anyone but ourselves, but we can often guess accurately what someone is thinking. Such empathy may be based on small hints that we are not aware of. Sometimes people do not really feel empathy. They project or attribute to others the traits that they have themselves. Empathy ordinarily implies acceptance of the other person, if not everything that he may say or do.

The experience of being genuinely in touch with, understood and appreciated by another person is an important event. In many lives such communication is a rare event. For some it never happens. What does it mean to have someone with whom one can speak of anything, unashamedly, honestly? What would it mean right now to be able to speak

34

to that person? By contrast, most human encounters do not take place between people who are listening, who hear and who understand. Instead, in every life, most of the time, the apparent listener waits only for the noise of the other to end so that he himself may speak, only to be also unheard. The German existential philosopher Martin Heidegger described such everyday discourse (and average conversation) as a kind of "passing the word along," an idle chatter born of casual curiosity, the repetition of an "average" understanding, a speaking not as "oneself" but rather as a spokesman of an elusive "the they."[8] For Heidegger, this "passing the word along" is part of a pervasive, deliberate, relentless evasion of self. In Heidegger's terms, it is a turning away from one's "ownmost possibility," that is, one's own death. This is the purpose and goal of ordinary discourse and socializing. So it is no surprise that many encounters go something like this:

> "Hello."
> "Well, hello there. How are you?"
> "Fine, how are you?"
> "Poorly. I've just come from the hospital. I have cancer."
> "What else is new?"

By contrast, a participant in a genuinely empathic encounter speaks with the knowledge that he will be heard. Someone is listening! This is no everyday event. To be listened to, to be understood and to be acknowledged as interesting by a respected other is among the most encouraging and helpful experiences in the life of any individual. Carl Rogers feels that listening with the intention of hearing represents the most effective psychotherapeutic tool. Perhaps it is the only important one. Somewhat afield, Ralph Martin, author of the book *The Woman He Loved*, speculates that the Duchess of Windsor may have been the first person who really wanted to know how Edward felt about his life.[9] If you want to be a psychotherapist or marry a king . . .

Empathy is not an easily taught or effectively feigned posture. If a therapist is disinterested, dislikes or fears a patient or if that patient is simply the vehicle for making money, such will soon be clear. When people neither appreciate each other nor particularly want to share in each other's lives, it becomes apparent even if the words spoken seem reassuring and affectionate. What we are speaks louder than what we say.

35

But then what happens? Assuming an interpersonal relationship between a therapist and a patient or a family that is as free as possible of lying and pretending, what comes of it? Beyond less pain what is the goal of psychological help, existential variety? How does it end? The patient's words might sound something like these:

> When I came for psychotherapy, I had no hope other than you. When I found you, I felt you were the answer. Now, it is clear that you are not the answer and I must continue my search elsewhere. I came hoping to achieve an adjustment to life through you. Now I understand that life is not that way. One never adjusts. One keeps on searching. But I have hope. And I am glad for the chance to go on. I will miss you.

From an existential point of view, any other ending of psychotherapy represents, at best, a grand misunderstanding on the part of the patient, and at worst a folie à deux (a madness shared by two people) between patient and therapist. A therapist who seems to promise freedom from anxiety or that his message will be available to assuage the patient's anxiety in perpetuity misrepresents the world to the patient and to himself. He and the patient are "in the same boat." The world is and always will be filled with abundant reasons for profound anxiety. Whatever were the initial hopes for a perpetual link, the ending of therapy sees doctor and patient going separately, each living with the anxiety of being a finite being, each seeking elsewhere what could not result for either from the therapy. At the end therapy becomes or is revealed as "not it." "It" is what is sought as life continues.[10]

In real life, most disputes occur when two people are trying to climb into each other's laps at the same time (instead of taking turns). Even the most charismatic of authoritative persons will sooner or later discover the power (charisma) that resides in the helpless or dependent person capable of making the therapist stay charismatic and powerful all the time.

Gandhi was told, "It costs your followers millions of rupees each day to keep you barefoot."

CHAPTER 2

Health and Illness:
An Existential Point of View

INTRODUCTION

Judging other people is falling into disrepute. That is mostly for the good. The judges have ordinarily been privileged and self-satisfied and the ones evaluated were usually misunderstood. Since the judges then met with each other to compare notes and since they all wrote and thought alike, there was no way to discover that they weren't thinking straight. Something like this was about to happen at a meeting I attended which had been called to consider the problems of native Indians. A group of distinguished experts in the various social and medical fields from all parts of North America had assembled and were prepared to provide their findings concerning the extent of alcoholism, broken homes, venereal disease, school failures and dropouts, street drugs, automobile accidents, suicide and violence among Indians. But, before the first presentation one of the observers, an Indian man, interrupted the meeting and wouldn't let anyone speak. He had something to say first: "I want to thank all of you doctors and lawyers and people from the government who have come here to help my people. That's very good and we are grateful. And we do need help. But all these things you've listed in the program aren't problems. No, actually we Indians only have two problems. First, we have to decide what is a good life. That's easy. But then, we have to figure out how you get a life like that if you're an Indian. And that's impossible."

What is a good life and who among us is to say?

Some existential thinkers are deeply committed to Judeo-Christian

37

traditions of Good. Paul Tillich, Christian existential theologian, wrote of the life of Christ as the reason and hope for each person to live his life openly, passionately and hopefully. Tillich believed that the message of Christ's life was not that a fixed prescription as to how life should be lived had been established. Quite the opposite, he felt that his own and every person's life is a search and a venture and that biblical inspiration was just that, inspiration. No detailed, life-living road map had been charted. But there was reason for the journey.[1]

Similarly, for Martin Buber, Jewish philosopher, life is made richer, more meaningful, more alive by the discovery of God's presence in a reverent relationship with objects and beings that he called I and Thou.[2]

Later in this chapter, a long passage from Hermann Hesse's *Siddhartha* provides a moving summation of all religious existential thinking: the search, your search has worth and meaning. There is something to be discovered.

Many other existential writers find no basis for religious hope. Yet for them, the remarkable thing about man is that he keeps going, keeps looking, keeps trying. He is the one-legged man who hops, the blind woman who reads with her fingers and walks with a dog. He is the husband and king of whom the wife sings,

> This is a man who thinks with his heart.
> His heart is not always wise.
> This is a man who stumbles and falls,
> But this is a man who tries.[3]

Perhaps there is no better example of all this than Sartre himself. He is becoming blind. Still, he writes as he has each day of his life. And he writes that there is no purpose. And he writes.

AVERAGE, ORDINARY PEOPLE

There are those very special people, loving and capable, generous and wise, who are enthusiastic about living in general and their own lives in particular. Along with their reverence for others, they mostly do what they want to do, do it well and have a good time at it. There is a kind of ambience in their lives. They are persons who are admired in almost all cultures.

Health and Illness: An Existential Point of View

One wouldn't mind "being like" the kind of person described above. But, we are instead ourselves—less confident, less generous and living a life with many "maybes." In the average, ordinary state of affairs, the individual in all societies conforms closely to the standards of his peers. He believes what "they" believe. She does what "they" do. Both will look with suspicion at anyone who does otherwise. This conformity, this thinking, believing and behaving like the others is not without some very obvious advantages. It facilitates comfort and companionship in everyday life and allows allegiances and affiliations that offer satisfaction and safety. Further, being part of a "we" provides a structure for the perpetuation of ethical and religious principles and allows agreement as to the way the cultural and material legacy of the society is to be passed on to succeeding generations. In being surrounded by people who think alike and can be expected to believe in the same way, there is a sense of order, a feeling that "all is as it should be," and one can choose to be relaxed. Life will "take care of itself." Of course, there are dangers in all that homogeneity, all that sameness, all that trust of the others. One may himself disappear.

Heidegger described this process of losing self in conformity with "the they" in his extraordinarily technical exposition of the nature of life in "average everydayness." This is one of the major concepts in his classic work, *Being and Time*. Unfortunately, his complex formulation of existence as "being in the world" does not translate easily into the language of subjects (I, we, he) and objects, and the paragraph that follows suffers some distortion. Heidegger is writing of the actual experiencing of life in day-by-day going about one's activities. He is here describing the norm, the average, the typical way in which the world presents itself as one goes along:

> I myself am not; my being has been taken away by the others. My everyday possibilities of being are for the others to dispose of as they please. . . . I take pleasure and enjoy myself as they take pleasure; I read, see and judge literature and art as they see and judge; likewise I shrink back from the great mass as they shrink back; I find shocking what they find shocking. . . . I flee from myself.[4]

The typical man and woman do not look for trouble by finding contradictions between what they and the others believe. Nor do they seek out discoveries which would require change and thus dislocation from the others. The stranger, the strange situation and the new idea are soon viewed as suspect even if there is a brief initial charade of hospitality and interest.

In average, everyday living, people seek familiar, safe, neutral ground. Perhaps above all they try hard to avoid appearing foolish to their peers. So they choose the known product and they avoid uncertainty. Particularly suspect and frightening are reminders about the mysteries of life and death, about the ambiguities of our origin, about the certainty of our mortality. Such matters are kept as far as possible from consciousness. The average reader of the yellow pages of the telephone book is both dismayed and surprised if he or she accidentally falls upon the listing of funeral directors. There are many more listed than one would have imagined! Why?

Even when it, the dreadful, has already happened one can still, through ingenious maneuvers, postpone the moment of one's full awareness. The paragraphs which follow tell of the death of my aunt who had been very close and very dear to me:

> When I first learned that my Aunt Esther had suddenly died, I felt a falling, dazed, momentary confusion. The world spun away from me. Then, in a few moments, I collected my thoughts and alternated between memories of her and the practical business of her burial: She was as kind to me as anyone has ever been. Should the funeral be Wednesday or Thursday? From the time I was a little boy, she had loved me and respected me. We mustn't be shamed into buying an expensive casket. She was such a goofy, joyous woman, a kind of sixty-year-old pixie. We want to put it in the newspaper and we'd better tell that woman's group she spent so much time with.
>
> Two burial services; first, the religious service; and then, the Sisters of the Northern Star service. What is it?
>
> All through the religious service, I managed never to be quite with it. I was waiting instead for the service of the Sisters of the Northern Star.
>
> Now! A woman in a long red dress drops a red flower on the casket, tells that red is passion and commitment and Esther was passionate and committed. White dress, white flower, purity and loyalty. Esther, that. Then, a woman stands, blue dress, blue flower, oceanic love of mankind. Esther was. This concludes the Sisters of the Northern Star service.
>
> Oh my God! My Aunt Esther is dead.

40

MATURITY: AN EXISTENTIAL DEFINITION

No one is perfect. There are no people whose lives are not filled or at least surrounded by uncertainties. Over time, the similarities in people's lives grow as the law of averages catches up with individuals and with families. Within that human context, what does constitute maturity? What is growing up fully and well? Such a definition would be synonymous with mental health and would mean more than an ability to adjust to changing circumstances. Also, any definition that rested solely upon a particular national or regional system of values would be incomplete. This imposes very real problems. For what is held in high esteem in one culture may be viewed with disdain or indifference in another. For example, recall a 1944 high school valedictory address which closed with the following exhortative flourish:

> I do not know beneath what skies
> Or on what seas will be our fate.
> I only know it will be high.
> I only know it will be great![5]

And in contrast, read "The Secret" as revealed two thousand years ago by Lao Tzu:

> The secret waits for the insight
> Of Eyes unclouded by longing;
> Those who are bound by desire
> See only the outward container.[6]

The hope of developing a single measure of maturity which could reconcile such diverse personal and cultural values is probably a vain one. Neither is it necessary for a person from the West to travel to Asia to find differing views as to what is of value. The coming of a new generation is sufficient these days to assure drastic reevaluation of what is desirable in life. Three generations in North America saw the glorification of Horatio Alger, from rags to riches, fighting all the way, *The Man in the Grey Flannel Suit,* a reasoned turning away from glory to settle for $25,000 and a good family life, and Jack Kerouac, vagabond Pied Piper for the rootless life. A great many of the contemporary North American children of the vale-

41

dictorians who were predicting great things thirty years ago express harsh critique of such parental goals. "What you really meant," they say, "is to put down everybody else, climb up over them, get more than your share, kiss up, kick down, cultivate greed, fight hard to be a 'big man.'"

Things change, including definitions of what a good man and woman should believe and do, what one should want for oneself and one's family. In recent years (and perhaps even more in the time ahead) the description of what constitutes a family has undergone great change. Beyond the value of personal survival and a general reverence for life, there is probably no universal norm for maturity, for success and for achievement.

This notwithstanding, a definition of maturity and emotional health will now be proposed. Hopefully, it will serve as a starting place and reference point in thinking about the many different patterns of human behavior which are shortly to be described. It is a definition of maturity from an existential frame of reference. Specifically, openness to experience, a wanting to know what is true, the wish to choose and be responsible for oneself and a respect for the opportunities of others to experience and choose for themselves (love) are suggested as characteristics of emotional maturity. This definition is obviously not free of either national or economic bias. It adheres most closely to the system of values that are held in high esteem in the West and, more particularly, among educated individuals of the middle and upper economic classes. Elsewhere, in some Asian societies, for example, a different set of values prevails. There, a reverence for tradition, acceptance of one's fate in life, knowing the sayings and traditions of the ancestors and parents are the important measures of the educated (ruling) "man of quality." And, importantly, in both the East and the West, among those who are poor, less educated, less free to explore, less graced with opportunity, the ability to adjust and to survive in a very hostile environment is the only reasonable measure of personal development. Of course, people with uncommon understanding, uncommon compassion and a profound capacity to influence and enrich the lives of those who are around them arise in every culture, in every social group and in every economic class. There are highly intelligent, kind and loving people everywhere; uncommonly wise people are to be found in the highest social classes as well as among those who have never learned to read and write. There is in mankind—in every man and woman—a powerful thrust to make meaningful what he sees, to

42

understand what is before her, to create new meanings. And while the force of social conformity is very powerful, there will always be those whose intense personal experiencing and strong commitment to whatever they undertake allow discoveries denied their contemporaries.

This is probably what Robert Pirsig is writing about in his very compelling and sad book *Zen and the Art of Motorcycle Maintenance.* The heroic figure, Phaedrus, seeks Quality, equates it with the ultimate and is made desperate by whatever is shabby, haphazard and of sloppy workmanship. Meaning emerges in the coming together of man with the material with which he works. Its name is Quality. If others will settle for less—so much the worse for the world.

> Or if he takes whatever dull job he's stuck with—and they are all, sooner or later, dull—and, just to keep himself amused, starts to look for options of Quality, and secretly pursues these options, just for their own sake, thus making an art out of what he is doing, he's likely to discover that he becomes a much more interesting person and much less of an object to the people around him because his Quality decisions change him too. And not only the job and him, but others too because the Quality tends to fan out like waves. The Quality job he didn't think anyone was going to see is seen, and the person who sees it feels a little better because of it, and is likely to pass that feeling on to others, and in that way the Quality tends to keep on going.

And thus:

> The real cycle you're working on is a cycle called yourself. The machine that appears to be "out there" and the person that appears to be "in here" are not two separate things. They grow toward Quality or fall away from Quality together.[7]

Using the definition described above, the mature person is one who is open to and curious about the many potentialities which are in his or her life. He is willing to feel what he feels and wants to know what is true, not only in his own life but in the lives of others as well. He is not overwhelmed by the wish to conform, seeking instead Quality in his work, love, decisions. He is also aware that life does not go on forever and he treasures the moments that are his. For this reason, he wants to choose for himself which of his potentialities will be selected and which surrendered. It is here that the matter of love comes into his life since he covets not only for himself but for others as well the freedom to experience their own lives and to choose what is right for them. This love underlies his deepest value, a reverence for life.

There is yet another dimension of full human development, a quality most difficult to describe. It derives from the religious-existential perspective of Buber, Tillich, Kierkegaard and from the mystical thinking of Indian and Asian philosophers. Akin to a reverence for things that are alive, it is a particular perspective about life, its order, unity and continuity. It is described by Hermann Hesse in these remarkable words:

He took Siddhartha's hand, led him to the seat on the river bank, sat down beside him and smiled at the river.

You have heard it laugh, he said, but you have not heard everything. Let us listen; you will hear more.

They listened. The many-voiced song of the river echoed softly. Siddhartha looked into the river and saw many pictures in the flowing water. He saw his father, lonely, mourning for his son; he saw himself, lonely, also with the bonds of longing for his far away son; he saw his son, also lonely, the boy eagerly advancing along the burning path of life's desires, each one concentrating on his goal, each one obsessed by his goal, each one suffering. The river's voice was sorrowful. It sang with yearning and sadness, flowing towards its goal.

Do you hear? asked Vasudeva's mute glance. Siddhartha nodded.

Listen better! whispered Vasudeva.

Siddhartha tried to listen better. The picture of his father, his own picture, and the picture of his son all flowed into each other. Kamala's picture also appeared and flowed on, and the picture of Govinda and others emerged and passed on. They all became part of the river. It was the goal of all of them, yearning, desiring, suffering; and the river's voice was full of longing, full of smarting woe, full of insatiable desire. The river flowed on towards its goal. Siddhartha saw the river hasten, made up of himself and his relatives and all the people he had ever seen. All the waves and water hastened, suffering, towards goals, many goals, to the waterfall, to the sea, to the current, to the ocean and all goals were reached and each one was succeeded by another. The water changed to vapor and rose, became rain and came down again, became spring, brook and river, changed anew, flowed anew. But the yearning voice had altered. It still echoed sorrowfully, searchingly, but other voices accompanied it, voices of pleasure and sorrow, good and evil voices, laughing and lamenting voices, hundreds of voices, thousands of voices.

Siddhartha listened. He was now listening intently, completely absorbed, quite empty, taking in everything. He felt that he had now completely learned the art of listening. He had often heard all this before, all these numerous voices in the river, but today they sounded different. He could no longer distinguish the different voices—the merry voice from the weeping voice, the childish voice from the manly voice. They all belonged to each other; the lament of those who yearn, the laughter of the wise, the cry of indignation and groan of the dying. They were all interwoven and interlocked, entwined in a thousand ways. And all the voices, all the goals, all the yearnings, all the sorrows, all the pleasures, all the good and evil, all of them together was the world. All of them together was the stream of events, the music of life. When Siddhartha listened attentively to this river, to this song of a thousand voices; when he did not listen to the sorrow or laughter; when he did not bind his soul to any one particular voice and absorb it in his self, but heard them all, the whole, the unity; then the great song of a thousand voices consisted of one word: Om—perfection.[8]

THE ORIGINS OF MENTAL ILLNESS

Individuals vary greatly in their approaches to the everyday experiencing of their world. Some are cautious people. They are wary of taking a false step. They are frightened of what lies ahead. They devote a good deal of attention to keeping control. When such a person finds himself outside the ordinary situations of his life, that is, in a new space, on new ground, in unfamiliar territory, he is likely to feel restless and uneasy. Such people's view of themselves, of others and thus of their world is one which emphasizes their personal fragility and vulnerability.

Not surprisingly, these people have often grown up with a deep mistrust of their own bodies as well. And the mistrust is of the very deepest kind. They have learned not to "trust their guts." They feel that following their feelings will lead them astray, will direct them into trouble and discomfort. And so, they are likely to be particularly wedded to the way of the others and if interrogated as to how they feel about one thing or another, they reply, "I feel just exactly the way we all feel about that." Such persons are obviously very restricted and handicapped as they live their lives. There are many places they cannot go, things they cannot hear, visions they will never view. In the attempt to fuse with what is "normal," they suffer the great estrangement of being cut off from themselves. They are constantly turning away from their own feelings.

While catastrophic events at any period of life can seriously modify any individual's attitudes, the early years of life are particularly important in setting the way an individual feels about his world. Attitudes about self, key other people, the safety of feeling what one feels and the general hospitality of the world in which one lives are established very early. In the process of personality development, the child is learning how to avoid anxiety, prevent shame and minimize guilt because these emotions are associated with uncomfortable bodily states such as restlessness, sweating, muscle tension, cramping pains and the other bodily manifestations of apprehensiveness and anxiety. The child's personality is a summation of those attitudes, beliefs and ways of relating that provide the most pleasure and fullest satisfaction, which is consistent with freedom from anxiety and bodily discomfort. This summation is continuously changing throughout life as new experiences occur. However, early life events and attitudes appear to exert a lifelong influence on the relative preponderance of security-seeking versus satisfaction-seeking parts of personality. The more pressing were the childhood needs to develop protective techniques, the more contingent, the more restricted, the more tentative is the child's and subsequently the adult's freedom to move in his life. "Safety first" seems to be a well-entrenched human principle. In the early years, one learns what is good (safe) and what is bad (to be shunned). Once learned, these lessons tend to be remembered always. As such, they shape subsequent learning.

One far-reaching implication of the simultaneous early and fairly permanent development of one's sense of "who I am" and "what my world is like" is that, to a large degree, one is one's world and one carries one's world along no matter where one is. It seems not to happen that a person is open, optimistic, friendly, confident and fun-loving while living in a nasty, unrewarding, dangerous, critical, shame-filled world. And physical migration to another spot doesn't usually help things very much. Further, insofar as sense of self and feelings about the world are in substantial part related to a variety of bodily tension states, the psychosomatic nature of experience and the consequence of experiencing on body function are inevitably linked. Body, sense of self, ideas about world, attitudes toward others, are part of the same whole person. And they stay that way throughout a lifetime.

The child with many fears is less likely to be as experimental, as curious or as willing to take risks in exploring the surrounding world as the child who has a more secure (and thus optimistic) early start. And if the early fears are severe and pervasive enough, "keeping safe" by pushing away (and out of one's mind) any threat of change or even variation in routine may become the individual's all-consuming concern. Nor is it simply the people and objects of the "outside world" which may come to be feared and thus avoided. The very manifestations of one's humanness, that is, one's feelings of love, anger, admiration, jealousy, curiosity, one's appetite for touching, sexuality, food, security, one's own body parts, may all seem unfriendly, unattractive and to be shunned. A man can come to despise his tender feelings as well as his anger if those tender feelings led him in the past to experience shame, repudiation or anxiety.

WHAT IS MENTAL ILLNESS?

Opposed to the openness, freedom and expanding life of the healthy and mature individual are the varieties of experiencing and reacting which are described as the symptoms of mental illness. A diagnosis of mental illness suggests that for a given person at a given time there will be anxiety and/or other forms of psychological or physiological discomfort unless very careful precautionary steps are taken as that person leads his life. These precautionary steps are in the nature of avoidance techniques or mechanisms for controlling, denying or substituting one's feelings. There is, as a consequence, less freedom to experience, less comfort in selecting from among one's various possibilities and a lessened ability to savor vicariously the joys of one's family or fellows. The individual is often mistrustful of his own competence and/or doubtful of the friendliness and accepting nature of the environment. His or her world is one in which there is a constant danger of encountering severe anxiety and/or humiliating self-doubt and much attention must be devoted to avoiding these dangers rather than to the hearty experience of life events. Indeed, such persons often come for help to a mental health professional specifically because they feel they are missing the good things life has to offer.

If the sense of disappointment and fear of further anxiety reach intolerable levels, it may become necessary for the individual to turn away from the parts of life shared with others and to develop instead an increasingly narrow and self-centered focus of attention. Or, in the face of overwhelming disappointment and intolerable anxiety, he or she may even determine that life is not worth living, may attempt to commit suicide or develop symptoms incompatible with life.

Sexual awareness and sexual impulse are ordinarily experienced with interest, curiosity and delight. Yet, for a fearful person a sexual feeling may be akin to a dangerous enemy coming closer on a deadly mission. In this latter instance, the sexual feeling, although it arises from the person himself, may be dealt with by a kind of exteriorizing (pushing aside) process in which the person makes himself a stranger to his impulse and thus to himself. The inability to trust one's own feelings or, for that matter, even to acknowledge them as one's own results in a progressive narrowing of the world of experience. Such narrowing can reach disastrous proportions.

In the first of the two case studies that follow, a very desperate interval in the life of a young boy and his family will be described in some detail. The way he came to feel about himself and his reactions to those feelings led to a time when his death seemed a real possibility. He presented a genuine medical emergency. During the course of his hospitalization and in the period after, hundreds of physical, neurological and laboratory examinations were conducted. For a time, his physical condition had deteriorated and the doctors who were caring for him were themselves obsessed with the fear that some serious physical abnormality had been overlooked. None was ever found. I think I understand what happened to him, but I'm not positive. For, while I value very highly the theoretical formulations offered earlier in this chapter and view them as extremely useful in directing one's thinking about people in trouble, they go only so far. Theories are about people in general. In work with any specific individual, one must always keep clear focus upon that person and let the theories come along after. This is one of the reasons I much prefer to talk with a person before reading somebody else's reports about him. Person first. Theories second. Sometimes, you never do find out for sure what was wrong.

Case Study 1: *I I must must not not make make a a*
mistake mistake

Jeremiah Rogers, thirteen years old, was admitted to the psychiatric hospital in Vancouver, British Columbia, on May 24, 1973, because of his incapacitating fear of being dirty. His difficulties had developed gradually over the preceding six months, beginning with tearfulness and anxiety when faced with any pressure at home or in school. Finally, his withdrawal became quite extreme. He refused to go to school, and at home he was exclusively preoccupied with the need to bathe and cleanse himself. Eating meals became a prolonged torture because of his extreme caution in order to prevent food from touching the outside of his mouth. He felt that any food on his lips was contaminating. His body weight dropped from one hundred to seventy pounds during the half-year before his hospital admission.

On initial examination, he was fearful and robotlike. He walked in a taut, stiff-legged fashion in order to prevent his undershorts from rubbing up against his anal area. This was one feared source of contamination. There were many others. The history and the physical examination made clear that the change in him was a profound one. Every concern in his life had been eliminated except for his overwhelming preoccupation with keeping clean and avoiding various contaminations. Nevertheless, in stark contrast to his general fearfulness and deteriorated physical condition, he answered all questions in a particularly sophisticated and adult manner: "Good afternoon, Doctor. I am delighted to meet you. I have heard a great deal about you. Where is your couch? I thought that all psychiatrists had couches."

In the hospital his condition deteriorated. He refused to eat because "food makes bowel movements." Gradually, he became mute, his weight dropped to sixty pounds and he was near death because of his precarious state of nutritional imbalance. He was fed by the nursing staff with several hours required for each meal. He received large dosages of tranquilizer medications in the effort to help him relax and intravenous feedings were instituted in the face of his

49

life-threatened, almost moribund condition. He slowly began to respond. Over the next two months, his weight very gradually increased to eighty pounds and he became somewhat more active and cooperative. However, his preoccupation with cleanliness remained, and he required the full-time attention of a nurse for feeding and cleaning him. Bathing, which the patient requested almost continuously with a pleading, barely audible "bath, bath, bath!" required two to three hours each day. Each bowel movement, accomplished with anguish, was followed by an urgent plea for an immediate bath. At one period, the patient spoke by repeating each word two or sometimes three times. He explained, "I I have have to to say say each each word word twice twice because because I I don't don't want want to to make make any any mistake mistake Doctor Doctor."

The family history revealed that the patient was the oldest of three children. His father, vice president in a very large, family-managed department store chain in Washington state, was a tall, handsome, somewhat distant person, a marine officer during the Korean War, a graduate of an Eastern Ivy League college. He was rational, authoritative, attentive to detail and very preoccupied with the demands of his business. His composure was never shaken. He was always quite logical. He tried to remain objective and usually succeeded. He was, in short, a quite formidable man.

Jeremiah's mother was a very attractive, carefully dressed, tall (five feet, ten inches), excessively polite woman. Although she was more emotional than her husband, at no time was she ever seen with a hair out of place, with a wrinkle in her dress or with any sign of wear and tear despite the enormous burdens of her child's illness. She herself was the second oldest of nine children born in a working-class Eastern European immigrant family. She wanted to go to college, but because of the severe limits of family finances she left after one semester and went to work in one of the department stores owned by her future husband's family. He was sixteen years older than she. His parents were staunchly opposed to their relationship, opposition that was continued openly up to the time of their marriage and subtly afterwards. Following her marriage, the mother set out vigorously to establish her role in the newly won social circle.

She tried very hard. She became active in a great many civic and church clubs. It was not, however, until after her first child's birth, approximately three and one-half years after the marriage, that she had any sense of having any real chance to "make it" with her husband's family. Jeremiah was a model child. Indeed, in his mother's words, he was "a perfect child." He was deeply devoted to his mother, was something of a surrogate parent to the two younger children, was deeply religious, scholastically successful and generally very adult centered.

The onset of Jeremiah's difficulties appeared to be related both to his difficulties with the other boys in his grade school who resented his "sissy ways" and to the beginning of puberty and sexual interests. One of the first manifestations of the difficulties that were to come was his request for help from the minister in order to rid his mind of "filthy thoughts." He was very troubled by an urge to look at pictures of partly naked women in magazines. He was approximately twelve and a half years old at that time.

It is not possible to say for certain what caused Jeremiah's retreat from his life. However, certain aspects of life within the Rogers family might be discussed. There was an intense relationship between mother and child, accentuated by the mother's social insecurity and her use of her oldest child to acquire acceptance and status. Jeremiah was hers—was her—and the paternal grandparents' access to Jeremiah could only be through her. The mother's needs for Jeremiah to be a certain kind of child, to think and behave in a relatively restricted fashion was thus very intense. As Jeremiah grew, his mother generally babied him, addressing him frequently at twelve and thirteen as "my big boy" or "my dear one" or "Jeremy darling." By contrast, there was a substantial psychological distance which mother and son alike maintained with the strong, silent father. In some ways, the mother was a kind of older child of the father and Jeremiah was a younger child. Jeremiah was clearly his mother's favorite. With the father it was hard to tell. What was, however, most clearly evident about this family was that from early days on there was considerable pressure on the child to be not himself but rather to fulfill certain requirements of the family situation. Perhaps the task of living in compliance with all of the demands placed upon him

51

became impossible for Jeremiah when he was faced unexpectedly with emerging sexual feelings which had absolutely no place in his psychological view of himself. It then became necessary for this "model child" who moved so skillfully in an adult-centered world to cut down sharply on his openness to life experience, an openness already severely restricted by his overdeveloped sense of responsibility to behave perfectly. He tried desperately to maintain the integrity and order of his world, and thus his self-esteem, by concentrating upon the matter of cleanliness. Maintaining absolute cleanliness and making no mistakes were his sole concerns. These commitments necessitated a life-and-death struggle and, at several points, the struggle nearly cost him his life.

He narrowed down his world of experience in a last-ditch effort to maintain his self-esteem, to be the kind of person that it was so desperately necessary for him to be. He was "doing the best he could" under the circumstances to assure his survival as a self-respecting human being.

At this writing, one and a half years after Jeremiah's initial hospitalization, he has improved greatly and has entered the first year of high school. Family psychotherapy with Jeremiah and his parents continues and all medications have been discontinued for half a year. Jeremiah remains a fragile, rather obsessive person, serious about everything, but occasionally he shows warmth and spontaneous humor. His father is trying hard to develop a better relationship with Jeremiah and this means a great deal to everyone in the family.

Mercifully, most of the problems that come to a psychiatrist's attention are less catastrophic than the ones presented by Jeremiah Rogers and his family. They are often, however, complex and challenging nonetheless. In some instances, an individual patient or a single family will present an interlacing variety of difficulties including a definitive mental illness, deteriorating interpersonal relationships, complicated financial and social problems and, as well, those hard-to-articulate matters associated with a lack of meaning in life. There seem to be more such patients in recent years. This may be one of the consequences of the rapid social changes which have exsanguinated the meaning from the words "forever more" and offered in their place the more watery "for the time being."

Case Study 2: *The Couple Who Consulted a Builder and a Psychiatrist*

Martha Vincent made a suicide attempt, swallowing fourteen of her sleeping capsules all at once. She and her husband, both in their middle fifties, had had another of their frequent arguments and she locked herself in the bathroom, took the pills and thirty minutes later came out and told him what she had done. They rushed to a hospital emergency room for treatment. The next day the family doctor suggested a psychiatric consultation and the psychiatrist asked that both husband and wife come one day later for an appointment. The husband thought it would be better if he didn't come, so he didn't attend. Mrs. Vincent was promptly sent home from the first consultation to get him.

When the consultation finally began, the Vincents were both very tense. But they warmed up while talking with the psychiatrist who was, like them, middle-aged, upper-middle class, a little overweight and sociable enough to offer coffee to the two of them. Mrs. Vincent was quite depressed, cried easily, expressed ideas of hopelessness and described a many-month period of increasing sadness, sleeping difficulty and agitation. She was also pouting and her conversation was full of pointed digs at her husband whom she felt was tired of her, thoughtless, wanted a younger woman or at least a chance to run around.

Mr. Vincent, a moderately successful auto sales company executive, was quietly supportive and dealt with his wife's accusations in a calm way, trying to be reassuring to her. But when he was asked to talk about himself, he became very serious and talked with much feeling about the emptiness of his life. He was not much interested in his work any more, not very happy about their two children. Their twenty-six-year-old son had quit college for the third time and was of late searching for a legendary guru in northern Mexico. Their eighteen-year-old daughter, a dropout from the final year of high school, had just moved in with her new boyfriend. He said that life was flat for him in general and he didn't know whether to expand or contract, that is, to make more money or less, to spend more time in his sports car, to buy a bigger car or to give up the expensive hobby altogether, and so forth.

Both agreed that the quality of their relationship had deteriorated in recent years and each tended to blame the other. They agreed as to the events that had provoked Mrs. Vincent's recent, severe depression. Specifically, four or five months earlier, Mrs. Vincent became angry and depressed when her husband was too solicitous and danced too many times with another woman at a country club party. As usual, everybody had had a lot to drink. Mrs. Vincent left the party on her own and when her husband arrived home a few minutes later, there was a hysterical scene with Mrs. Vincent running for the aspirin bottle and her husband forcibly restraining her. The next day, they made up and had a serious talk about their lives. They decided that they should pull back from their social commitments, spend more time together, make love more often, sell their big expensive house and build a smaller place. They had their home appraised and were told that it would bring $90,000. They bought a building lot the next day and Mrs. Vincent contacted an architect and described the needs she and her husband would have in the decades ahead. The next three months were good months for the Vincents. They had more sense of purpose than they had experienced for some years. But when the bids for their dream house came back, it became clear that their alternative to a $90,000 house was a $90,000 house. He was angry. She was depressed. Things deteriorated between them, and two nights earlier, following a party where there was a great deal of alcohol, Mrs. Vincent attempted suicide.

There are several ways of looking at the events in the lives of this couple. One could focus on Mrs. Vincent and decide that she is the patient and that her depression is the illness that needs treatment. And indeed, her symptoms were severe and one could not ignore her immediate need for "something." Mental depressions almost always feel worse than they might appear to someone who isn't depressed and many times depressive symptoms, once begun, are extremely persistent. Very often, depressive symptoms persist or worsen even if the apparent cause is removed. They develop a kind of life of their own. In this instance, I felt I had to treat this depression actively. Treatment included careful assessment of the likelihood of another suicide attempt, a serious effort to let Mrs. Vincent know that I understood how very bad she felt and institution of a specific antidepression medication regime.

At the same time, it would have been hard to overlook the complex interpersonal problems present in this family and between this couple. She had organized her life around him and them—and they were drifting apart and he didn't care. She worked at it but didn't feel particularly pretty any more and her husband's clearly diminished sexual interest seemed to accentuate her fears. She was also disappointed in the children both because it didn't look like they were going to do much with their opportunities and because her husband blamed her for the way they were turning out. She blamed him too but felt very guilty. Perhaps, above all, she was haunted by the fear that he would leave her. She had never been alone and the thought overwhelmed her. So she found herself trying to read his mind. And the thoughts she read were not very reassuring.

Mr. Vincent had his problems too. He had been strictly reared, taught to work hard and to be intolerant of those who failed. And now he had a houseful of "failures," including, to a certain extent, himself. He viewed his wife's sexual approaches rather as if she were a baby kangaroo trying to jump into its mother's pouch and the more desperate she became, the stronger that image came to his mind. His children troubled him very much both because they seemed well on their way to going nowhere and because he felt very uncomfortable explaining what they were doing to his own still-critical parents and to the other couples in the Vincents' social group. Some of the latter appeared to have children who were very successful and Mr. Vincent felt increasingly uncomfortable with them. He also had some problems at work although he was reluctant to acknowledge in the presence of his wife that he was a poor third in a company with one hundred employees and that the number-four man was coming on strong.

One might also look at the Vincents in terms of the role designation that both had so totally taken on in their early youth and wonder how it had worked out for each of them. Mrs. Vincent in particular had burned a lot of bridges behind her in accepting an identity as wife and mother in a home where father knows best. She had come from such a home and in her early years had no encouragement to prepare for anything except caring for her future children and helping her future husband. It wasn't quite that bad. Sometimes she read, sometimes she went to lunch with friends, summers she played golf. But those were "portal to portal" parts of her life and her investment of self had been in husband, son and daughter. She was fifty-six, very frightened about the matter of money, particularly when she compared the earning potential of her husband ($30,000 plus per year) and herself. She could type but not well. And more important, she didn't want to type well. She felt somewhat guilty that her daughter seemed to be heading the same way and was planning to talk with her about finishing high school and going on to college.

Mrs. Vincent "despised the kind of woman who is a women's libber" but was beginning to think they were right.

Viewed somewhat more broadly in an existential frame of reference, the Vincents, individually and as a couple, were finding it hard to believe in the older meanings in their lives and at the moment they lacked the courage, imagination and hope to find new ones. The house incident was a good summary statement of the spot they were in. In their attempt to solve a problem, they were confronted with themselves. That confrontation could in theory have been a very stirring and creative opportunity. But it wasn't. They blamed each other for the lack of meaning each experienced. They were probably lucky that they didn't go on to build the new house. The Vincents had only the unused plans for the house and no answer. A good many other couples in the same boat have no answer plus a new and expensive house.

Part 2

THE THREE GENERATIONS: LOVE, RESPONSIBILITY AND PROPERTY

To a large degree reality is whatever the people who are around at the time agree to. We think in the plural. Female identical twins in their mid-twenties, cousins of this writer, were married within a short interval. When I saw one of them a few months later and asked, "How's married life?" she replied, "We like it fine!"—meaning she and her twin. It's like that for sisters, sorority sisters and sisters-under-the-skin. And brothers as well. And sisters and brothers. We like to agree. We even like to agree that a subject is important enough to disagree over. We use each other to validate our world and then to relax. To turn one's back on someone is a more cruel rebuke than to dispute them, however forcefully. So, everywhere there are clubs and societies and people who are "in" and those who don't qualify. In most of those societies and clubs, the worst one inside, once in, is more intimately and tenderly held than the best one outside. With the passage of time, the insiders develop "language," history, battle scars and children for whom "in" status is sought. The separation from those outside then becomes greater. So, there are families, coreligionists, social class allegiances, national and international bonds. There is also talk of a brotherhood of mankind, but it is hard actually to grasp what that means. It is a little like thinking about one's grandchildren's grandchildren.

Our world has grown much smaller in recent decades. However, the away-from-home attractiveness of one's conationals is surprisingly consistent. For verification, check the lobbies of the Tokyo, Delhi and Addis Ababa Hiltons. This writer spent several very interesting years talking with international students on North American and Asian college campuses in the late 60s and early 70s. Most remarkable was the almost exclusive cohesiveness of conationals when overseas. That is, Asian students stay together with other Asian students from the home country while in North America. Equally, despite prior plans and expectations, most North Americans group with North Americans while in Asia. The explanations offered by each of the overseas student groups took the form of identical criticism of the host nationals whose sincerity, depth, honesty and motivation when hospitable was questioned. Unstated but at the heart of all who were disappointed (and all were) was this: "They don't seem to recognize what a special person I am. My Phi Beta Kappa key and ready smile mean nothing to them. Don't they know about Amherst College?"[1] And for the Asians in North America, there was the almost universal experience of being invited for Thanksgiving dinner, being offered an instant and intense cross-cultural friendship—"but they never called again." In the normal course of things, we tend to associate with individuals whose training and experience is most like our own, people able to understand and appreciate our efforts. This is not surprising. In the words of J. M. Thorburn, "All the genuine, deep delight of life is in showing people the mudpies you have made; and life is at its best when we confidingly recommend our mudpies to each other's sympathetic consideration."[2]

One of the important characteristics of any group is the nature of the agreements as to what should take place between the generations. Social change, when translated into life experience, means alteration in the ways of relating between parents, children and grandparents. The change from rural to urban society meant that the children didn't work with and for the parents any more. The changes brought to postwar Japan by the American soldiers meant that the children didn't have to pay so much attention to the parents' ideas. The recent mobility in North America means, among other changes, that the parents don't have to pay for the grandparents any more.

All changes cost something and the magnitude of social change has been enormous these last decades. One can assume that the costs may not yet be fully counted. Nor is it clear precisely where to look in taking measure. Yet, for this writer it seems likely that change in relationship patterns between the three generations may prove to be the most important of all.

In the three chapters that follow, the domination of family and group values over individual consciousness will be considered in some detail.

The Three Generations: Love, Responsibility and Property

The first chapter describes two versions of a cruel society, a selfish arrangement of three-generational living that allowed those with power to keep it as long as they could. Perhaps the words *cruel* and *selfish* are too negative and one-sided. The clarity of values and the strict assignment of role in these cultures did serve to relieve people of the need to think much about the meaning of life. Chapter 4, "No More Grandmothers, No More Grandfathers: Learning from Peers," and Chapter 5, "Living as an Older Person," consider the manner in which two decades of social mobility and rapidly changing social values have influenced the way people of differing generations feel about each other, and thus themselves.

CHAPTER 3

Once Upon a Time, Old People Didn't Like Young People: A Legend

Once upon a time the world was populated by many different races who closely resembled contemporary man except that the older people didn't like the younger people. They were suspicious and jealous and fearful of them. The parents and grandparents not only didn't like children from other families, they didn't even like their own. There were minor differences from family to family and nation to nation and in some places the hostility was more overt than in others. But fundamentally, there was no doubt about it. All over the world, the older people didn't like the younger ones. It was a time which calls to mind what the writer Jacques Prevert said about husbands, wives and others who lived together. "If all the people who were living together were in love, this globe would light up like a shining star." But ages ago, the lack of love was between parents and their children, between older people and the generation upcoming.

In general, the antipathy between the two groups began early in the life of the children and its extent was often extreme. Extraordinarily coercive steps were taken to effect complete regimentation of the thoughts and actions permitted young people. More ominously, the need to control them led to the contrivance and manufacture of wars against other nations' young people (whose parents in turn readily accepted the challenge). The fundamental purpose of the adults on both sides was the control and redirection of aggressive impulses born of the interaction of the two generations. Outside wars prevented the young from turning on the old and along with other customs, traditions and religious prohibitions preserved the power of the parents' generation an extra fifteen to twenty years, even to the period of enfeeblement or death. Then, since children almost always emulate their parents no matter what the nature of the relationship, the struggle was repeated anew between the former children, now parents, and the third generation. In this way, the process continued for a very long time.

THE EASTERN (ASIAN) PATTERN

At a certain place on the Eastern continent, the relationship between older and younger people was extraordinarily cordial until the children reached school age. At that point, the carefree, indulged, essentially playful life of early childhood was abruptly terminated. The children began a disciplined process of control of thought and behavior which, overnight, obliged them to become serious. Each child was taught to manifest a depreciation of self and other young people while at the same time demonstrating an exaggerated respect for all older people. Childhood hours were devoted to putting to memory the rules, sayings, traditions and expectations of the older people by means of tedious copying and mindless recitation. From the beginning of primary school, for seven or eight hours each day over a period of many years, the child would repeat, repeat, copy, copy, repeat again. Tedium, discipline, order, control, regimentation, suppression of laughter, denial of impulse and the development of an extensive repertoire of self-effacing bows and self-critiques occupied each child's attention. Deviation from what was taught was unthinkable; questioning the ideas of a parent or a teacher was intolerable. Above all, the children were taught, "Never trust your own feelings unless they tell you to serve and honor your elders and to accept your responsibilities as assigned."

There were many of that older generation to serve. In addition to teachers, parents and grandparents, the "extended family" tradition established a hierarchy containing countless aunts and uncles, great-aunts and great-uncles, older cousins and older friends of the family, all of whom lived within the same house or nearby. The child was obliged on every possible occasion to demonstrate respect to each elder. Furthermore, the intensity of the allegiance of the older people to each other made an affront to any one of them an affront to all. To contest a parent, teacher, aunt or uncle was an extreme offense. The power of the system

63

enforcing reverence to elders was so great that it was policed not only by the older generation but by group action of the younger people themselves. The child who attempted to deviate from the set patterns was descended upon from all sides by teachers, parents, grandparents, great-aunts and great-uncles and, no less, by brothers, sisters and classmates. Accordingly, deviation was rare.

If the influence of old over young was to be sustained, emerging sexual impulses needed to be controlled and channeled in a manner that ultimately reinforced the authority of the parents. In practice, this was done in the following manner: After early childhood, boys and girls were separated and kept separate until the time of their marriage. Friendships between the sexes were not allowed. Dating was unknown. The "divide and conquer" system imposed upon the boys and girls was further reinforced by the psychologically effective mechanism of marrying older boys to quite young girls. Since usual marriage took place between a boy in his mid-twenties and a girl some six years his junior, boys and girls had no future with peers of the opposite sex. Thus, at the time deemed appropriate for marriage, the parents determined all details, including choice of the mate. The marriage of children served as a basis for linkage between groups who sought an allegiance with each other. It is insufficient to say that the wishes of the children with regard to the mate were rarely decisive. Rather, the entire social structure of the society placed full authority in the hands of the parents or older people.

Even after marriage and indeed because of the marriage, the power of the older generation over the younger remained very great. Ordinarily, the young bride came into the home of her husband's parents where she frequently endured a low status and at times became the scapegoat of her husband's mother. The acceptance of this role by the young wife was, of course, guaranteed by the kind of educational experience and role models presented to all girls in early childhood and adolescence. In ordinary circumstances, girls were given precisely that education which assured that they would perform the role of obedient wife and obedient daughter-in-law. In this kind of society, the suppression of women was very great. However, it should be viewed not primarily as the power of men over women but rather as a necessary ingredient in the maintenance of superiority by older people over younger people.

The older people maintained a regular state of warfare with neighboring nations which they obliged the young people to fight. They also developed a system to delay distribution of resources and wealth which preserved for themselves power and control long after the young had matured. The wars, though continuous, were more often than not gratuitous; that is, the decision to go to war was by no means mandatory. Over and over again, a gratuitous war, an elective war, was undertaken by the older people and fought by the younger people. Of course, the leaders of the country, the older people, never described any of the wars as unnecessary. Instead, a precipitant such as a religious affront or a threat to national honor provided the necessary rationalization. Many writers in commenting upon these once-upon-a-time wars have suggested that there might have been fewer conflicts if older people had been obliged to fight them personally. Such writers, however, ignore the fact that an important cause of war during that particular time was the hostility of parents toward their own children. War was a technique by which young people's strength and purpose was dissipated.

It was not only through control of the education of the young, restriction of youthful sexuality, separation of the sexes, parental decision making in marriage and the establishment of gratuitous wars that young people were held in check. The whole of the civilization—its laws, its folkways, its religious beliefs and the system for passing possessions from generation to generation—all served to discourage young people from contesting the authority of their elders. The religion called for worshipful respect and devotion to one's homeland, to one's living parents or dead ancestors and to an ill-defined but essentially unifying cosmic presence. Filial piety was thus equated with both patriotism and spirituality and was the cornerstone of the basic belief system. Daily ritual visits to the parents as a form of daily prayer were made by the young children, young adults and adults with surviving parents. This kind of devotion necessitated a denial of aggressive or acquisitional tendencies and provided a psychological state of mind consistent with delayed receipt of family wealth or assumption of decision-making power. The power, the money and the position of respect remained in the hands of the older people until extreme enfeeblement or death overtook them. Then and only then, the "young person," grown to middle life, at last "came into his own." He prepared to sustain his power against the threat of premature readiness to rule on the part of his own children. He used the words and actions of the children's grandparents to justify his behavior.

In general, the process was effective. It continued for a very long time.

THE WESTERN PATTERN—CLOSER TO HOME

The once-upon-a-time Western society differed in certain respects from the Eastern. There was more industrialization and substantially greater wealth. Individual family units were smaller. There was more apparent freedom of movement and expression granted to the children. However, the essential antipathy of the older to the younger generation closely approximated that present in Eastern lands. The once-upon-a-time Western education did not crush the spirit or regiment the children as thoroughly and relentlessly as did schools in the East. Nevertheless, Western schools were generally mediocre and uninteresting. From generation to generation, the boredom of the primary and secondary education was endured, then passed on essentially unchanged to the next group of children. In Eastern society, it was fruitless for the child even to consider protesting the educational system. In the West, children were free to contest the system but never strong enough to modify it. A modicum of freedom led to many open protests. However, sufficient power resided with the adults to defeat the children and maintain the status quo. A similar situation existed within families. Because there were only two adults per family, Western parents lacked absolute authority over the children who, as a consequence, launched rebellions in late childhood or adolescent years. Such rebellion, however, provoked an escalating series of social forces mounted to restore order. Four kinds of social agencies enforced conformity. They were:

1. Enforcement functions and disciplining responsibilities among teachers in the primary and secondary schools.
2. If the school disciplinary force proved inadequate, juvenile probation and correctional institutions were available, primarily for children of the lower social class.
3. Private military or boarding schools and professionals such as psychotherapists and counselors served as additional social controllers among rebellious children of the upper classes.
4. Ultimately, for males, assignment to the military service and/or to war

was available whenever youthful protest began to amass sufficient power to threaten genuinely the authority and power of the older generation.

How this Western system worked to sustain control of the children and young adults by the parental generation is illustrated in the following family history. Since all social phenomena tend to be more direct, explicit and less camouflaged among the poor, the family to be described is from a lower social class. Similar relationship patterns were to be found year after year in tens of thousands of homes throughout the once-upon-a-time Western world.

In addition to the mother and father, there were three sons, two of whom were to have very difficult experiences during their adolescence and young adult years. There were also two daughters, one of whom was to become pregnant while still a high school student. Both parents worked in laboring jobs, neither having completed high school. They were church-going, hard-working people who tended to see things in the rather inflexible fashion that they were taught. Although their authority weakened as each of the children grew older, the parents were obliged to maintain the children's behavior as it "ought to be," that is, in accordance with the prevailing morality of the community. There were no aunts, uncles or grandparents around. The parents lived alone with their children.

The oldest boy did relatively well in school until he reached the age of thirteen. Then he began to react against the authority of his mother and father and as well against an eighth-grade teacher. The father responded with threats and occasional physical beatings. Within the school system, the boy was grouped with several other "rebellious students" and he found himself increasingly isolated from the average members of his class. This situation reached intolerable levels in his junior year of high school and following repeated truancies, the legal officer of the juvenile court was called in. The boy faced a consolidation of adult figures against him—teachers, the principal and assistant principal, parents, the minister, and then the juvenile court officer and judge. On his seventeenth birthday he damaged the family automobile while truant from school. This set off a series of mounting difficulties. The father struck the son who very nearly returned the blows. Instead, the boy expressed the pre-enlistment sentiments voiced before and since by countless others: "If you ever raise your hand at me again, I'll knock you on your ass even if you are my father." One month later, with the permission of the parents, the boy enlisted in the navy.

The Three Generations: Love, Responsibility and Property

The next two children were a boy and a girl who adjusted to the requirements of the family and the school without too much difficulty, but the fourth and fifth youngsters, a closely spaced boy and girl, presented enormous problems. The rebelliousness and resentment of the oldest son was pale indeed when compared with the third son, a boy who didn't like the school system, fought with his siblings, feared and hated his father and was openly contemptuous of his mother. At fifteen he was on probation for truancy and fighting in school. At sixteen, he spent three months in a boys' and young men's "correctional institution." There, he found himself among other poor, aggressive, largely uneducated youthful males who handled their resentments of adults by direct assault. Ninety-five percent of the other young people in the once-upon-a-time prison matched this general description. He learned angry and mean things in his brief stay in boys' and young men's prison. Following his release, there was a fight in the family in which he struck his mother and his father and the police were called. After some further deliberations involving the family, the minister, a judge and a school principal, this son also elected to go into military service. There he had a very difficult time for the first several years and spent some months in a military stockade. Ultimately, however, he acquiesced to the authority of his officers and after four years he left the service honorably and with a much greater acceptance of the authority of older people. When released from service at twenty-one, he demonstrated a kind of subdued resignation to his own life. He regretted being unable to complete high school but went to work in a service station and was soon married. In this lower socioeconomic family, a spirit of "one penis to a household" prevailed and it was ultimately necessary for the rebellious sons to leave for the military.

The youngest child, a girl fourteen months her brother's junior, began to have difficulty with the father and mother at approximately the same time as her next older brother. She, however, left the family at the age of seventeen because of a premarital pregnancy. For a daughter in this kind of family, most of the tensions existed in the area of sexuality. In Western schools, the boys and girls attended classes together and individual friendships were not particularly discouraged. However, from early days every girl was admonished that premarital pregnancy would bring unthinkable shame upon her and her family. And it was in this manner that the power of adults over their daughters was sustained. In Western culture, boys and girls studied and played together in such a way that no matter what the amount of prohibition or restraint, a certain number of the girls inevitably became pregnant out of wedlock. Whether the percentage was one girl in thirty or one in ten made little difference. The example of each girl's social martyrdom was widely heralded throughout the society. It was a very effective system. Social and sexual taboos inscribed in religious writings were passed on from the old to the young. A certain percentage of the young violated these tenets and the severest sanctions were imposed. Each seventeen-year-old girl's pregnancy, painful though it was, served a vital purpose in the maintenance of the power of older people over younger people. She became an example of the consequences of contesting parental authority or wisdom. She was obliged to leave school, family and community to bear an unwanted child in another setting among strangers.

The arrangement was not dissimilar to that described in the Shirley Jackson short story "The Lottery," in which an unnamed society annually selected by lot one from its midst who was then stoned as a sacrifice to the gods.[1] The pregnant but unmarried girl's plight, though short of death, served as a grim warning to others not to contest the authority, wisdom and power of the older generation.

The Western gratuitous war played an important role in controlling the lives of the young people. The society had an average of one war every ten to fifteen years and, including periods of mobilization and demobilization, approximately 20 to 25 percent of the history of the period was spent in preparation for or recovery from warfare. The wars were varied in nature. One took place within the geographic boundaries of the country and two were initiated against neighbors. A fourth war was actually started by the older people of two other countries. But the leaders decided, "Why not join in?" So they did. As methods of transportation improved, it was possible to launch and receive assaults from great distances. This was important because improved transportation systems also served to increase affectional bonds between neighboring countries and it became necessary to select enemies in more geographically remote settings. Every attempt was made to assure equity in the selection of soldiers. In each village, the older people were called upon to select which of their young men would go to war.

There were a variety of "industry by industry" and "profession by profession" rules which also served to preserve the requisites of older workers and professionals. For those young people working toward professional roles, the educational process was dragged on as long as possible. To become a doctor took fourteen years or longer after high school graduation. Achieving status as a psychoanalyst required a record twenty years of study after high school. To receive an advanced degree in the study of the humanities required, on the average, from six to nine years of work beyond high school, occasionally twelve years. For those in academic careers, a probationary period of three to six years was imposed before they were judged by their older colleagues with regard to competence for tenure. In general, younger teachers with strong allegiance to students fared very poorly when judged by their older colleagues. Young teachers were obliged to choose where their loyalty and commitment rested—with students or with older professors and administration.

In industry, a seniority system was maintained which guaranteed that younger people would not be employed until all older persons who wished to work were secure. From time to time discussions centering on the favoritism toward older workers took place, but old and young accepted the explanation that "life would be intolerable if special security, special honor and special reward were not reserved for those who are older. The thought that our own children could replace us would be very unfriendly indeed. Who would want to have children under such circumstances?"

In the West, as in the East, the old held onto power and money as long as possible. The manner of distribution of Western wealth was of paramount importance since the society heavily interested itself in money and material possessions. Money and the power that it brought were largely reserved for older people and the giving and withholding of money as a bribe, bait and medium of behavior control was well developed in Western society. Some young people organized their lives around the matter of receiving money from their parents from early childhood until they reached their fifties. Some parents even succeeded in controlling the money left to children after their own death, establishing trusts so that money came only in small amounts until they, the children, had grown quite old.

THE BEGINNING OF CIVILIZATION

While handwriting as we know it had yet to be invented, for Ajote, who was now age thirty-eight, it was unmistakably on the wall. He slept uneasily in his cave, feeling closed in, surrounded, trapped. In the early morning hours, he often thought of the afternoon some thirteen summers before when he had stealthfully slain the headman of the tribe in which he lived. A few discreet weeks after the murder, he had taken the cave of the headman and with it leadership of the group. He ruled during the succeeding thirteen years. But now, Ajote began to cough and to spit red which was a certain beginning of a loss of strength and power. For a headman, such loss meant death. Ajote, frightened, had attempted to do a little political friend making, trying to warm up to some of the younger men by making friendly gestures on the hunts. But, as is usually the case with appeasing gestures motivated by fear, these efforts made him only more afraid.

He thought of fleeing, but to where? The extent of his world was only the hunting area of the tribe—the caves in which they lived, the lake below and some fifty square miles of forest bounded by the far hills. He was restrained from penetrating those boundaries, recalling the murderous treatment he had afforded a strange man who had fled from those far hills and come toward their lake three summers before. His apprehensiveness mounted as he recalled that the murdered stranger had been, like himself, an older man. Why had he come?

One day, while Ajote was coughing and spitting he saw the most agile and unfriendly of the younger men watching him. He felt he had no hope and decided to flee from the group. That night, while the others slept, he left the cave, carrying food and a weapon. He reached the far hills at dawn and an hour later lay hidden one hundred yards from the central gathering place of the tribe who lived beyond the hills. Several of the young men in this group resembled the older man who had been slain. Ajote experienced great fear and decided to return to his own tribe.

However, he took four days to make that five-hour journey and when he returned he had carefully practiced this story which he told with great feeling to the people of his tribe: A dream had foretold imminent danger to the group. He had seen an image of many of their women and young people killed. He remembered specifically the crushed head of the strong young man who had observed him coughing. In the dream, a strange beast, half-mortal, half-animal, had led him, Ajote, to the far hills to avenge the slayings. On awakening he had immediately gone to the far hills as instructed and discovered that the people there were making preparations for an attack as had been predicted in the dream.

The Three Generations: Love, Responsibility and Property

The events that followed made Ajote the leader of the group as never before. He had foretold the grave danger. He had caused his tribe to send its younger men over the hills in time to head off the assault. In that war, the strong young man who had observed Ajote's coughing was, as foretold in the dream, killed. Ajote subsequently made known to all what was necessary to preserve the group against other enemies. All the other young men were very respectful to Ajote. This was the beginning of once-upon-a-time civilization.

CHAPTER 4

No More Grandmothers, No More Grandfathers: Learning from Peers

When his remaining two grandparents died in close succession, twelve-year-old John Lorton told his father, "You're next, Dad, and then me. Our Grandmas were a screen that shielded us both. I'm afraid."

And an ancient Chinese blessing is the wish: "That the Grandfather goes first, then the father, then the son."

For generations and generations, almost every individual's sense of "who I am" has been cast within the broad frame of "Thomas, son of John and Mary who were in turn son of Martin and Louise and daughter of Sidney and Rose."

To be born outside that frame or to be orphaned was (and is) to be at great risk, at times to the point of death. Through the centuries, the privileged child was simultaneously grandchild, nephew, niece, godson, goddaughter, first, second, third cousin and/or betrothed to the daughter of my father's oldest friend and classmate. This order within relationships described the past and fixed the present as the route to a pre-arranged, understood future. The lineage of kings was both proud legend of what had been and a promise of certainty in a world fraught with ambiguity.

In many stable, long-established societies, grandparents provided a preserving, conservative input, one emphasizing traditions and telling the history of "our" people. They both offered a reinforcement of the authority of the children's parents and yet attenuated the tension between parents and children through love and advice offered to each. The matter of love is still important because all too often that which makes life bearable is the fact that somebody loves you no matter what you do.

73

You can earn respect and affection in the street gang or with one's peers, but you have to earn it everyday. Unconditional love is sometimes easier for grandparents than parents because they have less complicated responsibilities and because they may see more clearly the continuity of their life in the grandchild. Further, in extended family situations, grandparents often provide more flexibility for struggle within the family (without leaving it) for children who come to feel that their job in life is to get rid of their parents.

Grandparents assumed responsibility for inculcating, reinforcing and romanticizing belief systems which form the basis through life for the young person's understanding of:

> *This* is who *I* am.
> *This* is what I believe.
> *This* is why I choose to behave as I do.
> *This* is what I believe in even if my
>   appetites, instincts and fears
>   would lead me elsewhere.

Perhaps more important than the teaching of specific rules for behaving was the fact that an environment was provided in which *the child learned to believe in believing, learned attitudes that might facilitate survival in the face of the most disheartening and disillusioning events.* The continuity of grandfather and grandmother through parents and through children is inherently reassuring. There is promise of more to come. Traditional systems taught not only rules. They made clear that life is continuous and that life and believing are synonymous.

We take for granted that everybody believes or could believe in something. This is not the case. The complex nature of both *belief itself* and *belief in believing* has been articulated by the distinguished American psychiatrist Jules Masserman in a remarkable 1953 paper, "Faith and Delusion in Psychotherapy."[1] He pointed out that the life of almost everyone now living and everyone who ever lived has been made more comfortable and satisfying by faith in the validity of one, two or three deeply held beliefs. First, many hold to the existence of a transcending God or Gods, a divine spirit who offers meaning, inspiration, guidance and hope for everlasting life. Other persons demonstrate faith in the inherent worthwhileness of the work of man, his industries, her writing, his farms, her science. They see obvious purpose in developing this planet and even in efforts to repeat the process on some other star satellite. The third major belief is in the essential truth of brotherhood, love, sexuality, loyality, fidelity and the communion between fellow beings.

An overwhelming majority of people in every society are deeply committed to the "reality," the "correctness," the "proven" status of one, two or three of these ideas, that is, God, work and/or love are *real.* But not everybody. Many of those who are called "schizophrenic" live lives in sharp contrast to the majority of their family and neighbors in that they refuse to believe in such assumptions. They behave as if they believed, and sometimes they directly say, "No God, no work, no love. Outright lies! Or at best, trivial." Such individuals are very threatening to others. For verification of the power of such threat, the reader might ask, "How would I feel, personally, about someone living in my midst who believed neither in a meaning to life nor in the value of any person's work or could never appreciate and demonstrate how good it is to be together?"

Masserman pointed out that all three of these fundamental beliefs may actually be "delusions," the vain hopes that enable the "normal" men, women and children to lead anxiety-free lives in villages and megalopoli around the world. When an individual has repudiated or abandoned the beliefs and the style of life that others lead, the possibilities of living together are diminished. No less, the possibility of living with oneself and life itself may be equally threatened. What would transpire in a world of societies where the individuals either believed in very little and/or where there was little sharing in what they did believe?

Inevitably, life is not easy. There are moments in every person's history when the very best one can do is to hang on to hope, to await another day, to be optimistic or stoic or inwardly turned or to seek another to hold one's hand. Even the most successful person will face despair if he encounters all of his personal critics on the same day. Most who are in jails, many who drift into the skid row areas in contemporary cities, most who contemplate taking their own lives, many who become sick with the symptoms that are called mental illness, are individuals who lack either the talent, the experience, the instruction, the internal resources and/or the faith (belief) to:

Keep trying
Hang on
Await another day
Be optimistic
Be stoic
Be speculative
Turn one's thoughts inward
Seek release from anxiety that
   accompanies a clasping of fingers
   with another person

In the moments when the best one can do is not give up and/or not make bad things worse, memories of what grandparents had to say and demonstrate can become very important: "We made it through bad times by sticking together, by believing in ourselves, by helping each other, by showing love, by working incredibly hard and by living the life that we believe in." The finest technology in the world diminishes not one whit the importance of a personal value system which guides the individual, group and society through moments when the exigencies of life strip away all that is casually worn. In every life such moments come. That suicide is now a growing choice of many young people in many Western societies is an ominous sign. It may reveal that freedom from the burden of the aged with their nostalgic messages may be more than the young can endure. Many have spoken of effects upon grandmothers and grandfathers of being separated from the succeeding generations. There is now growing evidence that such separation may be equally destructive to the young. The grandparental role in society has been an imprinting which taught the young person that living is living out beliefs. For many, that input has been largely interrupted. The family, which formerly included grandparents, aunts, uncles, great-aunts, great-uncles and godparents, has now become the two-generation (nuclear) family plus "friends." The "we" of young people is much more likely to be a reference to their own generation rather than to a family system of self, parents and parents' parents. Since many parents are busy and tired, divorcing in record numbers and not too certain anyway about what is of value, it is now the boasting of peers and the safe-adventure ditties on television that have largely replaced the stories grandparents had to tell. Those stories were forcefully and repeatedly told from the child's earliest days. They were

76

reinforced by believing peers, amplified by ritual, choice food, song and dance and ultimately personally consecrated in some initiation rite.

THE CHILDREN OF THE 1950s, 60s AND 70s

No summary statement encompasses all that has happened to the 225 million people living in North America in the last twenty-five years. Almost all of us have lived through and been changed by the extraordinary events of the times. Even those who attempted to barricade themselves and their families from surrounding events found no way to stem the tide of change. Our curiosity as a species is too great. Someone is always turning on the television and then you're in the middle of it. Television makes it difficult to live quietly alongside the carnival while the rest of the world rides the roller coaster. While the barricaders are working on the walls and the moat, the small children sit in the living room twenty hours per week watching the animated screen. Still, there are families who to an extent have sustained their traditional way of life without much concession to all that was going on around them. The family stayed cohesive. The mother stayed home. Religion remained important. Everybody had their jobs to do. The hierarchies stood. The parents carefully monitored the children's associates. And, of course, at the other end of the continuum, that is, among very poor and marginally educated people, changes are always slow in coming.

Most young people growing up in the 1950s, 60s and 70s differ in important respects from their predecessors of earlier generations. To begin with, there are a great many of them. Half the people who ever lived live today and half of these are twenty-two or younger. Many of the children who grew up in North America are among *the first in the history of the world* to be educated by people neither approved of nor supervised by the local people—parents, teachers, religious leaders, school board, tribal or city council. These children learned to trust what they saw on television because of the dependability, tenderness and honesty of Captain Kangaroo and Mr. Green Jeans, Winky Dink, story ladies and Sesame Street. Two decades later, they were watching Walter Cronkite and the TV specials on the shootings at Kent State, the funerals of Martin Luther King, Jack and Bobby Kennedy, the ugly story of My Lai, Vietnam and the still unfolding tales of Watergate, FBI and CIA. Not only were they greatly influenced by what they saw but the mode of presentation made the on-the-spot history lessons different from the ones their parents had received twenty-five years before. Television says, "Here are the facts we have and here are the pictures. Some things aren't certain. These you will have to decide for yourself."

The "extended family members" introduced by television also served to demonstrate to young people how they have a "right" to be treated in the home and at school. No injustice to a child is left uncorrected beyond the second commercial.

The children of the 1950s, 60s and 70s have been more on their own. Affluence, the move to the suburbs, working mothers and smaller homes to care for, all made the labor of children seem less essential. Children weren't part of the work force. They were free to travel, play or whatever. There weren't many things they *had* to do. Their parents were busy. Teachers were no longer particularly feared. Sundays were given over to watching the football games. There was, in many families, a lessening of executive functions of the older people with regard to the children. In families where father continued to "know best," the children were faced with classmates and friends who raised questions and offered attractive alternatives. Of course, the more than six hundred thousand children whose parents obtained divorces each year were often among the group thrown on their own.

The "Cult of the Wonderful Adolescent" began in the 1950s, reached a lofty high in the 1960s, then retreated abruptly in the 1970s. It was an intoxicating era in which the music of the Beatles, Bob Dylan and Coltrane, the generation of writers after J. D. Salinger's *Catcher in the Rye*[2] and the young film makers following in the tradition of Bergman, Fellini, Antonioni and Warhol all starred the young hero. The "progressive educators" who carried the message of John Dewey, Columbia University Teacher's College and the givers of advice who came after the durable Dr. Ben Spock all kept a spotlight on the young. They were contributors to young people discovering, "I'm very important." For many of these young people the intoxication, group intimacy and heady blend of drugs and lots of leisure supported the illusion, "I'm creative as well." And, since many young people knew more about drugs than their parents, teachers, doctors, ministers and police critics, it was possible to feel, "There's a lot I could teach them."

78

No More Grandmothers, No More Grandfathers

These "everybody is equal" forces, augmented by writers like Ginsberg, Mailer and Vonnegut, and above all, the process of growing up with other liberally reared children, also greatly reduced the level of shame and guilt about sex and the body that has so dominated the adolescent and later years of most now grown to middle age. This is quite an important matter. Guilt over sex and shame about one's body have been traditional among educated people for a long time. If the art of making people ashamed goes out of style, what will happen?

As a case in point, if a bit stylized, consider the following paragraphs taken from a mischievous book called *Plain Facts for Old and Young*. It was written by a doctor. Thousands and thousands of copies were sold. It was passed from generation to generation. It added to the level of misery and unhappiness of most who read it.

CURE OF THE HABIT

The preliminary step in treatment is always to cure the vice itself if it still exists. The methods adopted for this purpose must differ according to the age of the individual patient.

In children, especially those who have recently acquired the habit, it can be broken up by admonishing them of its sinfulness, and portraying in vivid colours its terrible results, if the child is old enough to comprehend such admonitions. In addition to faithful warnings, the attention of the child should be fully occupied by work, study, or pleasant recreation. He should not be left alone at any time lest he yield to temptation. Work is an excellent remedy; work that will really make him very tired, so that when he goes to bed he will have no disposition to defile himself. It is best to place such a child under the care of a faithful person of older years, whose special duty shall be to watch him night and day until the habit is thoroughly overcome.

In younger children, with whom moral considerations will have no particular weight, other devices may be used. Bandaging the parts has been practised with success. Tying the hands is also successful in some cases; but this will not always succeed, for they will often contrive to continue the habit in other ways, as by working the limbs, or lying upon the abdomen. Covering the organs with a cage has been practised with entire success. A remedy which is almost always successful in small boys is circumcision, especially when there is any degree of phimosis. The operation should be performed by a surgeon without administering an anaesthetic, as the brief pain attending the operation will have a salutary effect upon the mind, especially if it be connected with the idea of punishment, as it may well be in some cases. The soreness which continues for several weeks interrupts the practice, and if it had not previously become too firmly fixed, it may be forgotten and not resumed. If any attempt is made to watch the child, he should be so carefully surrounded by vigilance that he cannot possibly transgress without detection. If he is only partially watched, he soon learns to elude observation, and thus the effect is only to make him cunning in his vice.

In adults or youth a different plan must be pursued. In these cases, moral considerations, and the inevitable consequences to health of body and mind, are the chief influences by which a reform is to be effected, if at all. These considerations may be urged with all possible eloquence and earnestness, but should not be exaggerated. The truth is terrible enough.[3]

How has it worked? What happens when children are out from under the relentless imprinting of values that grandparents, uncles, aunts, ministers and parents formerly provided? What happens when the shame, guilt and fear associated with sexuality is largely lifted? What happens when the principal teachers of young people are young people? What happens when young people decide to decide for themselves?

In many families, the effects of all these events have been devastating. I think that as a group, the North American children of the 1950s, 60s and 70s were among the hardest to raise of any in this (or any) century. The general disappearance of grandparents as ultimate authorities, the pace of life and variety of activities of contemporary parents and the Pied Piper effects of identification with youth culture has taken a considerable toll.

Many, many of the middle-aged individuals who have come to my office to talk over their divorce plans or their sense of purposelessness are people who have lived through dreadful experiences with their children. Drugs, sex, police, violence, wandering off, quitting school, challenge and lack of respect on the part of young people have led to the dissolution of many contemporary families. Disappointment about what has happened to their children caused many parents to blame each other. People like to stay with and return to people with whom they have shared victories and celebrations. Ex-partners in bankrupt businesses avoid lunching together. In thousands of families, the consequences of overwhelming social change after World War Two were shattered hopes and plans of parents for their children.

Not so long ago, I was asked to serve as a consultant to an ongoing family psychotherapy program that wasn't working out very well. The therapist had started with one of the teenagers, then expanded the program to include the parents and older sister, and, at my suggestion, had asked the grandparents to participate as well. They were strangers to me but I recognized them by name as members of a prominent local Jewish family. I walked into the room where they were all sitting and realized that someone was smoking marijuana. It was the daughter, about eighteen. The younger boy, seventeen, wore a large crucifix. The grandparents were worried. The mother was nervously smiling. The father was slumped in his chair. I looked around and started to laugh. The mother said, "I feel exactly the same way. I'd be laughing myself if I wasn't so busy crying."

Other times, there was no possible way to laugh. Many youngsters who left home because there was no meaning there fared worse in a world of strangers. For some of them, the confrontation with what was missing in themselves awaited completion of a migration across the continent to the West Coast. Then there was no place to go. The suicide note reproduced below was left by a twenty-four-year-old woman, far from home. It was addressed to her boyfriend. One of how many thousands of final messages that came back to heartbroken families, to be read and reread, it said everything and nothing.

> Dear Tom,
>
> You must forgive me and carry on. You have so much strength in you and I would hate to see your ability go to waste. And never, but NEVER blame yourself for what has happened. My lows are so outrageous that I can't see living with them for the rest of my life. There would never be peace of mind for me. This was my own decision. I know I promised I never would but my soul never ceases to ache except when I am stoned or drunk. Please don't shed any tears for me. I know you will but please don't worry for long, because I won't be suffering. It is the best thing, believe me. Love you.
>
> Love,
>
> Jane

P.S. There's probably more I could have said, but I can't think of anything. Except forgive my selfishness and may God forgive me. Say good-bye to everyone for me.

Many of the millions of young people on the move, toward Vancouver, to California, to Kabul, to caves and communes in Greece or to unreceptive hosts along the Ganges River in India found themselves in water over their heads. Some discovered unknown strengths and learned to swim. Others couldn't. There have been many, many of those others.

A Sudden Silence at Mrs. Van Warren's Country Club Lunch

At seventy-four, Mrs. Van Warren is the last of the way it was and an invitation to one of her famous luncheons is always a mixed blessing. One's social status is affirmed during a boring, tasteless, ceremonial and overlong meal. Rich from birth, from marriage, from remarriage, Essie Van Warren has no way of discovering that she is not an expert on all subjects. So, she speaks only "ex cathedra."

The lunch, Sunday, after church, was to have been for eleven, but the Very Reverend Baxter's wife didn't come. She had to skip church to have an excuse, but that was small enough. She'd been to lunch before. Mrs. Van Warren, who didn't like the minister's wife anyway, was glad. Seating eleven people means you can't have alternate seating for man, woman. With ten, it's possible.

The guests included the Nolands, he the executive vice president of the town's major banking firm and she formerly a Duncan, a very good family. The Nolands, in their early fifties, had three young adult children, two of whom they would not speak of at Mrs. Van Warren's luncheon. The Wentworths, oil and real estate, were also there, hoping that questions about their only daughter would stay superficial and that the subjects of abortion, trial marriage, marijuana and something called "coke" wouldn't come up. The Richards, the biggest department store, in their mid-forties, wanted not to come. But they came because his dad told them to. That was something Mrs. Richards was going to bring up with the marriage counselor on Tuesday. The fourth couple were new, the Sloans, he a writer and the token outsider. But not really. Sloan's wife had formerly been married to a cousin of Mrs. Wentworth's. Very wealthy people.

Grace first. Then a frantic but hopeless dive into a second mild aperitif. A crabmeat cocktail. Then a jellied consommé with a garnish of sour cream and caviar. Then, the second sermon of the day as Mrs. Van Warren began to talk about the young people, their lack of morals, their poor dress, the weakness of parents of that kind of degenerate youth. Mrs. Noland spoke up about the way caviar improves consommé, and Mrs. Sloan was eager to agree. (What's she hiding?) Mr. Richards guessed the crab came from Mexico, but Mr. Wentworth thought California. Mrs. Van Warren continued to say that simple things, clean tastes are disappearing and that the leaders of the church should consider who should receive communion. A baked herbed chicken arrives. And then, like a bomb, she asks, "How are all your children doing?"

There is a sudden silence at Mrs. Van Warren's country club lunch.

Social, educational and religious institutions were a major locus of the generational upheaval in the 50s and 60s. Many contemporary North American churches became battlegrounds. The minister was the usual victim. In all likelihood, the most difficult professional job in the 50s and 60s was that of minister in a small church where race, war and the struggles between old and young compounded the definitions of Good and Faith. During those years, I came to know a number of ministers and their wives who became caught in a crossfire of bitterness and scapegoating between their changed-mind parishioners and the more conservative and traditional group who paid most of their salaries. I count some of these clergymen and their wives as among the most impressive people I have ever known.

Case Study 1: *Praise the Lord and Denounce the Children!*

Thomas Spencer, Jr., seemed ideally suited for his calling as a minister. He had never considered any other work. He was friendly, gentle, kind and not afraid to let people know he liked them. He was a devout Christian who felt that he had been personally "saved." His commitment to Scripture was more literal than allegorical. He was selected by his graduating seminary class as the outstanding member of the class. That was in 1960. His first congregation had greatly appreciated him and he was viewed in his own circles as "a comer." Though relatively young, he had been selected unanimously by one of the largest churches in the area as the new minister. The former minister had left under fire.

In the spring of 1966, one year after assuming leadership in his new congregation, he was caught up in a bitter civil war. Two of the ten-member governing board had resigned, accusing the minister of "un-Christian radicalism" and disregard of the Bible. These individuals were long-time members of the church, major contributors, individuals with considerable influence with their coparishioners. The critique of the minister extended to the minister's wife and the level of assault on this couple was petty, cruel and full of innuendo. Nor were the two of them particularly good fighters. So it came to pass that among the complaints about the minister was that he turned the other cheek.

By twentieth-century standards, Rev. Spencer and his wife were not militant radical leaders. He had voted to invite a black minister from a neighboring community to join a local ministers' study group and had spoken from the pulpit often about communication between the generations being a two-way street, even on issues that included war, sex and drugs. He also declined to sign a "love it or leave it" petition aimed at critics of the American war effort in Southeast Asia.

After two years in his new post, Rev. Spencer developed a peptic ulcer and was hospitalized. During that hospitalization he began to prepare a series of sermons entitled "Thou Shalt Not Bear False Witness." He had decided to fight back. His physician felt he should change churches instead. I was asked to talk with him at this time and found him to be a very sincere and impressive man. He knew what he was getting himself into—to the extent that anyone in 1967 understood how much upheaval and struggle would take place in the United States in the next five years!

In the three-year period between 1967 and 1970, it seemed that

84

all the hostility, divisiveness and anger generated between old and young, conservative and liberal, fell upon Thomas and Wendy Spencer. Before his resignation from the church in the summer of 1970, there were three congregation votes of confidence, an "independent" review from the national organization and continual questioning of the character of Rev. Spencer and of his ability to "heal the wounds." He was identified with those who wanted to convert the church to a youth center, to turn away from godliness and to compromise between right and wrong. As the country heated up on the subject of the student protests of the Vietnam war, the moral character of the minister became a topic of discussion and there were vulgar stories about his having had to leave the last church because of scandal.

I saw the Spencers during that difficult interval partly as a friend and partly to help them deal with their stress-related problems. Wendy Spencer was clinically depressed at one point and since vacations, talking things over and practicing "speaking her mind" hadn't helped, I placed her on a regime of antidepression medications which helped a great deal. There were also two recurrences of bleeding from Tom Spencer's ulcer. But, as distressing as anything else, the long struggle was very hard on the Spencers' relationship with each other. They each sometimes felt the other trusted "the wrong people" and both were given secret advice at times as to the trouble the spouse was causing. Mostly, the constant stress and the personal attacks on each of them were painful and exhausting and caused them to withdraw from each other as well as from their accusers. Their irregular psychotherapy sessions may have helped them with that particular problem. They felt they needed an outside friend.

The Spencers finally left the congregation although, even at the end, a small majority of the group still voted approval of the minister. After a hiatus of several years during which Rev. Spencer did primarily administrative work, another church selection committee convinced the Spencers to come back "into a fold" where, in 1976, they were a greatly appreciated pair. The church they left in 1970 seems still to have trouble.

The Three Generations: Love, Responsibility and Property

The 50s and 60s saw a trade-off of independence, equality, candor and mobility at the expense of a sense of continuity, tranquility, order and ritual. Has it been worth it? Time will tell. Certainly, the young people, as they finally grow up, bring qualities that should make for a good life for themselves, their children and their neighbors. In particular, their allegiance to and affection for each other is impressive. They don't seem to experience the kind of rivalry with (against) each other that marked earlier generations. In my own growing up, so much loyalty was demanded by parents and other adults that there wasn't much left over for peers. I owed it to my parents to succeed, to study, to work harder than my contemporaries and to surpass them. By contrast, very few of today's young people are reassured when their peers do badly or fail. And, it is with their peers here and around the world that they will need to live and work and share.

The return of the pendulum (a bit) in recent years is related to a growing awareness of the limits of life that were forgotten during the last decades. To a considerable degree, this is a multigenerational, continent-wide rediscovery. Energy and oil are growing scarce. We can't keep running. The first of the postwar children have grown up, the jobs aren't there and the revolution didn't come. Marriage is suspect but life in a single-parent home is often miserable. Drugs went only so far in making life good but it's dreadfully sad to witness what drugs do to a certain few. We didn't build the supersonic airplane and it doesn't even matter.

Most parents would say that they have changed and grown too.

If it would all slow down for a moment there might even be a reconciliation.

CHAPTER 5

Living as an Older Person

For someone reared in a society that respects, elevates and honors older people, the aloneness, relative poverty and sense of irrelevance of so many aging North Americans seems unthinkable. A young Korean physician who was about to return home came to talk with me about his feeling about the separation of the generations. He had lived for three years in the United States.

> What is hardest to understand is how your countrymen treat old people. I think it is very cruel. We are a poor country but no one would put his mother or father in a different home to live out their old age. It is our responsibility to take care of our parents. Didn't they take care of us when we were young? Think how they must feel living away from their children and grandchildren. My mother lives with us and even during the war [the Korean War] when we had little to eat, we were glad to have her. My father died in the war. Every morning I go before his picture and pay my respects to his memory. I don't think I would like to be an older person here. Many other ages would be fine, but not old age.

Among the quarter of a billion people on the North American continent there are many different kinds of "older individuals." No single description is sufficient. For some *very few,* old age is the finest period of life. It is a time for enjoying life, a time of mattering, a benevolent period of living fully to the very end. For such persons, old age brings its own rewarding variety of joys, deeper understanding and interpersonal fulfillment. But this does not happen often. And it does not happen automatically. Older people, like everybody, need others who care about and admire them. How a person feels about himself is also not easily separated from such matters as income beyond social security payments, the quality and location of housing, the ability to climb stairs, chew food and move without fear of falling. And above all, their sense of well-being may depend on whether the mate is living.

Many of the changes that have taken place within society during the last three decades have been very hard on older people, separating them from everyone else. Migration from the farms to cities, the breakdown of three-generation family living, the rapid obsolescence of technical skills, the mobility in the business and professional community and the tantalizing opportunities for the young to go off on their own early have all tended to penalize older people. These developments count against the possibility of older people having significance to anyone except themselves.

WHEN OLD AGE GOES WELL

There are special satisfactions which may come in later years, particularly if both members of a couple are living and in reasonable health. Not many achieve all that they had hoped for in their youth. Few who aspire to such positions rise to the very top. But the discovery that life offers satisfactions and joys even when one's goals are "scaled down" can be very reassuring. Older people usually come to understand the absurdity of the person who methodically and painstakingly plans all things. They learn about a tombstone in a Miami cemetery that lists 1925 and 1969 as the dates of birth and death and bears this inscription: "Man plans and God laughs." They have learned that "this too shall pass" and serenity may come in their lives. If they are among the lucky parents whose children stayed married, there is the reassurance that "he has a wife and she has a husband to look after them now." It's as though school let out and vacation has started.

Among the joys of the older years may be the rediscovery of one's mate. Couples who have lived with the pressures that accompany rearing children, including PTA, bad grades, other children's angry parents, the first accident with the family car, "What is she doing out past 2 A.M. with *that* boy?" "You're quitting college?" "You lost your job and your wife is pregnant!" and so forth, often have fallen out of touch with each other. Their reacquaintance may be very meaningful to both. And a long-kept secret about older people is that their life together often includes a part that is sexual! Children have traditionally had a great deal of trouble accepting their parents' sexuality. This is true whether the child is fourteen and the parents thirty-eight, the child is twenty-four and the parents forty-eight, the child thirty-four and the parents fifty-eight, the child forty-four and the parents sixty-eight and yes, there are sometimes parents in their late seventies whose relationship includes active sexuality to the discomfort of their fifty-four-year-old children (whose sexuality in turn is denied by their thirty-year-old children). When both mates are alive and when the physical and financial realities are not overwhelmingly negative, then older people can say, "All of life is worthwhile, but I cherish in a special way these last years since the kids are raised and we are back together and we get along so well." Obviously, the loss of such a relationship through death of a mate is a particularly cruel experience, one likely to place enormous stress on the survivor. The loss of a mate is the ultimate test of a person's wish to go on living. The frequency with which the deaths of long-married individuals occur in rapid succession attests to the fragility of life without another. Sometimes, however, even the loss of a mate does not rob an older individual of his sense of relevance and meaning. Some very fortunate families enjoy relationships which span three and four generations, enriching the lives of young and old alike.

My family was graced by the presence of grandparents and great-grandparents. We celebrated three golden weddings. These people were very important in my life and in the lives of my children. I came to know a good deal about "geriatric medicine" from my family experience. When I was a second-year medical student (with a new blood pressure cuff and stethoscope) I was consulted by several members of the family who were worried about Grandma Molly, age sixty-eight. Grandma had been somewhat apprehensive about the presence of unfamiliar workmen in the house and had hidden her money in a purse which she put into the oven. At supper time, some unexpected smells were produced. "Medical" assistance was sought.

I gave Grandma a thorough examination, noted her high blood pressure and paid particular attention to her problems in solving certain mental tests which I gave her. For example, she did poorly with the task of remembering numbers. I would call out a series of five or six numbers and ask her to repeat them. She often forgot one or mixed up the sequence. A bad sign! On another task designed to reveal waning mental prowess she did equally poorly. This consisted of the simultaneous recitation of the alphabet and numbers (A1, B2, C3, D4, etc.). Grandma's mind seemed to want to go in one direction or the other and the task of switching back and forth from letters to numbers was difficult for her. Grandma acknowledged the memory trouble that I was discovering and then, as was often the case with her, she began to tell me in great detail about some events in her early childhood.

One of Grandma's favorite tales, told over and over during the last two decades of her life, was an "audience participation" story and concerned an event that happened when she was eight years old and a second grader. The teacher asked a question that Grandma alone in her class was able to answer. The question was this: Which word should be emphasized in the following sentence: "Is God upon the ocean as well as on the land?" Each of those queried by Grandma over a thirty-year period, her daughters, sons-in-law, doctors, lawyers, businessmen, family friends, and others, always guessed wrong! Perhaps forty times during her last twenty years, Grandma challenged me to solve that problem. I would guess *is, upon, ocean, land* and then go into the small articles and prepositions until finally Grandma, with glee, would declare, "No! The word to emphasize is *God!* You see, you aren't so smart."

My medical report to the family was rather dire. The future was clear and all too ominous. Grandma gave many indications of organic brain damage. The problems of senility and deterioration were imminent. We were all sad.

Twenty years later, in her eighty-eighth year, Grandma Molly, alert, imaginative and great fun almost to the end, passed away.

At family parties during those years, Grandma was always in evidence. Two or three times each year, she could be counted upon, rather shyly at first, like a young teenager, to step into the middle of the living room to sing and dance "After the Ball Was Over" with my father, with me or with our friend Harry Myers. And each time, on the second or third chorus, we would all join in; Grandma, Grandma's children, her children's children and her children's children's children. We knew we were sharing something very special.

We took very good care of Grandma. She was "under doctor's care" over the years and things never got out of control. She was on blood pressure medicine steadily for twenty years. Once, she became very depressed as a side reaction to one of the blood pressure medicines and she was promptly switched to another. She was always busy and she lived in her own home. She had help with cleaning but she herself was the one who was responsible. She cooked most meals for herself and sometimes for the whole family. She had many stories to tell and she instilled a sense of the history and folklore of our family in her descendants.

Of course, affluence also makes some difference, making it possible to construct a life that camouflages losses which are more obvious in the lives of those who lack mobility. Difficult personal qualities such as obstinacy, resentment of change and inflexibility are more easily tolerated, perhaps not even noticed, in grandparents who fly north during the summer months than in those who live upstairs. And, of course, people with money rarely become totally irrelevant no matter how old and obstinate they become.

BITTER OLDER YEARS

Most grandparents and their families aren't as lucky. Rather than an emphasis upon what is right with them, many live with a sense of self that emphasizes their losses, their loneliness and their growing incapacity. For them, old age is the time when things go wrong. Above all, in an increasingly urbanized, progress-oriented and affluent society, one of the things that went wrong is that they are *poor*. One-third of the nation's older people live "below the poverty line"—they are poverty stricken! Older people also are poor in terms of prestige, influence and power in an affluence- and youth-oriented society. They lack voice. Sit-ins, protest marches, strikes and voter registration campaigns are not the concerns of older people, even if they are the concerns of the times. Living separately from younger people, away from "where the action is," they lack information that would make the contemporary society of interest to them. This separation from the growing part of society is costly. The contemporary historian and balladeer Bob Dylan reminds us, "The times, they are a-changing." And he adds, "Them's not busy living, them's busy dying."[1]

Overshadowing all losses are those that make for loneliness. The world fills up with strangers. The death of old friends and the migration of others leave giant gaps in place of people who admired, reaffirmed and understood. Whether one is seven or seventy, having someone your own age to talk to and play with is of importance. Friends listen to us, nod their heads, laugh at our stories and affirm our judgments. As a case in point, consider a few events in a day in the life of a young, married, successfully employed thirty-five-year-old man.

> I leaned forward to give Marie a perfunctory good-bye kiss but she didn't let it go at that and instead held onto me for a whole minute. I muttered something about being late and having to run, but I really liked it.

> They were all waiting for me when I finally got back to the office wondering whether I had gotten the order from the old goat or not. When I told them we had made it, Jack, Lou, John, Nancy, all of them toasted me with coffee. They called me the "dragon killer."

> The salesman wanted to pay my check at lunch, but I told him, "Never mind this $2.38 check. Wait till I get to the home office and you can take me out for a night on the town."

> In the middle of dinner, the kids got so noisy that I couldn't hear myself chew. So I finally yelled out, "Everybody shut up and listen to me." And by God, they did. I got to talk for almost two minutes.

> Marie took a long shower before she came to bed. And when she arrived in our bedroom, she shut the door and, sort of with a laugh, said, "Are you asleep?"

In all probability, the most impressive lesson of the twentieth century relates to the discovery of large, unnoticed, undervalued and deprived social and racial groups in our midst. In each instance, better food, better clothing, better opportunity and greater acceptance made it come to pass that others were more like us than we had realized. There were the mentally ill, the mentally retarded, the poor people, the black people. Now we are discovering the Indian people and the old people. Next, perhaps, the people in jails will begin to look more familiar. In every instance, the human and social needs of each person and group were just about what common sense would have suggested.

In most large cities, there are various social programs for older individuals sponsored by the city, state, province or church organizations. We prefer to believe that these programs are useful in meeting the needs of older people. However, a dissenting view follows. It was voiced by a social worker, a therapist employed in a "Golden Age Center" in New York City.

I wish I had never gotten into this work. It terrifies me. This is the seventh year that I have been a recreational therapist here and I can tell you that there is nothing golden about growing old. It's not very pleasant. Oh, among the thousand or more people who we're involved with each year, there are twenty or thirty who are like the ones you see on television, lively, happy, with something to give, and able to laugh. But believe me, they're really the exception! When you talk about old people, forget the word *happy*. The lucky ones are those who are able to manage and who are content, I mean resigned.

Old age is mostly a time of fear. There is fear of dying, of being alone, of being sick, of having no friends, of not having any money. And loneliness is the most terrible part of old age. Little by little, they lose their friends. People move away. People die. Even the neighborhood changes. The little shops are torn down and up go high rises. There is nothing familiar left. Another problem is the muggings and the holdups. Most of the older people I know are poor and they have to live in a tough part of the town. Then, because they're not able to fight back, they are a good target for the kind of thug who would kill anyone for $1.35. All of them are afraid to go out at night. They are prisoners after dark.

Our center provides almost every service you could think of. The most popular is a doctor who comes in to take people's blood pressure. And there's a newspaper that's published, the *Golden Years*. We have a lot of dances, birthday parties, discussion groups, workshops in art, needlepoint, singing, card playing, bus trips, guest speakers, a small library, a financial counselor and just about everything. And, there are ministers from every denomination who work with the social workers. But, like I said, there are only very few old people who seem to have a good time at the center. Most of them don't. They come hoping for the greatest thing in the world to happen to them. What is that? It's for someone to listen while they talk about their ailments, tell how lonesome they are and maybe brag how wonderful the children they never hear from are.

I'm fifty-eight and obsessed with the notion that one day I'm going to be like them. I don't think I'd like to live like that. But as bad as it is, even though their lives don't seem to have much meaning, very few of them want to die. I guess I'll feel the same way. So will you. Just to be on the safe side, take care of your teeth.

HEALTH PROBLEMS OF AGING INDIVIDUALS

As life proceeds, transient and minor bodily difficulties usually progress to a point where they are persisting health problems. The body is rediscovered, but this time in a nostalgic way. The value of teeth, of freely movable arms and legs, of unclouded vision, precise hearing, easy digestion and plenty of energy are best appreciated by those who are older. Their bruises heal slowly and recovery from a fractured bone takes an eternity. Accordingly, older individuals have an understandable protectiveness about their bodies. As one great-grandfather said, "When I'm asked to do something, I not only have to decide whether I want to do it, but also whether my body wants to. Sometimes, we disagree." An older person has to take into consideration matters that would never occur to a young person. Can I digest that? Will I be able to see that fine print? Can I hear the actors' voices from the balcony? Can I, and should I, walk those steps? Is the journey worth the tiredness I will feel when I come home?

Certain kinds of physical illnesses are particularly devastating. Conditions that long immobilize and require placement in an unfamiliar institution are very difficult. Consider for example, the consequences of a fractured hip. There is the injury itself followed by transportation to the hospital, a series of X rays and ultimately the bad news that hospitalization of weeks or months is necessary. Further, the individual may learn that at least two operations will have to be performed. Even worse, the outcome is uncertain. Life inside a hospital means enforced dependency, separation from loved ones, sharing living space and the most private matters with strangers and an unfamiliar and often uninteresting diet. Pain often grows worse at night and disrupts sleep. There are also the personal slights that are inevitably experienced by those who must be cared for by three shifts of nursing and medical personnel. The very indignity of being a man or woman deprived of erect locomotion is in itself a considerable affront.

Individuals who are immobilized, whether by fracture, stroke or heart attack, are particularly susceptible to the mounting level of anxiety, narrowing of personal interests and loss of hope that accompany mental depression. Depression superimposed upon a preexisting physical illness is extremely demoralizing and its development makes the diagnosis and management doubly difficult. Depression also impedes recovery from physical illness by taking away appetite and decreasing cooperation. Perhaps more important, those healing forces subsumed under the heading "the will to live" are destroyed if depression is not treated. Vascular disease is another serious threat to older people and since blood vessels are a vital part of every organ, it is an enemy that may strike anywhere. The heart, brain and kidney are particularly deadly targets. Kidney disease is associated with elevated blood pressure which in turn makes damage to the heart and brain more likely. Damage to brain tissue produces unpredictable consequences, depending upon the place and extent of injury and the preexisting personality of the individual involved. The process may be very acute or quite subtle. If the changes are gradual, the individual can, to a certain degree compensate for and mask (for a time) the humiliating and confidence-destroying symptoms of memory loss, confusion, disorientation and mental depression.

Case Study 1: *A Man Who Held Power to the End*

Mr. Reginald Vance, Sr., was seen by a psychiatrist under rather extraordinary circumstances. He was seventy years old and chairman of the board of a large industrial corporation. He had decided to change his last will and testament in order to eliminate both of his sons whom he felt had turned against him. His attorney was uncertain as to how clearly his client was thinking and decided to ask for a psychiatric report at that time. Mr. Vance was not enthusiastic about subjecting himself to such examination but did so at the firm insistence of his attorney.

Reginald Vance was a very distinguished and impressive man. He spoke with assurance, looked directly at the psychiatrist and started out in the psychiatric examination as if he were calling to order a meeting with the junior staff members in his office. This impressive start notwithstanding, he was actually quite confused, disorganized and deluded. Beneath a rather haughty and disdainful façade, he was a man who was uncertain as to the date, the city in which the psychiatric examination was being held and the reason for the examination. He attempted to cover his first several mistakes by angrily accusing the doctor of trying to confuse him and he stood up to leave. He was persuaded to remain with great difficulty and then only after the doctor agreed to call in Mr. Vance's wife, who had been waiting in the outer room.

In general, Mr. Vance presented many of the classical signs of chronic and severe brain damage. These signs included a decreased ability to understand, to remember, to calculate, to judge and to learn. For example, when asked to perform simple mathematical problems he proved to be quite impaired. He demanded a paper and pencil before answering the question of how much change a buyer could expect if he gave the clerk a $5 bill and made purchases in the amount of $1.75. His final answer, $3.75, was incorrect. He was also unable to perform tests such as subtraction of serial 7s from 100 (93, 86, 79, 72, and so on). He did not understand the task for a time, then finally replied, "Of course, 100 minus 7 is 93. And 93 minus 7 is 84, and 84 minus 7 is 67. And 60 minus 7 is 53. 53 minus 7 is 56." During the examination, Mr. Vance became angry several times and at one point, after failing to answer a question, he began to cry.

Mr. Vance was struggling desperately to maintain an outward appearance that masked his sense of impending disaster. He was a proud man attempting against odds to maintain his dignity.

The suspicious ideas Mr. Vance had developed about his sons were "delusions"—fixed, false ideas that were not open to change. Specifically, he felt his sons were trying to poison him with gas released in buildings in which he walked. He stated that their purpose was to wrest control of the family business in order to assist communism. As he spoke, his wife, age sixty-eight, sitting slightly to the rear, shook her head negatively indicating her disagreement with the husband. She was, however, reluctant to disagree with him publicly.

His delusion about his two sons was not entirely without basis. They were both in his business and were soon to follow their father in leadership. But in the meantime, they were in the position of protecting their father while simultaneously reassuring exasperated employees who faced the confused, angry and accusatory old man. This dual role made it difficult for them to "talk straight" with the father. He sensed their "deviousness" and felt that it hid malevolent intentions. The delusion provided a kind of face-saving solution. He could maintain that the changes he was experiencing in himself were not the result of his advanced age and waning powers. Instead, they were the consequence of an evil plot, one developed by his own sons. He projected all responsibility outside himself. Otherwise, he would have been required to face his own fragility, loss of powers and impending death. This was not possible for him.

The problem of differentiating between mental depression and other problems of old age is a very difficult one and will be considered in the chapter on depression. But there were many instances in my own practice where an older individual was thought to be hopelessly senile when instead he was primarily depressed and the depression accentuated all other problems. In these many instances, effective treatment of mental depression, usually with medications, relieved not only the various physical and mental symptoms of the older person but eased considerably the problems between the generations which were thought to be unreconcilable. This fact, the prevalence of a treatable mental depression which compounds the problems of older persons and the people who love and care for them, needs much wider recognition.

SERIOUS ILLNESS AND THE DENIAL OF DEATH

When death impends, there are often powerful forces at work which conspire to rob the dying patient and the family and friends of what might be extraordinarily meaningful, life-enhancing experiences. The central fact is that in urbanized North America there are cultural taboos against any sign of recognition that a threat to life is signaled. The rules of good sportsmanship about death impose a tragic charade on those who are seriously ill and upon their relatives. Each must pretend not to know what is happening even though each knows full well. One need not go far afield for evidence of the powerful restrictions imposed on the dying and those who attend them. The dehumanization of the dying patient in the name of sparing feelings is very common. It happens in every hospital. Everyone knows that the patient faces a life-threatening situation, yet no one speaks of it—not friends, not family, not doctor or nurses and, ordinarily, not the patient either. Suspecting that he is critically ill and may be dying, the patient either does not try or is unable to get anyone to acknowledge this fact. Grotesquely, all the signs may be present that others await his death; diet restrictions are abandoned, the room is changed from ward to private, blood pressure is taken more frequently, visitors with swollen eyes are allowed beyond the ordinary hours. Yet nothing is said.

In effect, all concerned conspire to deny the reality of what is inescapable and pervasive. The effect of stripping the approach of death of its meaning, of pretending that such a palpable risk doesn't exist, is to treat the patient as if he did not exist—as if he were already a nonperson. His encounters are deprived of all human warmth and candor and the time that remains in his life is thereby rendered inauthentic and meaningless. Sometimes, however, it works out differently, as this story Dr. Carl Whitaker told me reveals:

> I went to see Jake about a week after the operation. They had all told me not to tell him what he had, but I walked through the door and began to bawl like a baby. Jake looked up and said, "It's okay, Carl, I know." I walked over and took his hand and said, "You bastard, I'm really going to miss you. You're one of the few people I've ever been able to talk to. A big part of me goes with you." Jake sat up in his bed, smiled and told me, "It's good to have somebody to talk to. The rest of them buried me about two weeks ago. I don't have courage enough to tell them I'm still here for a few days." We talked for an hour, one of the best hours we ever had together. We cried a little and he laughed when I told him I was going to name a goldfish after him. He was dead a week later. His wife wrote me that he had talked a great deal about our being together and she wanted to thank me.

In a similar way, the next of kin are often ignored in hospitals until it's time to request an autopsy. All studies show, however, that they are a very high risk group, prone to a host of diseases, to severe depression, to suicide and to life-shattering, poor decision making during the mourning period.[2] The interval of the serious illness, the terminal illness, the time of death and the period of bereavement are parts of an inseparable whole. Honesty and candor in the relationship between doctor and patient, between patient and mate and between patient, family and doctor

98

during the earlier periods in the patient's illness will have real significance during the later (mourning) period. However, when the patient, the family and the doctor are successful in their denial of what is imminent and inevitable, the effect can be disastrous.

Case Study 2: *He Didn't Say, So She Didn't Ask*

Mrs. Florence Teague, age sixty-three, was admitted to the psychiatric unit of the University Hospitals seven months after the death of her husband. She was depressed, expressed a sense of hopelessness and was contemplating suicide. She was described as never having found herself after her husband's death. The husband's illness had begun five years earlier when he was discovered to have a prostatic cancer. Over the succeeding years, there were three major surgical procedures. Extensive radiation and chemotherapy treatments were given at several intervals and there was a two-month period of hospitalization immediately before death.

Mrs. Teague had a very dependent relationship with her husband which continued with little overt change during the illness and up to the very day of his death. *At no time did she or her husband discuss the seriousness of his illness, her fears about the prospect of life without him or even practical issues with regard to the payment of bills resulting from his hospitalization.* Nor was the doctor (or group of doctors!) useful in helping the patient and his wife prepare together for the consequence of his illness. Everyone kept his thoughts to himself. The wife who wanted (and simultaneously, didn't want) to ask her husband many things, to tell him many things, remained silent. On the day before his death, from his hospital bed, the husband filled out the checks for the monthly bills. This had been his custom throughout their marital relationship. He died without ever advising his wife on any matters, without acknowledging to her that he was dying. He had mentioned that his will was in his lawyer's office. That was all!

Kepecs, Graham and Chosey have developed a new kind of medical ward, one that includes, along with other therapies, attention to communication between patient, family, nursing and medical staff and also with other patients and their families. They refuse to leave to chance those matters relevant to the psychological and social needs of both the seriously sick patient and the jeopardized family. Patient and family are regularly and carefully apprised of the purpose of the examinations that will be held and of the treatments that will be undertaken. The impact of the illness upon the lives of all who are involved, its financial consequences, its implications for the future, and so forth, are discussed individually with each patient and family and in the ward meetings as well! As soon as the patient can move from the room, he joins the group. Sometimes, the bed is moved into the conference if the patient is bed restricted. These authors report that the use of group therapy techniques prove to be astonishingly touching and powerfully rewarding. The medical ward provides an atmosphere in which people learn and gain strength from each other; those unaccustomed to talking with their mates, parents or children learn from watching other families. This kind of experience also raises many questions for the helping professionals. Can a moment of illness ultimately enhance the quality of life through greater communication and understanding between people who care about each other? Can the upheaval of serious illness lead to deeper meaning in life and fuller appreciation of human experiencing? Can the frightening, lonely and somber moments in life offer a basis for a greater openness, tolerance and understanding? Such questions are ordinarily left for the chaplain, some friend or, more often, for nobody! Mostly, the coming together in hospitals of patients, doctors, families, nurses, attendants, volunteers, ministers, friends is a vast "what might have been but wasn't."[3]

A BRIEF REFLECTION ON THE FUTURE OF AGING

Several themes recur throughout this chapter. First, many social, financial and health variables influence the emotional stability of older individuals. Most older people are poor and some are very poor. They are preoccupied with worries about being able to pay for themselves, frightened by the very real physical dangers that are present in the deteriorating neighborhoods in which they live. Each year they seem to fall back in the face of the rising costs of food, clothing, dental care and other necessities. These concerns are often the most important determinants in their sense of well-being.

A second characteristic of the older generation is that it is very much cut off from the other generations in contemporary America. This is no one's fault. Every individual, every family, every generation has been caught up in a whirlwind of social change that has cast some off to the side. As the ones most often cast aside, older people have experienced dire consequences: it is sad to be unnoticed and unwanted. What is becoming equally clear is that the havoc associated with social change has not been restricted to the older generation. In the midst of national and international concern about the ecological balance in nature, there is growing wonder about the ecology of the contemporary family with its generational cleavages that make children strangers to their grandparents.

Where all of this will lead is uncertain. There is no going back to the three- and four-generational family farm. At the same time, it seems unlikely that grandparents and grandchildren are destined to remain strangers through very many generations. It costs everybody too much.

Common sense should make clear that to devote the first half of one's life to rearing, nurturing and investing one's passion and compassion in the young and the last half of one's life alone and lonely is not an ideal social arrangement. In the preceding chapter I noted that one of the lessons of television was that young people discovered early how they were "entitled" to be treated. I suspect that as they approach the halfway point they'll think of something.

Part 3

PEOPLE WHO FAIL, TROUBLE AND DISAPPOINT

CHAPTER 6

Violence and Weakness, Rebellion and Surrender

There is always reason for suspicion and doubt when one person evaluates and makes judgments about other people. Nobody's life is perfect. Quite often the harshest critic of the other understands neither the other nor himself very well. Still, there are many individuals whose lives seem overwhelmingly, almost unbelievably filled with bad luck, trouble and failure. Some emerge from the straight, detourless route of broken home, foster home, girls' or boys' correctional school, jail and prison. Over the years, they build or accrue nothing and instead involve themselves with drugs, alcohol, violence and unpaid debts. They offer little help, joy or encouragement to any other and in the process of making the same mistakes over and over, they are resigned to and accept failure.

There are millions of such persons in North America. They are largely anonymous strangers. The people who know about them are police, social welfare workers, bill collectors, hospital emergency room personnel, tavern owners, Alcoholics Anonymous workers, parole officers and such family as still keep in touch. They are people who fail, trouble and disappoint, all the way.

One can rationalize about them but almost nobody would want to live the life they lead. Since they are almost exclusively poor people, their life stories are hard for others to understand. As a result, even well-educated, well-read and well-traveled individuals rarely have much understanding of the life experience of people who fail and do so in a very complete way.

Many social institutions have been created to care for or deal with individuals who fail, trouble or disappoint. Their patients or clients are overwhelmingly those who have emerged from less privileged backgrounds. Whether one studies infants born with birth injury, badly burned children, battered children, the mildly retarded, school dropouts, inmates in juvenile detention, broken and disorganized families, inhabitants of the alcoholic skid row, individuals prematurely old, or convicts awaiting execution on death row, those from poor and deprived backgrounds are inordinantly represented. It would be an oversimplification to equate financial stability with mental health. However, it becomes clearer all the time that to be deprived of a full share of society's opportunities is destructive to personality and spirit. Of course, this is a matter that everyone clearly understands—but in just such a way as to forget. Most psychiatric textbooks skim or skip the subject. It is boorish to speak of it in most social circles. Selective inattention to the plight of life which is not "me and mine" is part of the madness of being sane.

The view from a psychiatrist's chair is a necessarily restricted one. But the psychiatrist who pretends that the social and economic realities that make so very many people miserable are not his concern is, in my opinion, not a psychiatrist.

Fifty years ago, Bertolt Brecht wrote:

> For even saintly folks can act like sinners
> Unless they've had their customary dinners.[1]

WHO NEEDS WHAT KIND OF HELP?

R. D. Laing is an English existential psychiatrist, writer and poet of great skill. He has allegiance to those on the "outside" and, in a way, he is their spokesman. He makes a virtue of nonconformity by pointing out the terrible things that some people come together to do to other people.

> He does not think there is anything the matter with him because
> One of the things that is
> the matter with him
> is that he does not think that there is anything
> the matter with him

106

therefore
we have to help him realize that,
the fact that he does not think there is anything
the matter with him
is one of the things that is
the matter with him.[2]

Throughout the centuries there have been those individuals whose styles of living confused, confounded, worried and infuriated their contemporaries. Sometimes they are called immature or antisocial, sometimes lazy or evil. Their selfish attitudes, unwillingness or inability to exercise control, unwillingness to work, unusual sexual interests or inordinate use of intoxicants place them apart from their peers. In other instances, they are simply one of a whole group of poorly regarded people who fare poorly in the society in which they are minority members. Still others are the black sheep who know what the white sheep expect of them but they don't come across.

An individual so designated is usually understood as someone with whom something is wrong. Depending upon the favored theory as to what causes evil, deviance or inadequacy in the particular era, the explanation chosen will vary. During the Middle Ages in many parts of Europe there were men, women and children who were thought to be suffering from bedevilment in the concrete sense of the word. The task of "redemption," that is, their forced conformity, fell to spiritual leaders who began by trying to drive out and, if necessary, burn out the devil. Different eras have different devils who, nevertheless, work, as devils do, to produce behavior and beliefs unacceptable to the majority. In the contemporary period, many causes of deviance have been detailed. There are genetic abnormalities, complex sociocultural factors and interfamily and interpersonal struggles and tensions that are offered as explanation of the behavior of those who don't adapt to family and societal hopes for them.

Psychiatric diagnosticians have attempted to sort out what it means to fail, trouble and disappoint. In the process, they have had to wonder what it means to succeed, please and come across with what others demand. As a case in point, consider the young man described below who grew up to become a psychiatrist. He does not fail, trouble or disappoint. He "treats" some of those who do. But . . .

Case Study 1: *From Little Boy to Psychiatrist in a Straight Line*

He is a boy of ten and his potential is boundless. His parents are educated, have money, love each other and love him. There are so many things he can do and be and feel. As to career, his future seems without limitation. He can be a doctor, a lawyer, an athlete, an engineer, a minister and indeed, at various times in his thoughts, he is all of these. Without knowing why, he knows he must be "a useful and successful person." His personal wishes at age ten are likely to conform closely to the ideas of those who are most influential in his life, that is, his parents, his minister and his teachers. He meets people and they say to him, "How old are you?" and "What are you going to be when you get older?" They seem to care about his answer and about him. To which college should he go? He begins to ask the question while still in grade school. Perhaps his college will be Harvard or Yale, Indiana or Stanford, McGill or M.I.T., Wisconsin or Chicago. And later he chooses. And in doing so he makes a certain surrender. He moves further in a life plan, the outline of which was sketched by the people he loved when he was a child.

The broad, general educational possibilities at the university allow him to sustain into his second semester the potential for all the careers. But then there comes another point, a moment in which he must choose again. He chooses medicine. In this choice there is much surrendering and he does not make the choice easily. Perhaps he slightly hedges the commitment, planning to combine law and medicine in forensic medicine by subsequently adding the law degree; or he resolves his conflict between the ministry and medicine by deciding to study medicine to become a medical missionary. But still, he chooses. And, in doing so, he moves within a life plan conceived with family and friends.

About this time, another matter captures his attention. His determination to stay a bachelor, play the field and marry at a mature thirty-five is tested in his twentieth year by a young woman, she also a student in the college, perhaps in music or the arts. She is sweet and soft, not unlike his mother. He discovers she is fun to split a steak-for-two with. Soon he feels she is getting too serious, repeatedly warns her against this. Six dates a week are too many. They each should see other people. He urges maturity, good judgment, even offers to help her find other dates. Instead, she arranges her own. And then, in a long, solitary, soul-searching day of considering bachelorhood to thirty-five, playing the field and being practical, he chooses her. He hedges the surrendering slightly. Perhaps their engagement will be a long one. Perhaps she will work over the years and the baby or babies will be delayed until after he is able to complete his medical training, his internship in Hawaii, his training in obstetrics at Johns Hopkins or better, psychiatry at the Sorbonne.

The first baby, his exhilarated parents' first grandchild and his proud grandmother's first great-grandchild, came at the end of the first year of medical school and the second during the early months of his internship. His surrender of the possibility of studying obstetrics at Johns Hopkins or psychiatry at the Sorbonne followed an interview with an insurance man, the one who sells "insure now and pay later" policies to protect "that lovely wife and those two swell babies of yours."

Some things were not surrendered but were traded. The year of internship in Hawaii was traded for the second child, Annie; the year at the Sorbonne was replaced by the coming of the third child, Susie. And the notion of yet another year of psychoanalysis for himself, this time with a woman analyst, was abandoned in favor of a house and an acre in the suburbs.

At age thirty-two, his training over, he is a physician and a psychiatrist. He pays the insurance man for the years of coverage. There are many things that he is not. He is not an alumnus of Harvard, Yale or M.I.T. He is not a lawyer, engineer, minister, sociologist, professional musician, physicist, anthropologist or baseball player. Despite many things surrendered and many potentialities lost, there are also many positives in his world. He is recognizably the grown-up boy, once ten, who wondered, "What will I be?" He is proud of who he is, where he has been, and he is confident about where he is going. He enjoys his work and is conscientious about doing it well. He is encircled by family and lifelong personal friends and feels a closeness on many sides. In surrendering, in choosing and in caring, in following through, in staying with the plan, in fulfilling a number of commitments to loved and admired others, his life sustains its meaning for him. There is seeming continuity to it. There is a unity of past, present and future. For him, life makes sense. One does what one should. One works. One cares for the family. Perhaps his children will be doctors too. He wouldn't have it another way.

But is his a good life? Is this the way everyone should hope to live? Won't this rather conforming man look back and wonder why he was so obedient, so nonexperimental and so responsible? Won't he ever want to raise a little hell? Should he have accepted so totally the values he was taught? And how good a psychiatrist can he really be with his straight and serious approach to everything. Could he ever truly understand people who fail, trouble and disappoint? Could he—who lives his life in intervals of years—possibly understand a person who lives from moment to moment?

In contrast, for many individuals who fail, trouble or disappoint life is different. There is no logical life plan and instead feelings of the moment rule existence. Rightness and wrongness are related more or less exclusively to feeling states. Symptoms may vary widely. He or she may be very, very passive, angry, constantly or never loving, withdrawn, hyperactive or inert; he may never leave home and parents or he may leave in earliest adolescence. He may never love, may love a much older woman or a much younger girl. He may posture as if the most virile of men or may furtively wear the clothing of a woman. He may ingest quarts of alcohol, candy in gluttonous amounts or may subscribe to the cultist adoration of the human body. Viewed beyond the fog of success and failure, good and evil, sick and healthy, a disconnected, moment-to-moment kind of life without a sense of unity of past, present and future will be distinguished. The urgency of the moment rules. The future and the past are submerged by the *Now*.

LIVING IMPULSIVELY, LIVING VIOLENTLY

Some persons handle tension poorly. An uncomfortable moment may seem to be an eternity. Unable to wait, to hold back, to control instincts, they act impulsively to relieve the tension. In the history of

110

many such individuals, there may be a long series of comparable moments, that is, moments when they were overwhelmed with the need to fight or to flee! In a life that is interrupted repeatedly, one never fully develops a sense of continuity of personal history. The urgency of the demands of those moments is so powerful that it is impossible to feel a sustaining sense of responsibility to others or to prior goals. Instead, life is characterized by its discontinuity. The individual's relationships are interrupted by an apparent disregard for promises. His or her future is sabotaged by an almost continuous surrendering of potential. This kind of moment-by-moment existence is particularly characteristic of individuals who grow up in disconnected, deprived, broken or stormy families. In the following case histories, consider the lifetime *absence* of "input" suggesting a purpose of life, a sense of continuity and the feeling that "I am among friends." The first was a young ghetto dweller who was interviewed while in jail awaiting sentence after his conviction for the fatal stabbing of a policeman. Contrast his life with the life of the young doctor just described (or with your own). What follows may seem like an extreme example of deprivation and its consequences. However, it is only extreme. It is not unusual. There are many, many thousands of such individuals.

Case Study 2: *A Young Man Who Always Landed the First Blow*

John Washington, age eighteen, jailed, awaiting sentencing after conviction for stabbing a policeman to death. According to testimony in the court, a policeman walked toward a group of young people standing on a street corner at 11 P.M. and asked, "What are you boys doing out so late?" Whereupon John pulled a knife from inside his shirt, ran toward the policeman and stabbed him six times. The others in the group, his friends, pulled John off the policeman and he tried to stab one of them. John was jailed and convicted of murder.

He was of uncertain parentage, raised by various aunts and grandmothers, and from the very beginning there was no home that he felt was his home, no room that was exclusively or dependably his own. There were many males in and out of the various homes where he stayed, but he had a sustaining tie to none of them. He was on the street a great deal, a street filled with aggressive, unhappy and neglected young people and with rats as well. At times in his life there was not enough food. When hungry, he seemed especially liable to misadventure. When he was eight years old, he was injured on the street, struck by a car and was unconscious for three days. In school he did very poorly and was behind two grades by the time he was eleven. When he was twelve he was arrested and placed in a correctional school for truancy and theft. No teacher ever liked him and no adults except his grandmother and one aunt ever talked at length to him about anything except what he had done wrong or what he was forbidden to do. He had been stabbed twice and beaten up many times in fights with other men, arrested a half-dozen times by policemen (white and black), had seen one friend killed and many taken off to prison. He viewed the entire white community with suspicion, fear and hostility. Girls he also viewed with hostility and suspicion because they frequently laughed at him.

Life for John Washington was very much a here-now sequence of confrontations, a series of "High Noon" showdowns. The future was the next challenge to fight. His past was a collection of humiliating memories. He knew for certain only that the winner of the fight was the one who landed the first blow.

Another person whose life seemed to center around the prospects for violence and avoiding humiliation was John O'Connell, a twenty-eight-year-old divorced and unemployed laborer who was admitted for the third time to the psychiatric unit of the Vancouver General Hospital in June 1972.

Case Study 3: *A Brawler Who Sought Approval from All*

He was a sturdily built, five-foot-ten-inch Caucasian man who weighed 225 pounds. He swaggered as he walked, scowled menacingly when encountering strangers; when relaxed among friends, he talked incessantly of how many people he had sent to the hospital after they had picked a fight with him. He presented himself in an emergency room at 2 A.M. in an intoxicated state and expressed the fear that he would kill himself or someone else. He was depressed because his girlfriend had called the police when he attempted to "talk to her." He was out on bail at the time after having scuffled with police. Two earlier hospitalizations had occurred under similar circumstances, times when he was having disputes with his former wife. There were two children from that marriage, but John had lost touch with them and did not contribute to their support.

He had grown up in a stormy, deprived family. His father was an alcoholic who died after a tavern fight. John was eight years old at that time. His mother remarried and divorced twice, then lived for a time in a common-law marriage which had been interrupted a few years earlier. She also drank heavily. Her mother, John's grandmother, lived in the same community and at intervals over the years she took over responsibility for John and his three older siblings, all girls.

From earliest years John was preoccupied with his sense of discomfort, embarrassment and fear of being singled out for humiliation. He endured the excruciating role of "the dumbest kid in class" and quit school when he was fifteen. There was only one thing he could do well during those years and this was his ritual of recess fights. He was physically large for his age and after he had fallen behind in school, he was bigger than all his classmates. He loved to brawl.

And in adult life the one thing he could do well was to bully and brawl. He had been out of school since the age of fifteen but had never held a job longer than four months. He had numerous arrests for being drunk and disorderly and had spent six months in the county jail for nonsupport of his children.

John was not a very versatile person. He was a repetitious and boring patient who seemed only to know how to pout, to storm around and to threaten. At the same time, his need for approval was very great. He wanted women to admire him and after being rebuffed in his seductive approaches to the nurses, he centered his efforts on gaining the attention of the female patients on the ward. He challenged one male patient to fight after a group therapy meeting in which a female patient had expressed her admiration for the qualities of the other man. His occasional helpful activities on the

113

ward were aimed at evoking admiration and praise. His motto seemed to be "Admire me and make me feel good—or fear me." At times, when confronted with having misbehaved, he could acknowledge his mistake but could not see how he could have behaved differently.

John Washington and John O'Connell are two of a large number of individuals with a low tolerance for frustration, lack of versatility, resentment of authority and a willingness to launch physical assault when angry. Over the years, such persons have been called "psychopaths," "antisocial" or "asocial" personalities, "passive-aggressive" personalities or, less dispassionately, "bad apples." They often cause a good deal of trouble both to themselves and to the people and institutions in their environment. They develop a poor record in school, with police, with employers and also in their close interpersonal relationships. Nor are they easily influenced to change their style of living by any of the "reforming" or "healing" agencies of society. In the year that followed John O'Connell's psychiatric hospitalization, he worked irregularly, drank continuously, tried several more times to make up with his ex-girlfriend and landed in jail each time. He had been offered outpatient appointments with a psychiatrist but he appeared only once, and then only to escape prosecution when arrested again for bothering his former girlfriend.

During the period of hospitalization, John was interviewed once in the company of his mother who commented, "John and I are a lot alike. I had a lot of trouble growing up till I was forty or so. I think in a few years John won't drink so much and will settle down." This is not an infrequent pattern. Indeed, if still alive and not a severe and chronic alcoholic ten years later, the "antisocial character" may well have become a rather conventional and usually law-abiding citizen. It is unusual, however, for such individuals to acquire much depth or breadth in their personalities. Maturity in an existential sense never happens. Instead, "settling down" follows the scattering or disappearance of the old gang, the extension and worsening of the hangover periods and, if the individual is very fortunate, a rediscovery of the woman or man who is still waiting at home.

We know enough to predict that our society could produce far fewer individuals who end up thinking, believing and behaving like John Washington and John O'Connell. This would require specific attention to

114

maternal prenatal care, avoidance of premature birth and birth injuries and the provision of adequate physical and psychological care for the infant and family. As the child grows, intellectual stimulation, loving (nonviolent) and stable maternal and paternal role models and youthful playmates would be needed. The school system that received the child would attend to the special needs of each and to the general needs of the group of children. Intellectual and emotional growth would be carefully observed without making the child feel like a failure. The child would receive careful yet tender indoctrination in terms of "what we believe." The violence of television would be drastically reduced. Racism would end.

Sufficient? A good start at least.

LIVING PASSIVELY

The person who attempts to live his or her life compliantly and with someone else in charge rarely achieves much personal maturity. There are many such persons. They have been variously labeled as "passive and dependent character disorders," "inadequate personalities," "constitutional inferiors" or, if particularly seclusive or eccentric, "schizoid personalities." They are often products of a disturbed, unhappy or broken family and it is there that narrow and nonassertive approaches to life are learned. Early life experiences teach the child what sort of person he is and what sort of people he or she can expect to encounter throughout life. One's essential trust in self and in others takes form very early, beginning with the discovery that mother and the important people who come later can be trusted to return. There is a basis for security in important relationships. There is no more significant lesson for the child. That kind of optimism about others is best learned in earliest childhood, reinforced when the mother goes away to the hospital and returns with a sibling, relearned with teachers and friends, firmly experienced in one's life with a mate and then reexperienced in a different light when one is oneself "the trusted other who returns" to one's own children. There appear to be critical cutoff periods beyond which the richness, meaning and generalizability of "the trustworthiness of the other" becomes sharply curtailed. The ability to trust another person, achieved in childhood, is the foundation for a lifetime of interpersonal relationships.

Similarly, it is with and from the mother, the father and young peers that the child learns the joy of making discoveries. He learns to "trust his guts" because she, the mother, and he, the father, trust him and are pleased by the discoveries made and reported. The child learns and discovers good things about himself. He or she is a person more likely to go right than wrong. The child fortunate to come from this kind of background carries a fundamentally optimistic outlook about his undertakings and as a consequence, feels freer to explore life's possibilities.

Of course, "stop," "don't" and "awful" are parts of the necessary learning of any child. Laing calls such learning a confrontation between "twentieth century mother and stone age baby."[3] And, from childhood on there is the hard lesson that everybody doesn't love you like mom and dad. For the lucky child, the earliest blows are cushioned in the familiarity and security of family, and later, in the circle of peers. Many children do not come from this kind of cushioned beginning and many of these are the poor and relatively uneducated children of poor and uneducated parents.

However, it is not exclusively through deprivations associated with poverty or "second-class citizenship" that the development of personality may be hampered. Just as there is a very high incidence of inadequate, asocial or antisocial behavior patterns associated with the lower socioeconomic groups, there is also a contrasting form of passive, ever-expecting, never-really-trying kind of attitude among children in certain upper social class families. Of such persons Hannah Arendt wrote:

> Necessity and life are so intimately related and connected that life itself is threatened where necessity is altogether eliminated. Necessity serves to prevent the apathy and disappearance of initiative which so obviously threatens all overly wealthy communities. Through the success and material provision supplied by the all-successful parent the struggles of life are diminished during childhood. The elimination of necessity, far from resulting automatically in the establishment of freedom only blurs the distinguishing line between freedom and necessity.[4]

Case Study 4: *A Man, Thirty-eight, and His Mother, Seventy-three*

Gerald Cotton, age thirty-eight, presented himself for "advice and counseling" at the university psychology clinic. He was enrolled as a graduate student in engineering but after one semester was thinking of quitting. Before leaving school, however, he sought an interview because "it seems like everything I start, I quit." A brief review of his job history and of his interpersonal relationships supported this description. He had graduated from college at the age of twenty-two, sixteen years earlier. During the intervening years he once returned to school for one and a half semesters and he had held nine or ten other positions. He had worked variously as a teacher, counselor in a boys' school, overseas administrative officer, personnel officer for a manufacturing company, assistant credit manager of a department store, and other jobs. He was never fired but always grew tired of the work and moved on.

He was a nice person, soft, gentle and very courteous. He had traveled widely, met many people, had many superficial friends but few intimates. He had contemplated marriage three or four times during his life but somehow or other "it never quite happened." He had experienced several heterosexual relationships, but none during the preceding year. He denied homosexual experiences.

There was only one significant human being in the life of thirty-eight-year-old Gerald Cotton and that was his seventy-three-year-old mother. She had been widowed for thirty-six years and had never remarried. Gerald was her only child. His complaints about her meddling were intense in contrast to his bland manner on all other topics.

At the request of the counselor, Mrs. Cotton willingly traveled across the country for a series of joint therapy interviews. She was a woman from another era, something of the "Grand Lady." She was the volunteer curator of a historical museum in the town in which she lived. She was also a connoisseur and advocate of the arts, gracious dining and all the other features of "living as one should." Her interest in her son was enormous and there were few details of his life about which she did not have an opinion. In fact, she had intervened on several occasions to help arrange new jobs for him when he became dissatisfied with the work he was doing.

Dialogue between the two was unusually spirited. It went something like this: "Gerald dear, if you had stayed with the job in the private school as I advised you at the time, I am sure that when the

117

headmaster resigned only one year later you would have been considered." To which her son with great anger replied, "The headmaster did not retire one year later. He died of a heart attack three years later. And the man who was chosen as the new headmaster was his assistant who had been with him for twelve years. I never would have been considered!" There was the quality of old married people about the two of them. Despite the frequent disagreements and arguments, they seemed very much to enjoy talking with each other.

Gerald Cotton was seen on five occasions before his mother's visit and seven times after her departure. At no time during interviews when the mother wasn't present did he evidence any amount of vitality, enthusiasm or commitment. He was involved, really involved, only when she was present! His approach to his life was one of limited commitments, waning interest and partial involvement. The one exception was his relationship with his mother. With her, he lived out a complicated ritual of inviting her into his life and resenting her intrusion.

The magnitude of Gerald Cotton's investment in his mother made it difficult to accept fully a second woman in the world. This is a form of Oedipal complex. As originally introduced by Freud and narrowly interpreted in this case, the Oedipal complex implies that this man's involvement with his mother included fantasized sexual (genital) contact as a consequence of which he lived with great guilt and fear. Viewed more broadly, however, one might say instead that his relationship with his mother contained both loving and angry feelings and that the intensity and strength of those feelings (plus and minus) was nowhere duplicated in his life. She was his main source of joy and anguish. It was hard for him to go on to other situations with much enthusiasm. His great moments were with or against, because of or in spite of her.

One could, of course, view Gerald Cotton's background as one in which, beyond the indulgence of his mother, there were also significant deficits. He lacked a father. Also, the oversolicitousness of his mother robbed him of the opportunity to be alone in his own life. She was always there or waiting to come in. He was always seven, six, five, four, three, two or one day(s) away from the time he would (or would not) make his weekly call to her. His many failures—his inability to prosper in a job, to marry, to complete school and so on—he accepted as a matter of course. They were a series of victories through defeat. But at least the defeats were his own. Any significant victories in life would undoubtedly have been "owned," that is, taken over, by his mother.

Viewed in an existential dimension, passivity and passive resistance allow the individual to answer any questions about the meaning of life by focusing on a specific person or group. No need to worry further. No need to think deeply. It's him! It's them! At times this form of relating in the world becomes rather complex and involves a large group of actors who are actually thinly disguised substitutes for mothers, fathers or an early love that went badly. The "problem" becomes the whole life.

Case Study 5: *A Man Who Suddenly Wound His Wristwatch*

Thomas Ryan was twenty-six. He was a very eccentric person. He was thin, small, often smiling through tightly clenched teeth. He did no work though for years he seemed about to get a job. Or, at least, this is what he reported by long-distance telephone to his mother during each weekly call. At the end of the calls, lasting fifteen to thirty minutes, he would signal the operator while the mother was still on the line and they would ask the telephone charges. Then she would send that amount through the mail. In that way her husband, Thomas Ryan's stepfather, wouldn't find out about the calls.

This young man lived the life of a hermit, but a hermit who wore a seersucker suit and carried a cane. He had no friend except his mother. He loathed his robust, outgoing stepfather and resented the athletic prowess of his half-brother and half-sister. His stepfather's mother—he called her "the witch"—he hated most of all. He visited her often in her nursing home and rubbed her hands because he knew how she would have hated it, and perhaps still did through a senile fog. He was a source of unending pain to his stepfather who was a minister in a large and affluent church in Washington state.

He, Thomas Ryan, was a master at making people with power or authority trip themselves up. He had developed the art of standing near a bus stop alone. Then, as the bus approached, he would move forward in such a way as to make the bus stop. Suddenly, he would look up as if surprised and walk on. One driver,

119

twice burned, jumped from the bus and chased him down the street.

Mostly he did nothing in particular. His mother sent him $200 monthly, possibly an inheritance from his father, possibly a bribe from the stepfather for living in Canada away from the family. The stepfather viewed him as "the worst boy who ever lived."

As a patient, Thomas Ryan sometimes kept his appointments and sometimes didn't. He liked me, more or less, and liked having someone to talk to. Also, the fact that the therapy was paid for by his mother pleased him even though he knew there was money for only one appointment per week for one year of treatment.

And that, essentially, was his life. Sleep late, get up about noon. Dress in a seersucker suit (he owned two) and go for a walk. In restaurants, he would play small games with himself predicting whether the waitress would select an "establishment face and physique" or take customers as they arrived. He attempted to convince himself that successful-looking people (like his stepfather and mother) were more likely to receive better service and thus "the world opens up for them." So, he was exquisitely attuned to whether the waitress filled his water glass, coffee cup and so forth. If he saw any suggestion of favoritism, he left no tip. Eating out was a tense experience.

Rarely, on a Sunday, he would get up early enough to go to church. Then, he would join the line of people bidding the minister a good day and when it was his turn, he would chatter on for a bit and then finish with some deflating sentence designed to make the minister feel bad or disappointed. He might say, "We couldn't hear the sermon in the back rows" or "I think you repeated yourself a little today" or "I think the drop in attendance is due to the weather."

Thomas Ryan made no apology for his life. He felt he had been treated brutally as a child, felt his mother should never have remarried, felt that he lacked the physical qualities of successful men and saw no reason why he should battle against destiny. He saw his therapy as a reasonable attempt on his part to clarify certain questions that would otherwise have been answered in normal family relationships and felt he owed no one thanks for putting up the

120

money for the treatment. In the end (after six months, one-half the time originally planned) the treatment ended when I insisted that the patient had to take one step (any step) in the direction of broadening his life. He could choose to find a job, return to school, make a friend, perform a voluntary service role, anything. Anything. He refused and the therapy ended.

Two months earlier, however, we shared what was for me one of the most remarkable therapeutic encounters I have ever witnessed. At my insistence, his family came for one joint session. We had spoken on the phone but I had not met them before. They were as described. The mother was rather beautiful at fifty, appeasing, hopeful. The stepfather was tall, handsome, strong willed, contemptuous of his stepson and long ago had given up hope that anything that included Thomas Ryan would be other than painful. The half-brother had refused to come for the meeting and Thomas's half-sister, newly a mother, brought her three-month-old baby along and managed to be busy if any questions were directed her way.

But Thomas Ryan was a different man during that hour. He looked harassed, his face was flushed, he sat restlessly on the edge of his chair. His attention turned rapidly from mother to stepfather and he countered any statement of either parent with an accusation. But he was clearly frightened and frantically trying not to be cornered. I had never quite appreciated the desperate other side of his life.

He always wore a wristwatch. It had never been wound or set before. But on that day, to my astonishment, his watch was set to the right time and he limited the length of this particular encounter. He furtively glanced at the watch many times during those ninety minutes. The rest of his life was timeless. It didn't count. It was portal-to-portal time.

Life became serious only when the real contenders were on the scene.

What does it mean to focus one's life so completely on the others? Does it make much difference whether the focus is primarily friendly or unfriendly? Certainly it matters a great deal to the recipients of the emotion. But the process of turning away from oneself and denying one's responsibility for life while simultaneously ignoring the existentiality of the other is similar whether following or pursuing another.

CHAPTER 7

Alcohol and Drugs: "Making the World Disappear"

Among the people who fail, trouble or disappoint, a very large percentage are heavy users of alcohol or intoxicant drugs. But the regular use of alcohol is also part of the life of a great many very successful and responsible people and many others who fall between. No simple summary statement about alcohol and the quality of life is credible. Here again, one talks of millions and millions of people. For some alcohol is a bonus. For many others alcohol is a poison that finishes off the drinker and permanently wounds all who stand near in three generations.

Alcohol and other intoxicating drugs are used because they temporarily change the way people feel. Any individual can "make the old world disappear" and in its place, new and often friendlier feelings about the self and others or about one's past, present and future appear. While wide variations occur at times in the same person, intoxication often is accompanied by heightened self-confidence, increasing conviviality and a kind of euphoria. Ordinary social restraints seem less binding and, instead, the events of the moment acquire preeminence. Alcohol is actually a central nervous system depressant, but its ingestion frequently produces a kind of high state. Alcohol provides a way of temporarily getting "out from under" worries, tension and anxiety. People all over the world appreciate this drug and feel that it enhances their life.

A substantial number of others, however, lead lives that are drastically altered as the result of heavy alcoholic ingestion and maintain a way of life in which alcohol and other matters interweave to produce profound restrictions. The World Health Organization's definition of alcoholism is as follows: "Alcoholics are those excessive drinkers whose dependence upon alcohol has attained such a degree that they show notice-able mental disturbance or an interference with their bodily and mental health, their interpersonal relations, and their smooth social and eco-nomic functioning or who show the promontory [early] signs of such developments. They, therefore, require treatment."[1] The drinking of alcoholic beverages becomes alcoholism when the ability to work or the ability to maintain interpersonal relationships is hampered or dependent upon the state of altered experiencing which accompanies the ingestion of alcoholic beverages.

Many factors may influence a given person to develop a depen-dence on alcohol. The *Henderson and Gillespie Textbook of Psychiatry* de-scribes the various circumstances in these words:

> Dependence on alcohol develops out of the interaction between social circumstances and a vulnerable personality; it is a psychopathological de-velopment, not a disease entity. Some of the determinants leading to alco-holism may be found in a disturbance of the individual's childhood environ-ment, in parental alcoholism and quarreling, and in the insecurity resulting from this or other disruption or deprivation of early child-parent relation-ships. Later there may be the influences of the individual's employment, business habits, friends and peers, social attitudes to drinking, the impress of the culture he lives in and all the incidents and mishaps of his life-history. The more social drinking there is, the more vulnerable people are placed at risk. Probably the previous personality is always faulty; it is sometimes grossly so. There is no single personality type which becomes dependent on alcohol. One finds amongst alcoholics inhibited, passive individuals, dominated by and over attached to their mothers. Others have prominent feelings of tension and social inadequacy; in some cases there is fear of being seen to have trembling hands, and the alcoholism is attributed by them to the need to control this physical tremulousness. Others again appear self sufficient and self confident, even omnipotent in their attitudes, having all the answers. Some have obvious difficulties in sexual adjustment. Some are self indulgent, others guilt ridden and self punitive. Some are keeping vague as it were, in their restlessness, conviviality and drinking, complexes of which they are only dimly aware, if they are aware of them at all. A considerable number are inadequate psychopaths, shiftless, irrita-ble and unable to form normal human attachments. Nor is this a full cata-log.[2]

124

Alcohol and Drugs: "Making the World Disappear"

Dependence on alcohol means that the individual organizes his or her life in such a way as to control experiencing, choosing intoxication over the other possibilities. Whether as a solitary or a group activity, drinking becomes more and more important. Meanwhile other matters lose their significance. Ultimately, "work difficulties" can break down to an inability to work, "difficulty in relationships" becomes estrangement or divorce. The ultimate consequences of prolonged and heavy alcoholic ingestion can make the once-versatile, competent person a shallow facsimile of his former self. After years of a narrowing competence, diminishing reliability and an increasingly shallow involvement in everything except drinking, he or she reaches a point of "no return." Heavy alcoholic intake can severely damage a number of systems in the body and it often happens that the alcoholic man or woman will suffer severe gastrointestinal illnesses, cirrhosis (damage of the liver) and/or a mounting level of brain damage. Damage to brain tissue may result in a great variety of clinical problems with symptoms such as extreme difficulty with memory, very poor judgment and in some instances a loss of coordination of bodily movement. The life expectancy of a person who lives continuously with excessive amounts of alcohol is diminished ten or more years. Such individuals are prone not only to severe physical and neurological illnesses, they are also prime candidates for suicide, for any kind of accidental injury and for automobile injury in particular. The drinking driver is responsible for one-half of the more than fifty thousand annual traffic deaths in the United States and Canada (and the hundreds of thousands of traffic injuries).

Individuals who are doing badly and who are drinking too much are quite often people who are remarkably hard to influence. And, ordinarily, only those who love that person very deeply stay with the helping effort very long. Alcoholics are discouraging on all sides—for therapists, family and above all, for themselves. Sometimes there is a half-conscious denial; often there is a very deliberate pattern of lies, pretending and hiding bottles under the car seat. Some professional people point their fingers at the mate of the alcoholic and claim to see a "cause" for the drinking in that the mate has a wish to care for a crippled or helpless person (and thus stand tall themselves). But I think this is one of those little (occasional) truths whose perpetuation spreads more lies than light. For every one spouse of an alcoholic who "needs" to be married to a drunk, there are ten who could do without the experience very nicely. What is true, however, is that years of being with a person who "fades out and away" is very hard on most mates and they show the consequences in their own personalities.

Case Study 1: *An Alcoholic Man, Forty-six, Who Smoked Marijuana Every Morning*

"Well, Doctor, you ask me why I always smoke a little when I first wake up. It's a kind of habit, you might say. My wife is constantly on me. She has such a lousy attitude. She doesn't understand anything. That's exactly what they told her at AA, but it didn't do her any good. You should see her doctor and try and talk a little sense into her.

"You want to know why I always light up a joint first thing in the morning. She doesn't sleep with me any more, so I'm there on the back porch by myself and since I'm not working much because of the economy, I may sleep a little later. Everybody is gone when I wake up about 10 or 11 [A.M.]. The last thing I do every night is lay out a joint on the stand next to the couch. And my lighter. When you first wake up, there will be a few moments when you are surprised it's morning, and you aren't just sure where you're at. Sometimes, you don't feel too good. Maybe your head hurts or you remember all the crap that went on the night before with her. Well, that's a good moment to light up and smoke. Just lay there and smoke. Then, in a few minutes—it's faster than a belt of whisky— I get up and use the john, brush my teeth and shave. Then I fix myself coffee. On the weekend, she's there and all the crap starts. You should talk to her, Doctor. Talk a little sense into her."

This man mixed his intoxicants. After twenty-five years of hard drinking, he had reached a point where he couldn't work. He was picking up momentum on the downhill ski slide. The quality of life of every member of his family was dreadful or worse. Neither I, nor the family, nor the police, the judge, the jails, the "dry out" centers, the mental hospital— nothing—could interrupt this man's plunge. To my knowledge, there is no regularly successful approach to alcoholism of this magnitude. We lack the cure or cures. Existing drugs, diets, psychotherapies, family interventions, social approaches, legal impositions, fail to change the outlook for many or most who are addicted to the intoxicating drug and the dropout life that it produces or protects.

When the therapy of an alcoholic man or woman is successful, it is usually because one or more of the following has happened: the patient sinks to but recoils from a kind of rock-bottom situation; he or she comes to a now-or-never moment of experiencing starkly and undeniably the expense of drinking; a serious physical illness develops and it is clear that drinking will soon mean death; there is a conversion to religion and/or to Alcoholics Anonymous, usually with the dedicated help of an AA group and/or a particularly persistent minister or doctor; the spouse or a close friend locks the outside door, throws away the key and makes it stick that "we stay here till you stop drinking or I die trying." Sometimes, even when all five of these circumstances take place simultaneously, the result is still disappointing. It isn't easy. Working with an alcoholic man or woman and his or her family requires enormous determination, an ability to live through periods of disappointment and the availability of support systems to sustain jobs, hope and family relationships. Alcoholics are people who live out the rule that "trouble comes in twos, threes, fours and fives." Most alcoholics (at least those of my acquaintance) never succeed in becoming social drinkers. They have to quit—as often as possible, as long as possible.

While alcohol is the drug most people use in modifying experience, it is not the only one available. And over the centuries, people have discovered and used various roots, leaves, flowers or plants and, recently, artificially synthesized chemicals to produce altered states of consciousness. Beyond a sense of relaxation and euphoria, some of these drugs produce states of altered consciousness in which there is a vivid and astonishing modification of perception. Some people feel that beyond temporary euphoria, such drugs offer an introduction to a new world of pulsating, vibrant color, richer texture, more harmonious movement and, ultimately, deeper personal understanding. Don Juan, the Yaqui Indian healer in Carlos Castaneda's *The Teachings of Don Juan* and *A Separate Reality*, exhorts his young, "square" apprentice to "loosen up," to give up his conventional mode of thinking, to enter into the "other worlds."

127

Don Juan insists that his protégé take a series of psychedelic drugs in order to learn how to "stop the world." "Stopping the world," a talent of sorcerers, makes all human prejudices about the nature of life and the nature of "world" irrelevant. When the world "stops," the person hears the language of animals, sees the life of vegetation, knows the links between the sky and earth. Everything that is "there" comes to consciousness. Abruptly, in a third Castaneda book, *Journey to Ixtlan,* Don Juan calls upon his student to forget the drugs and go on to experience the ambiguity, the mysteries, the dangers and the sadness of life. In the books— though not necessarily in real life—the drug experience removed blindfolds and made it necessary for the student (Carlos Castaneda himself) to assume more personal—rather than conventional—responsibility for his life. Ideally it would work like that.[3]

Before the contemporary period, drug abuse meant either the excessive use of various sedatives, particularly bromides and barbiturates, on the part of one or more immature patients of almost every doctor or an addiction to morphine, demerol and heroin by one of a small and tragic subculture living on the fringe of society. This latter group included many who turned to criminal acts to obtain funds to support their addiction. They were "a group apart," hopeless and incurable. This kind of drug addict was viewed as a latter-day leper, 1 percent sick and 99 percent depraved. It was not until the contemporary period when many young people began to take drugs that public awareness turned more carefully to how they work. With that attention, it has become clear that laymen, lawmakers and doctors alike knew little or nothing at all about drugs and the people who used them. Indeed, much of their (our) knowledge was false information. Most people don't go from smoking marijuana or hashish, swallowing LSD or taking uppers or downers to a life of crime, the breakdown of personality and so on. An estimated forty million or more individuals have used illegal drugs to produce transitory states of altered consciousness without serious consequences. Today a majority of the young people in their teens and early twenties have experimented with marijuana. Some go on to try LSD or mescaline a time or two, and most of those find that they have little or no wish to make drugs a regular or important part of their lives. A small number of their peers find the drug-induced experience to be a worthwhile part of their lives and intend to smoke marijuana "on the weekends" for a long time. An extremely troubling fraction of this group come to count the drug experience as a most significant part of their lives and they make all other matters subsidiary in importance. Drug intoxication becomes a daily ritual, coloring all life experiences. As with the chronic alcoholic, this kind of life can only be a narrowing, repetitive, self-centered and progressively less manageable existence.

The repeated use of drugs like LSD and the amphetamines constitutes a threat not only to stability and capacity to work but ultimately to the very life of the individual. This is even more the case with users of heroin. Heroin is a strongly addictive narcotic which is made from but is more potent than morphine. Users describe the drug as capable of producing an "extraordinary euphoria," unmatched in other human experience. One young addict, eighteen, hoping (vaguely) to break her addiction because she was pregnant and did not wish to endanger her unborn baby, described the meaning of heroin in her life as follows:

> It's really lousy that something as unbelievably good as the high of heroin has to screw up your life. People who aren't users don't have any way to know. I guess I have to quit—maybe about a month from now—not before. It's velvet. I will quit, about six weeks before the baby comes. My boyfriend says he might quit with me. After the baby comes, I'll try but I'm not sure. Heroin is Saturday under a warm quilt.

However, heroin is an addicting drug upon which the user becomes physically and psychologically dependent, and when it becomes necessary to withdraw from the drug, *extraordinarily unpleasant* psychological and physiological symptoms are experienced. Withdrawal symptoms include *extreme* agitation, restlessness, nausea, vomiting and, at times, delirium and hallucinations. Fear of being without money to buy the drug becomes the almost total preoccupation of the heroin addict. Other interests in life recede. Much of the prostitution, robbery and general crime of the cities is the result of addicts' desperate efforts to support their addiction. An estimated 50 percent of those passing through the large city jails are heroin addicts! The heroin addict is prey to his or her supplier and becomes trapped in the predatory world of the billion-dollar criminal drug trade. For some addicts, the only escape is suicide. A lesser but considerable risk is associated with dangers of infection, hepatitis and so on, associated with the use of a needle in introducing the drug into

129

the body. Once addicted and once ensnared in the life patterns of the heroin culture, the individual has largely surrendered free choice as a part of life. He "needs" the drug every day. To date, few of those once addicted to heroin and the heroin culture are ever totally free of major involvement with drugs. Terms like "caught" and "powerless to escape" best describe their lives. There is as yet no easy way out. Theirs is a life pattern that is almost impossible to live. Today in North America, there are an estimated 650,000 persons living a heroin-addicted life! No one knows what to do about heroin, the criminal life of the addict and the dreadful losses that accrue from and within the addict population. Some, today, feeling that there is no way effectively to stop a heroin addict's craving for heroin, advocate giving heroin on demand to addicts, hoping to eliminate the element of criminality. An alternate approach has been to provide a less addicting, more controllable drug, methadone, as a substitute for heroin. However, the most prevalent approach is the one that attempts to cut off the supply of heroin by arresting suppliers and arresting and imprisoning the user for up to lifetime terms. This "law and order" effort seems to have some limited effects, one being to force local addicts to move elsewhere. Where heroin is involved, everybody's choices are few, disappointing and humbling. One single hopeful note concerns that group of American soldiers who became heroin addicts while in Vietnam or Cambodia. Many, at this writing, particularly those who returned to somebody, appear to have successfully abandoned heroin upon their return. Nowhere else in Western society are there reported comparably hopeful results. In China, however, after the 1948 revolution, heroin addiction was eliminated through a program that included execution of drug sellers and an intensive program of rehabilitation of addicts.[4] Of course, controls of all kinds are much more stringent in China than in the West, and the introduction of such controls would drastically change Western life.

In any case, there is no more heartbreaking circumstance than that which faces the person who is a heroin addict or those who care about that person. It is dreadful! To date our therapeutic efforts are feeble. Loving, medicinal, social assistance and punitive approaches may, with luck, cure 10 percent.

While less regularly catastrophic than the life of heroin users, many who take the hallucinogens, LSD and mescaline, have suffered sustained periods of disorganizing intoxication and/or gross mental confusion. LSD, a derivative of ergot, is a potent drug which, when used in minuscule amounts, produces a profound alteration of the user's state of consciousness for hours, sometimes longer. There are frequently visual hallucinatory experiences such as vivid, pulsating and vibrant color sensations, distortions of space, alterations of the sense of one's own body and a considerable loss of time sense. Those who have had an experience with LSD intoxication describe it as a very moving and powerful one, for better or for worse. Some report the discovery of "new possibilities in life" as the result of states of altered consciousness associated with the use of LSD. For many others, an LSD episode was an extremely unpleasant experience.

The "older" drug intoxication problems of excessive use of sedatives like bromides and the barbiturates and the use of stimulant drugs such as amphetamines or dexedrine, while somewhat overshadowed by the widespread use of marijuana, LSD and heroin, remain considerable problems in themselves. The barbiturates, widely prescribed for their sedative and sleep-producing qualities, are a particular problem because they are so often used in suicide attempts. Prolonged use of the stimulant drugs such as dexedrine or amphetamines have led to disastrous periods of "disinhibition" with many instances of confusing, angry episodes in which all varieties of aggressive behavior, including murder and suicide, have occurred. And, in recent years, instances of permanent brain damage resulting in confusion, assaultive tendencies and, at times, murderous or suicidal acts have frequently occurred with use of amphetamines.

The barbiturates and the various stimulants have somewhat opposite mood effects. But, there are many individuals who use the various types interchangeably! In their flight from the nonintoxicated moments of their lives, they have discovered that "it doesn't make too much difference which road you travel, just as long as you get out of 'there' as fast as you can!"

Why do people drug themselves? And why don't people who are intelligent and who realize the damage they suffer from alcohol or other drugs stop? There are many reasons. Drugging oneself is above all a way of changing one's world. It is a mysterious event, uncanny. I am "a certain way" now. Yet I know that if I drink four ounces of gin, within an hour my world will be changed. For a while, things might seem better. The same with smoking a cigarette of marijuana or swallowing two amphetamine tabs. My world would be even more drastically changed by my own act if I took a minute amount of LSD or if I injected a narcotic like heroin into my body. This ability to make one's world change is a power, a dependable if not effective tool for the person in dealing with the joys, the fears, the sadness and the boredom of life. Taking a drug is something to do which will have an effect. Even the most resourceless, most impotent, most ineffective individual acquires a mastery of sorts through a constant resorting to intoxicants. With experience, one could even acquire a kind of expert status in drug self-dosing: "No matter what they say or do, no matter how frightening the world, I have the ability to change it all for a while." Many who drug themselves have few areas of functioning in which they retain the ability to change much about their lives.

Thus, "getting off" an alcoholic or nonaddicting drug habit requires the decision to surrender a dependable and frequently utilized "emergency exit" from life's most stressful moments of ambiguity, fear, pain or boredom. If the individual has other possibilities (loving, working, learning, meditating, praying, reading, playing, talking, hobbying), the process is as much trading and substituting as "giving up." Anything that rewards this act of substituting makes the trade a more likely success and so it is usually easier to believe in something along with key others who believe in you. Therefore, the endorsements of family, friend and/or therapist are always important and sometimes decisive in determining whether a person is able to break or modify patterns of intoxication. "Kicking a habit" means *believing* in something or somebody. Obviously, if that habit is accompanied by the intense craving of a physiological and psychological addiction and great discomfort accompanies the surrendering, the necessity for *believing* is even greater. However, those who have long been committed to a life dominated by alcohol or drugs are often the very ones who have stopped believing in self, in love, in work, in worship and, sometimes, in the value of their own life. And conversely, when an individual is beginning to drink to excess, something very important is taking place. That which they have been is in doubt and in jeopardy.

CHAPTER 8

Life in a Prison: Doing Time

All life events occur in the context of time and space. One thinks back and forward to people, places and happenings. And in each instance, it is "I" who was or will be "there." But at the end, when one dies, that particular process stops. There are limits to us. We are doing time and we try not to think about it. But the awareness is always at hand. So, the plight of the person who is already "sentenced" is all too familiar and haunting. This is probably one of the reasons that the life of a prisoner is hard to think about.

What takes place when a twenty-two-year-old hulking, brooding man is returned from the courtroom to the prison from which he tried to escape? How does he live with his thirty-year prison sentence? What will happen when three men are sent to prison and two have fifteen-year sentences and the third has only a five-year sentence because he gave testimony against the other two? Will the man who is a drug addict accept transfer from prison to a free-from-heroin rehabilitation hospital, or will he stay in the prison where drugs are plentiful and life can be lived from injection to injection? Why do most prisoners keep returning to prisons? What happens next in the life of the crazed, driven and hate-filled individuals who made chilling television drama until apprehended by a Cannon, Columbo or Kojak?

Life in prison is simultaneously tedious, difficult and dangerous. But there is one way to camouflage the lack of power of the individual in his own life.

Case Study 1: *The Prisoner Who Stayed Drugged for Twenty Years*

The public defender called me to ask if I could come on the very next day to testify on behalf of his client who was a prisoner well known to me. He thought my testimony might help to lessen the length of sentence from a threatened "life" to "only" ten to fifteen years. I was irritated about the short notice but didn't bother to complain. In the life of people like Farrell, the prisoner, all things happen in the same casual, as if by chance, manner.

Farrell was actually a very unusual person. He was intelligent, had a sense of humor, knew everything about prison life. I had known him to befriend and protect prisoners new to the system, and once he bravely acted to help a new security guard who didn't know the rules and had invited retaliation. The other prisoners liked him and the security force left him alone. He was forty-two years old and a kind of senior citizen in prison. He had been on the street only six weeks in twenty years! He had spent 1,034 of 1,040 weeks behind bars! While in prison, on seven days of each of the 1,034 weeks he took street drugs, illegal drugs smuggled inside. There were always barbiturates, marijuana, LSD, tranquilizers, and once or twice each week, heroin would arrive in the prison. Whatever was around, Farrell managed to take a share.

The court hearing was for sentencing as the result of his participation in an unsuccessful group prison escape. That unhappy event had been an impulsive, last-minute "joining in" for him. He was serving the last months of a very long sentence. But someone yelled, "Come on, Farrell, let's go," and he was on his way. That morning, a few hours earlier, he had taken three or four LSD tablets and his memory for details was a bit clouded. However, he dimly remembered thinking there was less to be feared from the guards than there was to be feared if he refused to join in the escape. He understood that everybody would be back together in prison sooner or later. The escape lasted nine minutes. Someone had shot a bystander, and someone had cut a guard. He was soon in solitary confinement and obsessed with the thought that he would return to court to face the victim, the prosecuting attorney and the judge. Of all events in his life, this was the most feared.

I wanted in my testimony to describe the way in which Farrell lived his life and to point out that intoxication was a part of everything he did. I hoped to say that Farrell was probably dazed and confused with LSD. I also wanted to ask this question: Is this vulnerable man, who has been locked in a drug environment called prison, fully responsible for drug-related behavior?

I gave measured, careful, honest testimony. The judge gave twelve years.

DOING TIME TOGETHER:
LIVING UNDER THE PRISON CODE

Twelve years. Twenty years. Life in prison. Life in prison plus twenty years to be served consecutively. What does it mean? How far away is endless? In which direction does it point?

The people who invented prisons and long prison sentences were probably hopeful that interminable confinement would accomplish two things: first, the person would grow older, weaker, less belligerent and would come to be without criminal constituency; and second, the prison's relentless no! no! no! no! would become internalized. This latter topic, the creation of internal restraint, is considered in graphic detail by San Francisco psychoanalyst Allan Wheelis in *The Quest for Identity*.[1] Wheelis tells a story about a father who is dying. He worries that he will not have time to teach his beloved child what must be learned for a meaningful life and he resorts to a desperate plan. The boy is told he cannot run free until the grass is cut, and cut with a razor blade. The boy begins the task with optimism, with false hope. Perhaps in a matter of hours he will be finished. But instead, the hours pass, then the days, the weeks, the summer. . . . What happened was that the boy's and then his adult world was never again the same. In the midst of laughter, there was the memory of the enormity of it all and of the sadness and endless toil called man's life.

Prisons don't seem to work in the same way. Perhaps it's because in the real-life prisons the father doesn't love the boy. Perhaps it's because the boy in the Wheelis essay had a good start in life and had the ability to incorporate the meaning of the experience. Perhaps it doesn't work in prisons because prisons are rarely a place where people are questing for identity. They are just doing time. There are a quarter of a million prisoners doing time.

One matter that separates all who haven't done time from those who have been prisoners is precisely that shared experience. One thing that all prisoners understand is that prisons are dangerous places and the first task is survival. Find a way to survive the boredom, the predators, the guards who want rewards, the young prisoner out "to make a name" for himself. Find a way to not think too much about the folks or the wife, the friend or brother. Find a way of not wanting to see them while hoping they will forgive and come without the prisoner taking the terrible risk of calling out for them. Perhaps, above all, find a way of doing time so that today is all one worries about. Don't look ahead. Don't look back.

All parts of prison systems have enforcers within them that ensure that the values and rules, written and unwritten, are faithfully observed. Some are those prescribed by the chronic prisoners. Such rules are called the "prison code." It is the most real of anything in prisons. The person who violates it is in immediate and lifelong danger. He discovers himself locked in at night with his own potential murderer in the same cell. There is no better reason for "going crazy" than the fear that accompanies being designated as a "rat"—an informer—within a prison system. That code also sets limits for the guards, and when necessary they are enforced.

One's physical size and strength are important in a prison. So are outside sources of income which may serve as the source of funds for bribes, protection or favors. The threat—or promise—of homosexual activity is an issue in every prison. And access to sources of heroin and other drugs is a special credential in any prison.

Yet, prisoners are human beings and much that characterizes people in other parts of the world characterizes those who live in prisons. There is a good deal of survival built into all people. In prison populations, despite all kinds of scarcities, intense overcrowding and many physical and psychological dangers, allegiances and loyalties develop. The "we" against "them" of cons against guards or cons against sex offenders provides the first opportunity many have ever had to think of themselves as part of a "we." The prison homecoming of the inmate who has violated

136

parole and is returned to prison includes a returning to one's old friends. And since prisoners in maximum security institutions have all been in other prison settings, one's record serves as a kind of introduction and a statement as to "who I am." There is a kind of fraternal tie to people with whom one has done time. There are also allegiances that develop out of one's respective place within a prison hierarchy. Those lowest (most hated and least respected by prisoners and guards) are the sexual offenders. British Columbia psychiatrist Anthony Marcus writes of them in his book called *Nothing Is My Number.*[2]

More highly regarded are those who have killed for honor and/or those whose criminal feats include such activities as robbing banks and the like. Having mentioned these allegiances, it is necessary to emphasize that affectional ties among prisoners or character-building circumstances should not be romanticized. These factors are present but in limited dose. They are more often than not overshadowed by other matters.

What does an imprisoned person think about during two decades of doing time? Some criminals are innocent of the specific crime for which they are sentenced. More often, alcohol was one factor in the criminal act and the event was a bit blurred. Also, those who are convicted and have years to think about what happened to them often have doubts about the adequacy of their legal representation. So, the promise of an appeal, a new trial, a reversal and/or continuing assertions of innocence or loss of memory tend to assume a central place in the thoughts of prisoners in maximum security settings. When one is sentenced to three thousand, six hundred and fifty dangerous days in a locked prison because of an act remembered dimly through an alcoholic haze (an act performed in a minute or an hour, on a day two thousand days before), there is inevitably an unreal, "Kafka-esque" dimension to the experience. That so much of one's contemporary life relates to an unpleasant event (that one wishes to forget) makes for an additional sense of unreality about everything. For most outsiders, it seems logical to assume, "That person committed a murder, or a rape, or a robbery. That is such a horrible thing to have done that they must think about it every minute for the rest of their lives, repent it, keep it alive and fresh so as never to do the same thing again. They must never forget what they did." The prisoner, perhaps understandably, does not wish to have a similarly intense focus on that single event. There is a limit to how long one can repent anything. Things fade.

137

Nor is this simply true of people with crimes to forget. Consider your own personal hour of least attractive behavior and then pretend that this behavior became known to all and is the predominant basis of your relationships with all others for the next ten years. All people defend against that kind of life no matter how badly they have behaved.

The individuals who have the hardest time getting people to forget the act for which they were sentenced are sex offenders. In a cruel setting, they are almost always the most cruelly treated. Everybody looks down on them. When they are part of a general prison population, they usually have to stick together both for protection and for companionship. Every prison code makes them the worst—except for a "rat" who helps the guards.

Of course, there is a wide range of troubling sexual behavior and those who do not directly touch or assault others are usually spared long imprisonment with a general prison population. Such individuals would include window peepers, exhibitionists (those who expose their genitals to children or strangers), obscene telephone callers or letter writers, those who steal others' clothing and use it as a sexual stimulant. There are the more aggressive individuals who touch or assault children or women of all ages. Among such a large group, there are obviously many different personality patterns. Many of these individuals prove to be very restricted in attitudes in all aspects of their lives and are not simply limited in sexual maturity. Those individuals who substitute some object or ritual in place of a warm and loving partner are quite often people with generally underdeveloped interpersonal skills. Their "once removed," indirect mode of seeking sexual satisfaction is, for them, the closest possible way safely to experience intimacy. Some men choose to come no closer to a woman than to steal a piece of her clothing for use in masturbation. For others, the only woman who may be safely approached is a thirteen-year-old girl, one who brings back memories of the peer he would never have dared to approach when he was her age, three decades before. The terribly shy, frightened, lonely, twenty-one-year-old boy who steals a woman's undergarments has taken an *object* and substituted it for a person. However, he has taken that object as a way of feeling close to a *person,* or rather, as close as he can dare. Medard Boss, in his 1950 book *The Meaning and Content of the Sexual Perversions,* emphasized how important it is to attempt to listen without rapid judging, to let the account of the

138

other person flow through you even if it is not easy to feel sympathy with his story. Only in that way can one learn how powerfully meaningful his sexuality is to him.[3]

WHO ARE THE CRIMINALS?

The people who commit violent crimes are very often the ones who drink and take drugs. This is true both of those who injure loved ones and of those who injure strangers and enemies. In some instances, the connection is simply that intoxication is the way of life of most habitual criminals or that crime supports a drug habit. For others, however, drugs or drink are taken intentionally when planning a crime because of their personal fear of apprehension or injury. Or, the intoxicants may unleash the hate and courage needed to threaten or injure another person.

There are wide gaps in knowledge about crime and criminals. This isn't too surprising. Those who commit crimes but go undetected aren't studied. Those who are caught are put away. The "bad element" are taken care of by the police, FBI, RCMP and the people who maintain the prisons. Those who do come to know something about how prisons work are ordinarily sobered, frightened and more or less indignant. *But, on this point, the friends of prisoners have much less influence than the guardians of prisons.* And the friends of prisoners are in constant danger of the public indignation that will follow the next brutal crime by a man or woman on probation. No politician can be an advocate for prison reform without appearing the fool when some inmate (ungrateful for the politician's efforts) kills someone in the middle of a campaign.

Who is the offender? By and large, the great majority of convicted criminals are young men, fourteen to twenty-five, who emerge from and live among the lower classes of society.* They come from broken or grossly inadequate homes. Because of what is missing at home and because of their own emotional instability, limited intelligence or specific learning disability, the school years are usually very unsatisfactory. Many were "the dumbest kid in the class." In communities where prejudices against minorities are strong and deprivations great, that group produces

*I have had little experience in women's prisons and the chapter, I regret, focuses on men. What I have read and heard about women's prisons makes them sound like the male counterparts, only worse.

many offenders. This creates a vicious circle of more crime, more prejudice and so forth. A substantial percentage of those imprisoned, 25 percent or more, suffer borderline mental deficiency or are so confused,
deluded or emotionally blunted that a diagnosis of "sick" or "crazy" is
made by fellow prisoners. Many of the others are severely handicapped
by inadequate, impulsive or addiction-dominated personalities.

Some who become violent criminals present a more complicated picture. All their brothers and sisters and almost all of their friends are more
successful. One can't explain their behavior toward other people as "what
they learned at home." These are disconcerting people; their crime and
their level of social achievement seem to go together. Newspaper head-
ings may raise the question while stating the facts:

> Judge's Son Arrested on Rape and Murder Charge
> Minister Charged in Deadly Assault
> Doctor Charged for Pistol Whipping Victim

The crimes of people who have a mother, father, apparent acceptance
at home, education, a chance for work and no obvious reasons to want
to hurt other people or take their things have always been a puzzle. Many
have been carefully studied by lawyers, psychiatrists, sociologists or, in
certain noteworthy instances, professional writers who make the criminal
the subject of article or book. A variety of explanations have been put
forward.[4]

Some psychologists and psychoanalysts have explained criminality in
persons whose family and friends are noncriminals through analysis of
scapegoating tendencies present in the families. If a mother or father
resents a particular child, sees "bad tendencies" in that child even as a
baby, then he is likely to behave in such a way that the fear becomes an
actuality. Sometimes, a story related by a parent about a child strongly
supports this theory of how criminals are made! The unhappy, defensive,
somewhat self-righteous mother of a fifteen-year-old boy who has been
charged with murder during an attempted robbery offered this explanation:

> I knew from the hour he was brought to nurse that we had trouble ahead.
> He was aggressive, you could see his father in him right away. When I
> brought his half-sister home from the hospital two years later, I had to

watch night and day to make sure he didn't harm her. I've known something like this would happen to that boy—and now it has.

In this situation one could guess that the mother's hostility to the boy's father, who had deserted her in the latter months of pregnancy, influenced her relationship with her son from early on. Children are ordinarily much more tuned into what their parents really think and feel than people realize. That is the child's major job. It seems likely that this mother's unspoken attitudes caused her son to see himself as capable of violence. A somewhat more speculative theory might emphasize the level of hostility this mother felt toward many people in her life. This would raise the possibility that her son acted out the aggressive feelings that overflowed from within the total family; that is, he acted for her.

Among those who commit violent or irresponsible acts, there appear to be a number who have suffered damage to brain tissue in early life. This may have occurred as the result of birth injury, prematurity, untreated nutritional disease, injuries from falling or accidents, encephalitis or other problems. These kinds of injuries to brain tissue may result in a decreased ability to control aggressive impulses or to exercise good judgment in the face of a stressful situation. Or, there may be no evidence of any impairment unless the individual takes alcohol or some other intoxicant.

At times, in the history of violent individuals one learns that there was impairment in the ability to read, to write or to perform mathematics in childhood. The resulting problems at school compounded everything else. Or, if there is a history of epileptic seizures, there are also the problems faced by all children who are known to have "fits." This interlacing and compounding of the various psychological, biological and social factors in maladaptive behavior make the matter of a thorough examination of all aspects of the person a very important issue. This is particularly true for young children who are doing poorly in their intellectual or social development. Dr. Carl Kline, a Vancouver child psychiatrist, and his wife, Carol, a reading therapist, have developed persuasive studies showing that many "problem children" suffer specific learning difficulties. They have trouble recognizing or working with various kinds of written or spoken symbols. This difficulty in turn puts the child in a disadvantaged situation which affects other aspects of his adjustment.

The Klines have developed techniques that center on use of young adult tutors who offer a variety of psychological, educational and social contacts as supplements to the deficits that the child's circumstances have produced. Once a child has begun the route of social trouble, school trouble and legal trouble, the problems compound each other at a rapid rate.[5] Most of us who never were the "dumbest kid in class" have no idea how awful it feels.

The electroencephalogram (EEG) is a useful tool in some cases in pointing to signs of subtle brain injury. But there is rarely, if ever, an absolute translation of any laboratory examination to a behavioral disturbance. The nature of the relationship of abnormalities of the brain to disturbed behavior has been a topic of intense study and disagreement for many years. There is a similar disagreement concerning the effectiveness of various stimulant drugs, antiepileptic medications, antidepression drugs, tranquilizers and more recently, lithium carbonate (a drug useful in the management of manic-depressive psychosis). All of these have been used with varying success in attempts to manage the impulsive, aggressive or disorganized behavior of children or adults.[6] Of course, a careless, casual or routine prescription of any kind of drug, especially for children, is a repulsive idea. No one would want to teach a child that he "needs" pills, that "pills and life go together." Also, the benefits of medication have to be weighed against the dangers of side effects, overuse and so on. But, without much question, many "hyperactive," restless, distractable children have been greatly assisted by carefully administered low dosages of stimulant drugs. Sometimes the same drugs are curative of bed wetting in children, apparently because they decrease a pathological depth of sleep. The decision about the use of drugs in children to modify behavior is obviously very much a matter for careful individual-by-individual consideration. But such experienced medical consideration is essential as *one* possibility in helping some young children who are consistently miserable, unsuccessful and learning to think of themselves as "losers."

Recently, there has been intensive controversy over proposed neurosurgical approaches to the control of extreme violence and impulsive, destructive behavior.[7] A similar controversy surrounds the growing application of a variety of conditioning, deconditioning or "aversion" treatments applied to control offenders (à la *A Clockwork Orange*). The friends of prisoners are wary in the extreme about experimental therapies for prisoners. I count myself among those friends. In choosing therapies the Golden Rule must be kept in mind, and this is known to be easier if one is dealing with family, friends and familiar people of one's own social class. It is best to exhaust the simple and least disruptive remedies first. With poor and uneducated people that doesn't always happen. This would mean developing rehabilitation or therapeutic programs for all prisoners that start with talking, learning a skill, reconciliation with family and friends, a job and a place to live in the early probation days. More complicated and experimental programs for men and women who are prisoners require the most scrupulous (outside) continuing consideration and supervision.

PRISONS: SOFTER OR TOUGHER?

People generally agree that we must be "tougher" with criminals. Given an opportunity to vote on the topic, two-thirds of the people support capital punishment. There is a call to put down violence violently. But this focus on the violent person obscures the many failing people and failing educational and economic institutions of which the criminal is a product. For most violent criminals, the family didn't exist or was a failure, the school hurt more than it helped, the reform school made things worse, the job market couldn't receive the person, the treatments for mental disturbances weren't available or were inadequate and the prisons simply increased the person's violence and commitment to drugs.

For several years now I have been a consultant to the Regional Medical Centre (R.M.C.) of Abbotsford, British Columbia. Its director is Chunilal Roy, a Canadian psychiatrist. It is a maximum security prison hospital, established as an experimental setting by the Canadian Penitentiary Service. Among the patients admitted to the center are some of the most unpredictable, violent prisoners in Canada. Many have committed murder, some multiple murder. The full inventory of violent and destructive acts are catalogued in the criminal histories of the several hundred men treated in the center each year. One prisoner-patient was murdered within the institution by one or more of the prisoner-inpatients. Once, four of the patients took a knife to the throat of a male nurse taken

143

hostage to force transfer of another patient off a particular ward. Some few prisoner-patients proved so violent, resistant and fear-provoking that they were returned to the status of prisoner and transferred to a maximum security section of some other maximum security prison. The effort at treatment (at that point in time) was a failure. Forty security guards, seventy nurses and five psychiatrists work there. It is—on the good days —among the most hopeful and inspiring working settings of my recent experience. Not easily described, it is for me a little like the Menninger Clinic in the 1940s, a time in psychiatry when there was more hope than there were data. When I listen to the men talking about their experiences at the center, I think about the *Diary of Anne Frank* and about the wonder of hope.[8]

Case Study 1: *How Can One Evaluate One's First Friend?*

Tom Morrant, thirty-four, had been in trouble all his life and in prisons or their junior equivalent since he was nine years old, unhappy, hostile, seclusive and now a murderer. He didn't know whether his second victim had also died. That was twelve years ago. Now he was afraid to ask. He had been sent to the R.M.C. a year and a half earlier because control in the regular prison meant continual solitary confinement. In the R.M.C. he had been almost impossible to manage despite drug therapy, fellow prisoner "buddies" assigned to help him adjust, visits and reassurance from a "friends of prisoners group" (the John Howard Society) and the assignment of nursing staff around the clock to help him settle in the center. I didn't know him in that earlier period but was asked to talk with him and his chief nurse therapist, Marcy Jones, about a year after his arrival. The problem was that Tom loved Marcy and resented her work with all the other patients in her charge. Also, Marcy was going to be leaving the center when her husband finished school and Tom wanted a commitment that she would write. Marcy wanted to keep things straight and clear with Tom and so the two of them came for a consultation with me. Marcy is Japanese, the mother of three.

Tom loved Marcy, but I should have gone on to say that it was Tom's first love and it had helped to bring about a miracle in his life. Before seeing the two of them, I had violated my own rule about

144

never reading other people's written reports before talking with a patient. Tom's history was as deprived as any I had known. But that was before, and now Tom was different. In the interview, Marcy talked about being his nurse, not his girlfriend, and Tom was saying that he could do better than her anyway. I asked Tom how good a friend Marcy was and he said he couldn't say for sure. He had never had any other and had no way to compare. He said he knew his demands were hard on her, but she had asked for it when he gave his word to her that he would never hit her (a year before). I asked him when he would become eligible for probation and he said 1988. Looking at Marcy, he said to me, in a most tender, sincere and open way, "But I have hope."

I have talked with a hundred of the prisoner-patients in the Regional Medical Center. They are treated with drugs, group therapy, relaxation techniques, "buddy programs," deconditioning efforts, high school educations and above all, with dignity and hope. They often tell me what I found in my interview with Tom and Marcy: something terribly important is going on in their lives.

Of course, there are reasons for doubt. Traditionally, behavior inside prisons is of little value in predicting behavior following release. And the necessary support programs for the crucial first weeks and months after release from a long sentence have yet to be provided by R.M.C.

Also troubling has been our inability to work out a satisfactory system for movement through sequences of settings within the institution which would allow the individual prisoner-patients to assume increasing levels of responsibility as they approached release. There are many other problems. One learns the hard way, quite often, that not everybody who is imprisoned is a nice person.

Consistently, we have trouble convincing the men to invite what is left of their families to come to the center to see how much that is constructive is left on either side. Unfortunately, a fair number of the families finally contacted want nothing to do with their imprisoned relatives. They have been burned before. For some of the men from such families and for the others for whom there is nobody, we are now trying to find substitutes. Sometimes we try to share the relatives of those who have them with the men who are alone.

145

We feel we have made some rather clear gains in the center. There is no need for a prison code. We do not ask one prisoner to betray another unless life is at stake. There are no drugs brought in from the street, something almost unheard of in any prison or prison hospital in the world.

I am optimistic as to what can come out of the work at the R.M.C. and thus guilty of convictions that go beyond the data at hand. It seems to me that the contemporary prison closely resembles the equally obsolescent, expensive, nonfunctioning mental hospitals of the 1940s and 1950s. In those days, things also seemed pretty hopeless. People wanted the institutions and the institution's inhabitants to be as far away as possible. Also, we didn't understand in the 1940s and 1950s that you couldn't treat mental problems unless you worked on a lot of other matters at the same time. One had to involve the citizens of the society, had to fight prejudice, had to eliminate job discrimination, needed to provide ways that would allow a person to slip back a little without having to start all over again. We had to learn how to reinvolve families who had abandoned the people who were in the hospitals. And we had to convert the hospital itself from a setting of hopelessness to a place of hope. We must do much of the same if we hope to improve the system that incompetently manages the people who become society's criminals.

There is no way that the present system can be justified. Its worst feature is that it makes crime an impersonal matter. The criminal's victim, his victim's family, his own family, his friends, are all stripped away from the event. He, the offender, has no accountability to any person for what he did. He is not asked to and cannot make a personal recompense to those he harmed. He isn't obliged to live in the mess he made, facing the people who have suffered. Quite the opposite happens. He lives among those who say, "You don't ask me and I won't ask you." Instead, the focus is on seeking a retrial, claims of police brutality and the prison life of we cons versus those screws. Psychiatrist Seymour Halleck in his book *Psychiatry and the Dilemmas of Crime* has pointed out that criminal behavior is often an effort to achieve psychological and social equilibrium by a person coping poorly with the stress of life on the street. Imprisonment is part of the "cop-out" on living.[9]

The prison systems that I know act directly against the hope for a future, noncriminal life for the prisoner. They are dehabilitating and

146

make repetition of criminal acts in the future more likely. As few people as possible should leave their home communities and the people they have harmed. Punishment, whenever conceivable, should mean working gainfully to pay recompense to the person harmed and his family. For those who must be firmly confined, small, manageable and more humane settings should be established as alternatives to the present-day large, out-of-control prisons.

Some day soon, constitutional lawyers are going to prove that you can't maintain these settings with locks on doors that keep people inside and holes in the doors where drugs are pushed in.

Part 4

NEUROTIC AND PSYCHOTIC PATTERNS OF LIVING

CHAPTER 9

Obsessive and Compulsive Living

A diagnosis of an emotional disorder can never be more than an approximating generalization which designates past ways of experiencing and behaving. And since life allows at least the possibility of feeling or behaving differently in the next moment, a certain or total description of any living being by a diagnosis is impossible. Only with death and the loss of possibilities can a diagnosis be in any measure complete. No person is ever simply "a hysteric," "a compulsive" or "a schizophrenic." Nor can anyone predict with certainty that the mannerisms, attitudes and ways of behaving previously characteristic of a person will be descriptive of him in the minutes, hours, days or weeks ahead. The cowardly man may come to live the life of a hero; the suspicious person may become trusting and relaxed; the girl who lived dependently and seemed so much a child may one day demonstrate conclusively that she is indeed a woman in the fullest sense. While knowing about, or better yet knowing, a person enhances the ability to predict how he or she might choose from among their possibilities, such prediction is never a certainty. Unpredictability is an inevitable characteristic of human beings.

However, there is a kind of person who experiences the uncertainties of human life as bothersome and as a source of sustaining discomfort. As a result, he often structures his life as if to deny as much as he can of such uncertainty. He seems to have a *modus vivendi,* a motto for his life that says, "So long as I keep in scrupulous order all of the people, all of the circumstances and all of the personal feelings that are important in my life, I will be happy and safe." He or she cautiously and carefully maintains a continual perusal of his or her carefully ordered and often narrow set of potentialities in life which have been staked out as important. He is not a person of whom it can be said that he is open to the full experi-

151

ence of life. Instead, the range of his meaningful personal engagement is sharply restricted. If the world of feelings, ideas, possibilities and relationships is a full field up to 360 degrees, this person may limit his range of concern to an area that is simply "that which is ahead." Certain activities are lifted out and placed above, assigned primary significance and faithfully attended. These possibilities may include earning approval, recruiting money or goods, maintaining a clean house, achieving a perfect record in something, living precisely as "they" would have one live, keeping perfect records and such. Other matters are assigned a subsidiary place in his life.

He may be a person who comes to a sixty-page newspaper day after day and, ignoring all else, turns to the page listing stocks on the New York Stock Exchange. On that page, of the thousand items listed, he concerns himself with two or three. These he studies, restudies, orders, tends to and then reorders again. In his life all other matters are subsidiary. The people in his life, other events, all the matters alluded to in the other fifty-nine pages of the paper, are bereft of the possibility of capturing his full attention. Indeed, he may be remarkably free of the ordinary anxieties that beset other men because he is unmoved by forces and events outside the narrow area of his concern.

Or, she may be a wife and mother, living in a home with agile, growing, changing children, who savors little of her day-to-day living because there is no time left after scrupulously attending to the tasks of tidying, cooking, counting, washing, saving, disciplining and worrying. Her life may be completely filled with the urgency of "things to do," responsibilities that are the first priority, deeds that must be performed. A departure from the regularity of her schedule makes her feel guilty and apprehensive. She is living the kind of life of which Sartre wrote, "She makes herself such that she is *waited for* by all the tasks placed along her way. Objects are mute demands and she is nothing in herself but the passive obedience to these demands."[1]

Or, he may be a serious, essentially friendless person of high school age who postpones having fun because of the urgency of doing well in high school in order to earn good grades, which would allow him to gain entrance to a fine college. There, still postponing, he will earn good grades, which will allow him entrance into a good graduate school. Once in graduate school, rigorous discipline, commitment and further postponing will allow him to establish a good record so that he may . . .

Obviously, it is not a simple matter to sustain this kind of narrow world view. Other matters keep pressing in. Keeping one's attention locked in on a designated area of life and putting aside everything else requires much effort. Threat to order must be put down. The irrelevant must be fitted in or extruded. The suppression of "irrelevant" experience may require denial, compromise, pretense, isolation, detachment, repression, turning away from or, finally, cutting down even more sharply the total area of life to which one is attentive. He says, over and over again, "There really is no problem, no basis for uncertainty. There will be no danger unless one loses his head. The secret is to stick to business, keep in order what is important." Thus, openness to the new, the unexpected, the unpredictable or recognition of the fact that potentials diminish and time slips away are all matters somehow overlooked, obscured from view or discounted. He tends his small garden, almost never leaving it. Occasionally, he must narrow its dimensions in the face of insistent pressure from the outside or in the face of his own diminishing physical strength. Death, a matter that makes all planning irrelevant, must be dealt with in a way that denies its reality.

Case Study 1: *The Physician Who Planned Everything*

A thirty-nine-year-old married physician who worked on a geriatrics ward in a large university hospital was extraordinarily attentive to his work, meticulously organizing myriad small details related to the management of his patients. He had prepared a daily "checklist" with forty items for each patient, and the nursing staff were asked to submit a list to him for each patient each day. He was, without question, remarkably dedicated to his ward and to his patients. The doctor who had preceded him was by no means as committed to the work. And the same was true of the doctor who preceded his predecessor.

In this aging and ill population, there were many who fell mortally sick. In such moments, the doctor was constantly in attendance, grimly battling to postpone, to head off death. The oldest, most incapacitated, most hopelessly ill of his patients received every possible medical assistance. When necessary, he introduced heroic efforts to win or prolong the battle with death. Yet surprisingly, he was never known to lose his composure when the battle to sustain life was lost. Instead, he would retreat at once to his office, the patient's chart in his hand. Once there, he would unlock a file drawer, extract a large group of cards and begin to make out a new card, one containing a compilation of all facts and figures about the patient who had just died. He would comment about this activity, "You see, in a way, they are not really gone. I have them here."

For the obsessive person, the need for structure, predictability and stability is very great. The journey through life is not a casual wandering. It is not a free-form dance. It is instead a series of planned, strategic and logical steps. Vagueness is poorly tolerated. Human events are judged in terms of their potential for disruption of the previously structured plans. The spontaneous nature of emotions makes them a potentially disruptive force and so they must be discounted, underplayed or even "disowned."

In a discussion about a young couple who had terminated their engagement on the afternoon of December 31, the doctor in the previous example stated, "I can't understand why they didn't wait until after New Year's Eve."

The need which this kind of person feels to establish consensus, order and certainty in his own life often governs his expectations of relationships with friends, mate and children. And, from time to time, he or she may be deserted by the spouse who is always a little bewildered as to why it is necessary to flee. The wife of the doctor was one such person.

> Of course, materially, we do have most everything I want. And he's not mean to me. He does remember our anniversary, birthdays and the like. But living with him is like living by the numbers. It's a long, dark, monotonous cave. It's no fun. Nothing is spontaneous. There are no surprises. It's like living trapped in ten feet of space. Walk three steps one way and the wall is there. Three steps the other way and there is another wall. I have to get out.

Her husband expressed great puzzlement as to what was troubling his wife:

154

I guess I have a lot of trouble letting go. I like to be sure, I try to think it out, sometimes write the pros on one side and the cons on the other. You wouldn't want to make a mistake if you could avoid it. Not that one mistake would be so bad, of course. Everyone makes a mistake sometime, but if you just go on making mistakes, then sooner or later you're going to get into trouble. But I started to talk about how hard it is sometimes for me to let go. My wife went out last week and bought a toaster and I was very upset with her. She just went out and bought it. I like to, well, to begin with, make sure that we need it. And then, I try to figure out the money for it. We do have a good income since both of us work. So, it's not exactly that we need the money. But I like to know that if we are going to spend money for a toaster that we'll get it back and save it by not spending for something else. Then, I like to be sure that we get it for the right price. I usually call one or two stores and look in the newspapers to see if there is a sale. Sometimes, I look in the want ads of the newspaper under used items. Of course, we've never bought anything like that that's used, but just to be sure. Then, I'll go over to the library and look up what the consumer magazine recommends. And I guess, if I feel we have bought the right machine, and at the right place, I feel, "A job well done. It's as it should be."

It remains a speculative matter to attempt to correlate early life experience with the development of overriding obsessive and compulsive approaches to later living. Many of these individuals in early childhood were taught that life itself is a long series of instructions as to "how things should be," what is good and what is bad, proper and improper, safe and unsafe. Instead of being encouraged to trust his own instincts and impulses, the child learns to seek comfort in ritualized behavior. Symmetry, counting, ordering and categorizing come to be the ordinary ways of reacting in the face of stress, vagueness or doubt. These kinds of responses are usually reinforced positively by "good grades." In school, the obsessively organized child may do quite well. But, of course, the child who is devoted to learning and participating flawlessly in adult-created behavior is somewhat less the child and is instead a small replica of an adult. And many obsessive adults have difficulty recalling much difference between their spirit and frame of mind as children and that which characterizes them as adults. They never really had much of a childhood. There is a kind of sadness in hearing such an adult describe his efforts to understand spontaneous behavior in his or her own children. Returning again to the doctor:

> I can't understand it when the kids gulp down their milk. I keep telling them to sip it slowly, to relax and finish their glass and then wait a minute before they fill it up again. And then, don't fill it all the way up. Just halfway up. Why waste milk? We didn't waste it when I was young, believe me! And even when we had plenty, my mother taught us to behave. That's a large part of what's wrong at our house. My wife refuses to limit and train the children.

"Training the children" in this instance would mean stressing that self-esteem and freedom from anxiety are contingent upon the very careful control of impulses and suppression of nonconforming trends.

Those with obsessive living patterns tend to resist change and the patterns tend to be rather durable. They often persist through an entire lifetime without disruption. However, this is not always the case. Certain life circumstances seem to promote a breaking down of obsessive living with a resulting anxiety that may be very intense. When this happens, pervasive preoccupation with fears about obscene, aggressive or shameful deeds (obsessions) may develop. Or, as if to divert himself, the individual may undertake some ritualized act such as hand washing, counting or listing (compulsion) which becomes a total preoccupation. The greater the threat, the more frantic are the efforts of the individual to reestablish order, perhaps by cutting down even more sharply on the dimensions of his life. Under stress he may ultimately retreat to a preoccupation with the thinnest conceivable aspects of human experience. He may eventually be totally obsessed with concern about the most apparently trivial matter which nevertheless completely fills his mind during every waking moment. The possibility of having done something wrong or incorrectly is constantly reviewed, relived, weighed, pondered. All other considerations recede in importance. Concern may center on some past sin, real or imagined, some past oversight, or he or she may be totally preoccupied with keeping clean. In the most severe instance, life's concerns may be reduced to the space between hospital bed and wash basin; life becomes only a ritualized treading back and forth. In this desperate way, the obsessive person continues the struggle to sustain some order so that life may be lived out. The events that accompany this kind of "decompensation" give a hint as to the dangerous elements which had always resided outside the narrow areas of concern that had previously been the "life" of the obsessive person. The characteristics of this outer world, the weeds from next door, which, with decompensation, overrun the well-tended garden, are dirt, shame, disease, disapproval, chaos, hate, failure and finally "my own death." With the collapse of the long-standing, defensive way of living all of these matters confront and terrify the person who for so long had evaded them. Many obsessive ideas and compulsions center on these areas in the decompensating person.

In a general way, three kinds of life circumstances appear to lay the groundwork for a breaking down of an obsessive and compulsive pattern of living. First of all, occasions do arise when even the most strenuous denial efforts cannot remove pervasive anger, resentment, disappointment or fear. Yet, there is no place in the life of the obsessive individual for direct expression of such emotion. In this kind of circumstance, the individual may flee from his anger (resentment, fear). At the same time, he is fleeing from himself. This is accomplished either by narrowing sharply his openness to the current aspects of his own life experience and/or by simultaneously developing some new ordering ritual as a way of reinserting stability and order into a world threatened with loss of control. With enough provocation or stress, the individual who had structured his life to avoid direct confrontation with his own feelings may find that the strength of those feelings makes "business as usual" an impossible mandate. Something has to give!

Another kind of life event that may produce a breaking down or decompensation of a previously stable obsessive pattern is, paradoxically, a promotion to a more responsible position. Because ordering, maintaining stability, tidiness, careful attention to paper work and neat office management are, in a general way, good business virtues, promotion to a position of higher authority is often bestowed on a person who has performed every act methodically. Success in maintaining rigid schedules, precise timetables and the like sees the obsessive individual promoted to an executive position calling for flexibility, the ability to tolerate uncertainty, skill in interpersonal relationships and, above all, the capacity to sort out the important from the trivial. A promotion from secretary-treasurer to president of the company, from teacher of introductory science to school principal, from physician on the ward to superintendent of the hospital, are all cases in point. The rigid formulas and structured life-style which worked in the lower situation are often unworkable in a job with many variables, uncertainties and constant change. The promotion of the man or woman who lives scrupulously by the rules to a post where the old rules don't work anymore then provokes anxiety followed by rapid accommodation to the new situation or rapid decompensation.

The person who avoids anxiety by keeping busy, keeping organized, working hard and keeping up a schedule faces an impossible problem as he or she grows older. Physical illness, in particular, poses an extreme threat to psychological equilibrium. The individual who feels that "what I am is what I do," on being deprived of the ability to do may experience a severe sense of depression and worthlessness. This is what happens to the woman whose whole life is devoted to husband and children and to "doing" for them, only to have this role taken from her by the death of or divorce from the husband and the ordinary departure of the maturing children. When this happens, depression, self-depreciation and anxiety occur along with an increasingly frantic preoccupation with obsessive or compulsive acts.

The matter of therapy, that is, helping the individual who has grown dissatisfied with all that doesn't happen in his life experiences or, conversely, helping the anxious individual whose obsessive defenses are coming apart, will be considered in more detail in a subsequent chapter. Some observations are appropriate at this time. Importantly, the obsessive individual is more easily described than effectively changed by known treatment programs. Effecting change in this kind of living pattern is notoriously difficult, often unsuccessful and, when attempted, quite a chore for both the therapist and the patient. The deficit in the patient's spontaneity, his inability to express his own feelings and his continual search for instructions as to "exactly what am I supposed to do now" are very discouraging, particularly if some form of psychotherapy is attempted. The tendency of the obsessive patient to routinize and remove spontaneity in life applies as well to his therapy. He attempts at all costs and at all times to eliminate vagueness, urging the therapist to outline areas that should be carefully explored, turning to other resource persons, reading articles in periodicals or in texts in order to discover what he should take up with his doctor. The possibility that useful discovery could come spontaneously in the relationship is ignored. Instead, he hopes the therapy will represent a safe and planned journey up a familiar, well-landmarked road. But that is precisely his problem!

The therapist, exasperated, tired of tugging at his patient in the attempt to divert him from ritualistic, relentlessly narrowing efforts, says, "Your estrangement from real human emotions and your refusal to look at your life deceives only you. Your blind search to find meaningless rules alters nothing. Your making of lists is absurd. You are mortal like the rest of us and while you are counting, your life recedes and disappears." There are times when the patient will reply, "Can't you see by the feverishness with which I work, by how much I surrender, by the heavy demands that I place upon myself, that I know all of the things that you say about me even better than you?"

CHAPTER 10

Hysterical Living

One of the most fascinating areas for study in medicine, psychology or the social sciences is that way of living, thinking and reacting to oneself and one's world which we shall refer to as "hysterical living." A thousand and more symptoms/complaints have been reviewed at one time or another under the general heading of "hysteria." They run the gamut from total bodily paralysis and complete loss of sensation, an uncounted number of unexplained physical complaints and/or a psychological insecurity and dependency resulting in lifelong invalidism. As early as the 1700s it was noted that some persons when worried or frightened could describe or demonstrate symptoms related to every bodily system and suggestive of almost every disease. These include abnormal movements such as tremors (shaking) of the head, arms and legs, a variety of tics and jerks, convulsive movements of the entire body, disturbances of gait, paralysis of the extremities suggestive of strokes, paralysis of the muscles affecting the vocal cords leading to an inability to speak. Such a list would also include disturbances in the ability to feel, including loss of sensation in one part of the body or in the entire body, disorders of the organs of sense including hearing, vision and swallowing, and pains of all varieties and in all locations including, not infrequently, pains of such magnitude and persistence that they lead to surgical intervention. And what is sometimes called "hysterical overlay" can produce a substantial exaggeration of symptoms of any and every organic illness. In short, the physical symptoms that may be experienced in hysterical living are many and varied, either reasonable facsimiles or grotesque caricatures of symptoms ordinarily referable to organic disease.

No less complex are the dependency, tears, anger, childish temper,

160

fainting, periods of confusion and sexual difficulties that are also frequently a part of this living style.

Who is this individual who may come to the doctor with any of the hundred symptoms listed above? Hysterical living in contemporary Western culture is more characteristic in women. This is governed largely by attitudes toward women and the rearing practices directed to little girls and reinforced as they mature. This is changing—though slowly. When the term "hysteria" was coined, it derived from the Greek word *hyster*—meaning uterus—and reflected the belief that uterine displacement or malfunction was involved in the symptoms and life-style of unhappy or physically ill women.

From an existential point of view, search of one's own history and feelings always reveals the basis for appreciating what is happening to another person. It is not some unknown or different kind of human experience that one finds in hysterical living. Rather, there is a different emphasis, a different degree, a different frequency with which certain kinds of situations are encountered. We have been there before, not only the dependent urge, but the murderous impulse, the homosexual thought, the wish to abandon everything, the grandiose fantasy, the covetous awareness of another's possessions or another's mate, resentment of another's success, the wish to be mothered again, the misperception that one's own name was being called, the fear when alone in the home, the resentment and mistrust of another race, the wish to hoard selfishly, the wish to take the most attractive portion of food from a family table —all these are not simply events in the life and consciousness of others. They are human experiences, many or most of which have been at one time or another in the consciousness of everyone.

OBSERVATIONS ON HYSTERICAL LIVING

Every person is, from time to time, given to a view of self or of self in relation to others which is characteristic of everyday experiencing in hysterical living. It may follow a sudden telephone call from one's boss with the crisp message, "I want to see you immediately." Or it may have been at a time when a woman was about to break her engagement and reveal that there was someone else she preferred. Or it may follow a call from a banker or from a bill collector or an unexpected message from the children's pediatrician. The sudden awareness of personal impotence or danger, the acute sense of being junior to another person and the overwhelming inclination to dependency are characteristic of the way life is discovered to be in hysterical living. To defend herself against the ever-present danger of anxiety, the individual tries to establish some kind of symbiotic allegiance with a stronger person or group of individuals. It is as if she believes that "so long as he stands beside me, immortal giant that he is, I am safe." Most of her life's problems recede or disappear when she is "tied in" with him. In turning herself over to him she must learn to suppress her own feelings about many things. This is compensated for, however, by the fact that she is not afraid while he is there. In the most intense and pathological form, her surrender of herself and her total trust in the other person's solutions represent a great personal delusion about the nature of the world. Hysterical living cuts her off from important aspects of her own life. She is first of all much less an individual. Her dependence upon him can make her shallow and superficial in many aspects of life. She tries to feel and say and do those things that she hopes will win his approval. She seeks a kind of safe, neutral ground, always watching him rather attentively for clues as to how he feels and, in particular, how he feels about her. It is not only that she is dependent upon him; rather, she structures her very existence in order to remain with him. She has a well-developed radar system in order to come to know what he is thinking and feeling almost before he knows himself. In this way she remains rather constantly on the alert. She is always "running scared" and in stressful periods may resemble a new member of a dance team, unfamiliar with the routine, hoping to bluff along by watching carefully what the other members of the troupe are doing. This dependency and turning to another makes her like Blanche, who in the final scene of Tennessee Williams's *Streetcar Named Desire* places herself and her destiny in the "hands of the gentleman." (In that instance, as in most, the trust was misplaced since the gentleman was taking her away to a mental asylum.)

Usually, in real life, the attempt to achieve a sustaining dependent relationship leads not only to loss of genuineness and surrender of personal destiny, but also to disappointment, humiliation and betrayal.

There is a fraudulence inherent in any person who places her destiny in another's hands. It requires a great deal of pretending on everybody's part. Her destiny is uncertain, but no more so than his. She is essentially as rich as he in terms of the potential for experiencing her life. If they are the same age, she is likely to outlive him! The hysterical living adaptation is her way of hiding or losing herself by using him to obscure her unwillingness to be responsible for her own life. His acceptance of that role accomplishes the same self-deceit in his life. Sooner or later, the pretending gives way. He may desert her despite years and years of promising, "Trust me. You need not concern yourself with responsibility for your life since I am here, and I will always be here to care for you. I am immortal." The facts of life will cause him to fail to fulfill this commitment. He may die and in that way desert her. Or he may tire of the awesome burden of her trust and betray her or abuse her in such a fashion that she simply cannot pretend that he is taking care of her. She may find herself caught between two strong men (or, occasionally, between a strong man and an equally strong mother) and be in great conflict as to where to entrust her own destiny. In this moment when hysterical living no longer works and she experiences her shield falling away, she may be flooded with anxiety. Or, following a brief interval of anxiety she may feel absolutely helpless and demonstrate her sense of inadequacy through the emergence of one or another of a thousand complaints about her body.

Even when her relationship with him remains more or less intact, there is inevitable dissatisfaction because of the limitations imposed by the role-playing in her life. At such moments, she may turn to the person who is to provide solutions to her problems and angrily declare that the world (for which he is responsible) is not perfect. Garbage is not collected. Mice abound. Bodily parts ache. Yet, he seems powerless. She experiences a kind of smoldering resentment, pouts, complains and accuses him of failing in his promises. Then he may come to resent her demands, and the time comes for him to opt out of the the impossible contract.

In gross form, hysterical living represents a great loss of human potential. Its pretended basis that "he is immortal," "that I am more fragile than others," "that he can stand between life's problems and me," gives way and reveals an overwhelming sense of being a child in an adult world and of living within a body one cannot trust. She must then move frantically in a chaotic search for how she feels, who she is and where she is going.

As I noted previously, in Western culture symptoms associated with hysterical living have clustered more frequently in girls and women. However, the essential attitudes toward life and developmental circumstances which predispose to such symptomatology can exist for a man as well. They include carrying from childhood into adult life a good deal of uncertainty about one's self and one's own body; a tendency toward defensive "fusing" with another person and the establishment of a dependent role with that person; a fairly hyperactive radar system maintained to discern the attitudes and feelings of the necessary other. Disruption of this pattern of living is often precipitated by abandonment, betrayal or abuse by the other or when an individual with strong dependency needs becomes trapped between two strong persons, each seeking domination. Decompensation is characterized by anxiety and/or somatic concern. Such events in the life of an adult male are illustrated in the following case study.

Case Study 1: *A Man with Chest Pain and Two Women*

Arthur Reynolds, a thirty-three-year-old unmarried schoolteacher, was seen in psychiatric consultation in April 1973 because of mounting anxiety about his heart. He had been repeatedly examined and had several normal electrocardiograms in the preceding six months. But he was not reassured. His internist decided to refer him to a psychiatrist. The interview revealed a friendly, somewhat passive man who was very anxious as he offered details about chest pains and other bodily sensations he was experiencing.

He had been teaching in the same school system for eight years, seemed to be an appreciated teacher and appeared to have a good attitude with regard both to the importance of his work and to his ability to perform adequately. His initial response to questions about his social life was that "everything is okay." Closer questioning, however, revealed the following information: His father had died some seven years earlier and he had moved into the mother's home where he was living at the time of the interview. His father's

164

death had followed a series of heart attacks which continued over a number of years. The mother was in generally good health but did suffer from "spells" at times of great pressure. During these periods she would withdraw to her bed for several days and her son assumed minor nursing duties as well as the tasks of straightening up the house, cooking and preparing a good deal of tea.

There was another woman in his life. For two and a half years he had been dating a woman six years younger than himself. She was also a teacher. He felt that he loved this woman but was cautious about marriage. He had found it necessary to return to his mother's home each night, preferably before midnight even though his relationship with the other teacher was an intimate one. Understandably there was little love lost between the two women despite the patient's strenuous efforts to maintain a peaceful status quo. That situation appeared to be deteriorating. A showdown loomed. Christmas was coming and his friend was anticipating a gift of a very small box with a ring inside while his mother was making holiday plans for her son to drive her eight hundred miles to the south so that they could visit her old friends.

Throughout his life, Arthur Reynolds had been a shy and uncertain person, the only boy in a family with three older sisters. He had been particularly close to his mother because his father had worked as a railroad conductor and was away from the family a good deal of the time. After graduation from state teacher's college he had lived happily in another part of the country, but his father's illness and his mother's wish for her son's return proved too strong for him to resist.

The patient was seen for eight hours of psychotherapy. His mother was present for two hours and his friend (who considered herself his fiancée) was also present with him for two hours. The therapist had proposed a meeting with both women present but the patient sought and received a moratorium to his doctor's request.

Both women seemed to have a similar effect on Arthur Reynolds. In their presence (in the consultation room at least) he was quiet, appeasing and inhibited. He appeared fearful of receiving a direct question and was very defensive when it was his turn to speak. He was frightened of provoking either of them. He was trapped between two strong women, both of whom had the capacity to make him feel anxious and guilty.

The therapist tried to be careful not to become a third strong person in the life of Arthur Reynolds. Instead, this very intelligent man was encouraged to look at his obligations to other people and his fear of provoking angry response from anyone. At times the focus was upon the psychological problems; at times the patient talked of his physical complaints. On occasion, the areas coincided:

> Patient: I've worried about mother's health for years. She's getting up there, you know.
>
> Therapist: She looks pretty robust to me. I figure she might outlive all of us.
>
> Patient: Well, fifty seven is up there. And if anything happens to her, I'd never forgive myself.
>
> Therapist: Pretty well preserved for fifty-seven. Looks pretty good. Maybe if you'd get off her back, she could get married again.
>
> Patient: (Pauses) My God! I just had that pain again in my chest.
>
> Therapist: That would really be cool. A double wedding. You could give each other away.
>
> Patient: Then you think my pains are . . .
>
> Therapist: I'm rooting for growing pains.

One pattern of hysterical living which called forth much interest, particularly several generations ago, was labeled "the grand hysteria," a condition that arose as if by magic or in response to the thunderous wrath of the gods: "And she was stricken with blindness"; "And suddenly, all the power left his legs and he could not move them"; "And as the train on which he was riding disappeared in the distance, she fell into a faint. When she revived, all memory of who she was had disappeared." Several of the patients with whom Sigmund Freud initially worked and who served as the sources for his original theories presented these gross kinds of symptoms.

Bearing in mind that the hysterical symptom is most likely to appear and persist in an individual whose life experiences and sense of self are congruent with hysterical living, the following case of "hysterical aphonia" (loss of voice), though very unusual in the contemporary Western world, may be illustrative of the kind of reality that allows or encourages the denial of self in hysteria.

Case Study 2: *A Disease That Magic Alone Could Cure*

Barbara Williams, age sixteen, was admitted to the hospital on November 9, 1973, because of a loss of voice which had persisted for two and a half months. All medical examinations of her throat were negative. A variety of therapeutic efforts had failed to restore her ability to speak above a whisper. She presented the picture of a calm and unconcerned, somewhat immature sixteen-year-old girl. She whispered answers to all questions but demonstrated little concern over her difficulty. She resembled closely the classical picture of "la belle indifférence" described one hundred years ago by Janet as characteristic of patients with "grand hysteria."

The patient's difficulties had begun at a high school dance when her eighteen-year-old boyfriend pulled on and broke a necklace that she was wearing. She complained that he had hurt her neck at the time and gradually, over a period of three days, developed an "aphonia" of sorts, characterized by whispering and moving her lips without making sounds. In the succeeding weeks, she received a great deal of attention from her family, teachers and classmates. The doctors were initially puzzled, then increasingly frustrated as the symptom resisted all treatments.

Although the patient and her family were products of a low socio-economic background, she was conveyed to the hospital in a chauffeur-driven limousine. It was owned by a well-known Mr. Green, a seventy-eight-year-old retired industrialist on whose estate the Williams family lived. The patient's father worked as a custodian. At the time of admission to the hospital, Barbara's mother proudly explained that Mr. Green was underwriting Barbara's expenses. It became clear that Mr. Green's relationship to the Williams family was an unusual one, perhaps something of a throwback to the legendary days of yore, of fairy godfathers, enchanted castles and such. The Williams family, mother, father and six children, had come north from Texas as migrant workers eight years earlier. The family was, more or less, adopted en masse by Mr. Green in the aftermath of a workers' strike against Mr. Green during which Barbara's father had sided with the old man and against the other workers. As a

167

result, the Williams family was moved into a custodian's home on the Green estate and the old industrialist, turned philanthropist to this family, assumed a kind of distant parental interest in them. Although actual contacts between the family and Mr. Green were stylized, formal and infrequent, this relationship was of overpowering significance within the family. The mother talked continuously about his occasional visits and what he had said to each child. Her chief technique in disciplining the children was to threaten to notify Mr. Green of their misbehavior, with the danger that the old man would withdraw their Christmas privileges and other things. The family was committed to the idea that "so long as he lives, giant that he is, we are safe."

Barbara was, recognizably, a child who had emerged from a family with this kind of perspective about life. She viewed herself as a child in a world where "things happen to you." She shared unquestioningly the family's superstitious commitment to belief in a spiritualistic religion; the notion of the hand from above reaching down was quite plausible to her. Her view of the world was one that seemed to say, "Of course, when your throat gets hit, you can't talk."

As a patient, Barbara repudiated the possibility of a psychotherapeutic encounter because of the participants. The initial intention of the psychiatric staff was to avoid dealing with Barbara in a manner suggesting that "big and powerful people were acting on little, passive and helpless people." That effort was not successful, however. In the end, after six weeks of hospitalization, to the disappointment of the staff but well within the frame of reference of Barbara and her family, Barbara was induced to speak through the use of an intravenous chemical, sodium amytal, a kind of "truth serum." The following day, in the presence of her family, again with sodium amytal, she was induced to sing a Christmas carol (it was that time of year). The following day, talking cheerfully, Barbara returned triumphantly home in Mr. Green's chauffeured limousine, prepared to join her mother in telling to all who would hear the tales of the miracles wrought by Mr. Green and his hirelings.

Some individuals present their complaints in a vivid and colorful fashion, demonstrate a broad range of emotions and with great convic-

168

tion and histrionically demand immediate attention by presenting all symptoms as if they were desperate indeed. Posturing of this kind seems designed to produce a stance by the clinician of excessive reassurance, the prescription of medications, the offering of gratuitous advice and so forth. But when this happens, the clinician has assumed a role facilitating the patient's dependency. This is a mistake as may be surmised in the following case study.

Case Study 3: *A Woman, Abandoned, Goes in Search of a Doctor*

The patient, a twenty-one-year-old woman, a former student in the university, sought treatment because of very profound anxiety, a fear of being alone, and specific concern that she might harm herself. Her symptoms developed after she had been abandoned by a rather dominating fiancé upon whom she had been quite dependent for two years. Symbolic of their relationship was the fact that she had given up her own schooling in order to live with him, had allowed her driver's license to lapse because he was critical of her driving skill, had taken on his political activism although she had little personal interest in such matters. In general, she overlooked his domination and abuse because, in her words, "I wasn't afraid of anything when I was with Jack." She had, in essence, adopted in her relationship with her fiancé a style of living that inauthentically said, "As long as Jack stands between the world and me, I need not fear; and our relationship is immortal." However, her fiancé abandoned her in favor of another girl and suddenly she was thrown back upon herself. She was filled with a variety of self-depreciating thoughts and somber fears. Old doubts about herself that had been out of her mind for some years returned to torment her. She was easily startled, cried with little provocation, slept poorly, was fearful of a nighttime intruder and, puzzlingly, for the first time since early childhood she was afraid at night that a mouse or a rat would enter her room. At the same time she was fearful of herself—fearful that she might harm herself or that in some crisis situation she would be paralyzed by fear and unable to seek safety.

She appealed to the doctor for immediate help, medicine and reassurance. But the doctor pressed on and asked for more details as to what she was feeling about the change in her life. He learned that she had, to her surprise, experienced some good moments in recent days, moments in which she realized that her fiancé had treated her shabbily. She reported that there was a part of her that felt glad that he was gone. She spoke of having felt dominated by him and wondered whether she might in the future have a greater chance at self-expression. She recalled her parent's disapproval of their relationship and the general disdain with which her fiancé's dominating behavior had been regarded by all of her friends. She tearfully asked herself why she involved herself with him in the first place, asked why she was "so weak and willing to be taken over."

Then, in almost the same breath, she said to the doctor, "I'll do anything you tell me. I'll take anything you'll give me. Perhaps you will want to put me in the hospital. You have got to do something."

The doctor viewed her symptoms and the pull they exerted upon him with very mixed feelings. He could reassure her, could offer medicines that would likely reduce the level of her anxiety or could hospitalize her, thereby guaranteeing that there would be no mice and that she would not be alone. At the same time, he did not want to reinforce the patient's tendency to escape herself by a pretense that "so long as he lives, giant that he is with his white coat, his pills and his mouse-free hospital, I need not concern myself about the meaning of my being."

In making the decision as to how to respond to the requests of his patient, the doctor tried to sort out in his own mind what he hoped would result from this stressful and unhappy time in her life. Freedom from anxiety was certainly an important goal, but she had been relatively free of fears while she was with her fiancé. Yet freedom from anxiety on the same basis—substituting a doctor for the missing fiancé—was not an appealing approach. That kind of comfort was won for her by a flight from herself. The price was heavy! Therapy, existential variety, would have to go a different way.

In the subsequent months of working with this patient (outside of a hospital), the doctor often felt that she wanted him to assume responsibility for *her*. Her message, disguised or otherwise, was, "You take care of me! You are bigger than I am!" She repeatedly presented to the doctor a series of complaints that added up to: "There's something wrong with my body. Do something!" Or, perhaps more fundamentally, she stated, "I've never really trusted my body. It's never been quite right. It requires attention and lots of it." In a way, the doctor's greatest contribution to this patient, by word and by act, by attitude and by manner, was to respond with the following message: "I trust your body. So can you. It's really okay. As a matter of fact, the same goes for the rest of you. You could really trust yourself if you'd give yourself a chance. I'm very curious how you will choose to live your life."

CHAPTER 11

Depressive Living, Mania
and Suicide

What is it like to be severely depressed? The average person's memory of transient moments of being "blue," disappointed or unhappy are misleading guides in answering this question. Mild depression, occurring as a now-and-again episode in the life of almost every person, is many levels removed from the experience of severe mental depression. The average reader would need to recall the period of greatest unhappiness and hopelessness in life, multiply its intensity by some factor of ten, stretch the interval of despair over time, not simply hours or days, but weeks, months, even years. Then, compound such experience by a relentless, every-night interruption of sleep beginning at 2 or 3 A.M. and continuing to dawn. There is no respite, no interruption. The depressed person's existence becomes a timeless ordeal. Each year, thousands of persons take their own lives in order to escape the anguish of depressive living. Beyond those who succeed, more thousands contemplate and attempt suicide. Profound depression is among the most catastrophic of all human situations. Yet, paradoxically, there is no tangible injury. There is nothing to show to enable another person to comprehend. There is only suffering without clearly evident reason. The sentence most commonly spoken by depressed individuals is this one: "No one knows how bad I feel. No one could possibly understand."

DEPRESSION

There is no natural course for depression. Often, changes in mood begin quite subtly, and it proves difficult to date their onset. Insidiously,

172

over a period of weeks, months or even years, persons, places and activities that had earlier possessed an aura of friendliness and pleasure become instead burdensome and to be avoided. Life experiences begin to lose their flavor. At the same time, episodes of anxiety and despair, unexpected and without apparent cause, begin to occur in situations that were formerly routine. As a result, the individual starts to withdraw, to hold back, to avoid, and there is a consequent narrowing of openness to life experience. In such a mood, old friends are avoided, work is postponed and religious services are shunned, even if each of these have been part of the patient's way of life since early childhood. When obliged to attend some public occasion, on entering the meeting room, the depressed and anxious individual takes note of all possible modes of exit, planning to withdraw even as he arrives. The same attitude marks interpersonal experiences. Such contacts are no longer engaging. Where before the individual lived in relative comfort in his or her world, he now feels estranged and made restless by it. There is a loss of harmony with things, with others and with oneself. Progression of the state of depression leads to extreme agitation and fearfulness, or, conversely, in some instances the individual may feel apathetic, tired, withdrawn and disinterested. Or, as depression grows, the individual becomes restless, impatient and agitated, while at the same time uninterested in matters that were formally very important.

One such matter, for example, is sexuality. Many who are developing depressive states progressively lose most or all interest in sex. If depression is developing in the husband, he simply approaches his wife much less frequently. If the wife is depressed, she is likely to find excuses and refuse, or her participation will be perfunctory. This is not to suggest, however, that the depressed person pulls away from the mate in all respects. He or she may become extremely dependent upon and prone to hang on and stay close to the mate. Sometimes this dependence is accompanied by a general reluctance to be alone, and the mate is obliged to assume almost full-time "baby-sitter" responsibilities for a spouse who had been very confident and self-reliant until that time.

Thus, over time, an individual's openness to his world may have retracted considerably. Relaxing and satisfying encounters occur infrequently. Friends become nuisances. The church, the theater or a large office building acquires dangerous dimensions. More mature aspects of the marital relationship become subsidiary to passivity and clinging dependence. Ordinarily, by this time, sleep disruption has begun and the patient's nights are dreaded as much as the days, ultimately more! The sleep disturbance is sometimes a characteristic early morning awakening. The day has been long and miserable and the individual is tired by bedtime and soon falls asleep. However, he or she awakens at 3 A.M. or 3:30 A.M. and is not able to fall asleep again. These early morning hours are a time of particular despair. He is tired, even exhausted, but his mind is beset with somber, ominous, hopeless thoughts about current life problems or about difficult periods in the past. He may focus upon wrongs done to him. Or at times, he will brood about his unfriendly acts to others. In those dreadful early hours, the noises of the home and the sensation and sound of his own heartbeat come heavily together. Worries about personal health or the health of the mate, children or grandchildren loom large; financial worries, real or imagined, are stark and overwhelming; the aggressive and ungrateful aspects of the world replace warmer and more tender sentiments. Everything is bad! Things are hopeless! There is no end to it! It is puzzling that some of these patients report that they do not cry. One man, who in the face of an exquisite level of depression in which he had twice attempted suicide, explained, "I wish I could cry. I feel like crying often. But no tears come. It's as if I'm dried up."

There are other times when depression does not begin insidiously over months and even years, but instead a specific traumatic event triggers a definable onset. There are individuals who can say, "I was in fine health, optimistic, doing my job, feeling good about things until moment X." Moment X is usually either an abrupt interruption of a deeply valued relationship through death, divorce, desertion, or it may follow a personal illness or injury. In the latter instance, the injury is frequently one that immobilizes the individual, restricting him to bed and making him dependent on others over a long period of time. Orthopedic injuries, major surgical procedures, heart attacks or strokes may precede and provoke depression. Coming during a convalescent period following injury or illness, depression may be very confusing to the patient's doctor, mimicking some form of "delayed healing." The patient and doctor may ascribe the unexpected discomfort, failure to gain weight, sleep disturbance and reluctance to return to a regular life situation as a continuation of the former injury or illness. Instead, a new problem and one of considerable magnitude has entered the picture. The patient with continuing incapacity despite "medical recovery" is often suffering an undiagnosed depression.[1]

Even when unrelated to other disease processes, the consequences of mental depression on general bodily health may be very profound. Depressed individuals may appear to be suffering from serious disease with weight losses of twenty to thirty pounds in a matter of weeks. Quite often, physiological manifestations of anxiety in the form of blushing, sweaty palms, rapid heartbeat, headache and tremors will also be present. Or some long-feared and ominous disease may seem to be developing. Because he or she feels so bad, only a diagnosis such as cancer, brain tumor or heart attack seems a sufficient explanation. Since any one of a thousand bodily complaints may be offered by the individual as the source of despair, a false clue may come from one of the laboratory studies that are performed to clarify the confusing clinical picture. In this situation, it comes to pass that the severely depressed patient is told by his doctor:

> I've been over you carefully and you are in good shape. Except, you have a very, very slight anemia. That is, your blood is a little thin, only slightly, but a little. And also, your pulse is a little fast. Now, neither of those problems is serious. I'm going to give you some iron pills for the blood problem and a little sedative to slow down the pulse. And in a month we'll see how you are.

The patient is misunderstood and the consequences are often serious. What is really wrong goes undetected. This happens often. It is a common medical error.

Most persons with substantial depression contemplate suicide, and a not inconsiderable number move perilously close to an attempt. The precise number of suicides in the United States and Canada is difficult to calculate. Many suicides are covered up, either by the patient or by the family physician. Family shame, religious prohibitions and insurance considerations lead to undercounting. However, a very large percentage of the yearly twenty-five thousand or more acknowledged suicides in North America occur as a result of a definitive depressive state. Many of these deaths are unnecessary since, when recognized, depression can be very effectively treated by the appropriate therapies. While no two people are exactly alike, the vast majority who are depressed will answer one question very clearly. When asked, "Are things different now than they were six months ago?" the reply is almost always, "Things in my life are as different as night and day! Things are much worse now! Things are worse than I believed possible!"

MANAGEMENT OF SEVERE DEPRESSION

Adequate management of the kind of severe depression that occurs very often in mature and older individuals requires that an experienced physician play a central role. *In the management of depression, denial of a medical approach with full access to antidepression medicines and, when necessary, hospitalization in a psychiatric unit is a serious mistake.* The therapeutic tasks call for the greatest personal and professional skill, and the clinician's first and immediate need is to reach out and make contact with a person who has become very much out of touch. This first task of "touching down" and bridging the patient's isolation is highly important. The severely depressed person has difficulty trusting anyone because he or she is almost always convinced that no one is in a position to know what is wrong or to offer assistance. The relationship between doctor and patient may be the last barrier to suicide when the patient awakens at 3 A.M. and contemplates until dawn what to do next. Establishing that relationship is both difficult and absolutely essential. I repeat the following as often as necessary; it must be heard:

> I understand how bad you feel and how hopeless everything seems. I've cared for other people who had a similar depression. I will work with you until you've recovered completely. I am going to ask your spouse to help us.

Including the patient's mate, or if there is no mate another responsible adult from the family, is almost always a constructive and sometimes a life-saving step. The patient, mate and friend should all be enlisted as allies and partners with the doctor in trying to find a remedy for the patient's difficulty. There are many times when you need all the help you can get!

It's best not to be vague about suicide and the doctor may well want to bring up the question directly: "I wonder if you have felt so bad that you have thought of taking your own life?" If the answer is an affirmative one, which it is with surprising regularity, the doctor, the patient and the patient's mate face the question of whether hospitalization is indicated. Frequently, the knowledge that a treatment program is being developed and that there is a firm contact between doctor, patient and mate makes it possible for the patient to remain out of the hospital while treatment continues.

In working with depressed individuals, the doctor will likely turn to drug therapy as an important part of the treatment. The patient's absolute cooperation and trust are essential. During the last twenty years remarkably effective chemical remedies have been developed, and even when the depression has reached a profound level, such medications frequently provide relief. However, a week or two or even three weeks of continued and faithful use of appropriate antidepressant drugs may be required before improvement occurs. The practical problems in this kind of situation are many. The patient, who may well be contemplating suicide, must be told that a long period of time will pass before relief comes. Even a day is a long time for a depressed person.

For the physician, then, in that first appointment there is a great deal to do, all at once. A solid contact with the patient and the mate must be established; the doctor must assure the patient that he has a sense of what is wrong, must emphasize the necessity of following exactly the medication instructions and simultaneously explain any possible side effects of the drug so that the patient does not stop his medication prematurely. Many of these drugs have mildly troubling side effects that are discouraging to patients. For example, a dryness of the mouth often accompanies use of antidepressant medications. Sometimes a slight skin rash develops. Occasionally, some dizziness occurs when one changes from a lying to standing position. And the first couple of days on any new medicine are likely to be worrisome and disappointing. In my own practice, at least 25 percent of patients will stop medications on their own unless we stay in very close touch, both by telephone every two or three days and with a visit at least every week. Obviously, prescriptions for large numbers of potentially lethal sleeping capsules are inappropriate.

Sometimes, the patient is so very uncomfortable and depressed that hospitalization is necessary. I have found from sad experience that once a decision to hospitalize has been made, the patient should be admitted at once. Changes in the plan such as a decision to move treatment to a hospital have led some patients to use the interval before admission for a suicide effort. This becomes more likely if the announcement of hospitalization is made and then the patient is left to worry and brood for a day or two. Once in the hospital, higher doses of medications can be given and supervision is more adequate. About one in ten of my patients who require hospitalization receive electrical shock therapy. The others respond to hospitalization, support and medications.

These matters will be considered again in Chapter 14, "Helping," but I want to emphasize one other important matter at this time. Specifically, by the time a depressive illness is established, the patient may be largely helpless to effect changes in his own feelings. He is almost totally incapable of self-help. I have worked with some of the world's most stubborn and determined people. But their maximal efforts to rid themselves of their depression achieved nothing. The urgings to try harder, work harder, work less, take a vacation, pray more, retire or what have you help not at all. The chemistry that underlies brain functioning is becoming more and more accessible to experiment and the pathological processes associated with mental depression are better understood in recent years. This is helping to explain how and why the various antidepression drugs work and why "more willpower" or "more faith" can't accomplish improvement. I find it very unfortunate that many already-guilty depressed patients are made guiltier still by those who have a simple plan. They just don't understand.[2]

DEPRESSION AND SUICIDAL GESTURE
IN YOUNG PEOPLE

In assessing depression and the risk of suicide, age is an important factor. For example, many young people who threaten or make suicide attempts do so in an impetuous way because of some here-and-now matter. They may have had no thought of suicide twenty-four hours earlier and if, mercifully, little damage is done, thoughts of suicide are forgotten a few hours later. Suicidal gestures in young adolescents and young adults are often a form of emphatic message of frustration or disappointment to a parent, sweetheart or employer. The message, in

178

translation, may sound something like this: "It isn't fair and I don't like it and won't stand for it! I will kill myself. Then you will be sorry!" Elements of frustration, rage, spite and a sense of impotence dominate the moment. The suicide attempt is often more gesture than anything else and little or no bodily harm is sustained. At times, the suicidal gesture leads to a change in a girlfriend's, boyfriend's or parent's attitude about some disputed matter. A bit of powerfully manipulative behavior may have worked. Of course, it's a dangerous game.

Not all suicide attempts by young people are unsuccessful. Neither are all such efforts perpetrated by impulsive, frustrated adolescents who simply needed to "do something" because of their pent-up frustrations and/or anger. There are times when the young person who made the suicide attempt remains depressed, expresses disappointment about recovering, offers no clear explanation of the circumstances that led up to the suicide attempt or talks in an incoherent, obscurely philosophical or morose manner. Or, if the individual utilizes a particularly bizarre, long-planned suicide method (such as a sixteen-year-old boy who attempted to kill himself with a bomb on which he had been working for that purpose over a period of two or three weeks), he or she is obviously a different kind of person than the impulsive, immature individual described previously. The young person who after a suicide attempt presents a somber, depressed or bizarre clinical picture must be viewed in a serious light. In that situation, steps need to be taken to protect the patient from himself, often through psychiatric hospitalization.

There is another kind of person who contemplates, threatens or attempts suicide as a well-practiced technique for controlling others. He or she may be somewhat older than most who play this game, but they have an essentially adolescent or immature spirit. They feel justified in utilizing the intimidating power that is in the hands of one who threatens suicide. Obviously, people who feel that "all's fair in love, war or what have you" can be a considerable problem for the involved family, for friends and for the therapist.

Case Study 1: *The "Helpless" Woman Who Could Tame Tigers*

Lynn Jefferson, twenty-nine, nursing instructor in a large municipal hospital, was referred to a psychiatrist by the dean of her school because of a spotty attendance record, several episodes of crying at work and the suspicion that she might be taking some kind of drugs. In the interview she presented an uneven picture. At times she seemed a rather sophisticated and intelligent adult woman. This contrasted with an initial set of demands which she tried to impose as her conditions for talking with the doctor. She insisted that the doctor promise never to contact her family who lived twenty-five hundred miles away (she was an only child and couldn't bear to hurt them), that he promise never to hospitalize her, that he agree to honor requests for medication and that she be free to contact him at any time she felt the need. She was assured that their conversations were private but was told that all the rest of her demands were childish. "Miss Jefferson, I'd be quite interested in working with you and I'd do my best. But I learned in 1939 that you can't do business with Hitler and I think your demands are those of a spoiled tyrant." She stormed out of the office but came back a few minutes later, pouted a bit and finished the first therapeutic hour on a cheerful note. She canceled the next appointment because she had a headache and appeared at his office without an appointment the following day. She was upset and disappointed when the doctor saw her for only a few minutes. Later that evening, she called to complain about an inability to sleep and requested a prescription for sleeping medication. The doctor offered to discuss that request at the next appointment. Lynn Jefferson slammed down the telephone angrily.

During the next several months, the patient alternately presented herself as a serious grown-up nurse trying to understand her problems and then as an angry, demanding child with an unending series of explicit and implicit demands on her doctor. In particular, she seemed to want contacts outside the ordinary therapeutic hours and wanted the freedom to call the doctor at home. She engineered several rather obvious attempts to encounter the doctor in a semisocial way, the most colorful effort being positioning herself at the bus stop next to the doctor's parking lot on a night when the temperature was ten degrees below zero. She was wearing no coat, stood shivering and looking helpless. The doctor, irritated at his patient but more irritated at himself for not driving on, drove the patient home. For the next several weeks, the patient seemed more at peace, less depressed, less demanding and more friendly toward the doctor.

Soon, however, her friendliness changed into an open wish to become romantically involved with her doctor who, she was certain, loved her as she insisted she loved him. The doctor offered interpretations and asked his patient to talk about her feelings rather than attempt to demonstrate them. She denounced her therapist for his rigidity. A few evenings later, a 2 A.M. telephone call from another nursing instructor brought the news that the patient had swallowed some twenty aspirin tablets. She was taken to a hospital emergency room and a gastric lavage (stomach pump) was used. She went home the same morning. However, she felt that because of her "suicidal feelings" she should be seen more frequently. When this request was refused, she resumed her nighttime telephone calls and staged a second, carefully preannounced suicidal gesture at 2 A.M. She called the therapist and announced that she had no choice but to kill herself because of the way he had treated her and she murmured, "Good-bye forever," hung up the telephone and refused to answer it again. The therapist paused en route to pick up an on-duty nurse from the emergency room and made a 2:30 A.M. home visit. Lynn Jefferson was moderately intoxicated, seductively arrayed in a nightgown and otherwise intact. On three other occasions during the succeeding year, the patient made overt or direct suicide threats, usually as part of some manipulative attempt to dislodge the therapist from what she felt was his cruel, aloof detachment.

She was a very trying person, who, despite relative chronological maturity, used the threat and the gesture of suicide as a powerful manipulative technique not only in her wish to control her doctor but also in her relationships with other important people in her life. The therapist repeatedly asked, "Is there any amount of reassurance that could convince you of another's esteem for you?" Or, "Does intimacy always present you with a need to test the other person?" Or, in exasperation, "When will you grow up?"

One step that proved very helpful to both Lynn Jefferson and her therapist was her agreement to allow her mother and father to join in for several sessions during one of their visits. They were older people (Lynn's mother was thirty-nine at the time Lynn was born and her father was forty-five), dignified and distant. Lynn's manner of behavior in their presence was about 90 percent "let's pretend." And they were the world's most civilized parents. All kissing, all hugging and all conversations were perfunctory. Her seventy- and seventy-six-year-old parents now, as when she was a child, rarely violated her "life space." They treated her in the psychiatrist's office as they had reared her, "aseptically." She grew up hungering for germs, lots of them!

In any instance where there is the suggestion of a threat to life, one must take it seriously. Where errors are made, they are better made on the side of overconcern and caution. There has been in recent years a concerted effort to develop predictors of suicidal behavior. Suicide prevention centers and/or suicide "hot line" telephone services have been established in a number of communities. Simultaneously, follow-up of all who threaten suicide over a one-, two- or three-year period has allowed some refinement in estimating probabilities. Of course, all such data refer to large numbers of people and provide only a general indicator of risk in any specific case. Most vulnerable are people who have lost a mate and live alone, those who drink heavily or take drugs, those who have recently stopped working and/or those who suffer manic-depressive illness or other psychiatric and physical illnesses.[3] I also worry a little more about people in whose family there have been one or more suicides. And I worry a great deal about patients who are depressed and respond slowly at a moment when I am about to leave for a vacation of more than a few days.

In the case of young, impulsive, immature individuals who have made an unsuccessful suicide attempt, it is usually a good idea to call for a family meeting with *everybody* present. Bringing young people and their families into the same room after a threatened or attempted suicide may open communication channels within the family that have been closed down for years. Such meetings bring into the open long-camouflaged fears and areas of misunderstanding. Equally, they also allow family members to make manifest the positive feelings they have for each other. A suicidal gesture represents a moment of crisis for the family. At the same time, it is a unique opportunity. The ultimate outcome can go either way. At worst, confronted by the threat to life of one of its members, the

182

family may grow more defensive, less communicative, more distrustful of itself. At best, "crisis intervention" may provide the discussion long desired by every family member which could not take place without crisis and the assistance of an outsider. However, a time of crisis represents a time-limited opportunity, that is, the potential for a constructive outcome is one that rapidly disappears. The clinician must carefully avoid sabotage of his own therapeutic effectiveness. This most often happens in one of several ways. First, the therapist undercuts the importance of the family conference by allowing a long interval to pass between the suicide attempt and the proposed meeting time. Or, a therapist can *guarantee* the failure of the meeting by agreeing to a conference at which one or more of the important family members are absent. For example, the father may be too busy working to come to the meeting about the suicide attempt of his son. Or the mother may feel that it would be better for the boy and his father to hold the interview. When this occurs, the purpose of the family interview will have been defeated. EVERYBODY has to come! Another way in which the therapist can undercut the effort is by assuming (or being placed in) a commanding, advice-giving, "charismatic" posture. Often the family arrives and says, "Well, doctor (or nurse), we are here. We want to know what to do. Tell us what to do." The therapist does well to avoid the honors offered and should instead seek only a partnership with the family in the effort to achieve an honest, open, direct level of communication. At the beginning of the discussion, neither the therapist nor anyone else knows what should be done. The therapist advises, "Let's find out what's going on. Everybody is going to have to help with that. Maybe something good can come out of this dreadful moment."

As mentioned earlier, there are times when depression in a young adult heralds a very serious emotional illness. Severe and sustained depression is contrary to the thrust toward life which ordinarily characterizes childhood, adolescence and the early adult years. When present, it often signals a very deeply fixed and not easily assuaged situation. It may be the beginning of a pattern of schizophrenic living or the first episode of a manic-depressive illness.

MANIC-DEPRESSIVE EPISODES

Sometimes, a pattern of recurring depressions may begin early and recur at intervals in later life. These recurring depressions may alternate with episodes in which there is an almost opposite state of mind, that is, an elated, hyperactive and profoundly enthusiastic "manic" mood. Or, depressive episodes alone may be present. The term "manic-depressive psychosis" describes this pattern of mood alteration. It often occurs in several family members. Genetic factors are important. Suicide risk is high. The depression of a manic-depressive cycle is often indistinguishable from other forms of depressive illness. Or, if there are subtle characteristics separating the clinical features of differing kinds of depression periods from the point of view of an outside, experienced clinician, the patient's level of suffering is still at the 100 percent level. But refinement of diagnosis allows a much more effective treatment program, one that offers a high probability of success in preventing recurrences. So, the most careful taking of personal and family history, the most thorough physical and neurological examinations and the most carefully evaluated treatment program are all essential. There is now much more reason for optimism in treating such problems than was ever possible before.[4]

Case Study 2: *A Woman Whose Life Changed for the Better in 1971*

Mrs. Annette Fisher had been hospitalized on a number of occasions because of recurring periods of depression and occasional periods of "elation and mania." I first saw her in 1971. She was forty-two years old, married, working as a legal secretary. Her difficulties had apparently begun quite early in her life. In 1940, just after her tenth birthday, there was an interval in which she was unable to go to school and instead remained home for about four months. At the time, the family doctor believed that she suffered some obscure physical illness, but on looking back at the episode Mrs. Fisher felt that it was the first of the recurring depressive cycles. The second came when she was sixteen years old. It was a very severe experience for her. At that point she felt so bad that she tried to hang herself. She was hospitalized. The doctors recom-

184

mended shock treatments but her family refused permission. After approximately six months, the depression lifted. At the age of twenty-five, the first period of mania occurred. It began gradually with a several-month period of growing elation.

The patient described that episode in the following manner:

"That first time when I got high, it started slowly. I'm not sure just when or how it began. However, after three months of being more and more elated and enthusiastic, I began to buy all kinds of things I didn't need and couldn't afford. I also began to make long-distance telephone calls all over the country at early hours. I had always been very restrained when it came to men, but during that time, I'm embarrassed to say, I dropped my standards altogether and I guess I had three or four sexual affairs in less than three months. And I wasn't sad when I broke up with each one. I happily went on to the next. I try not to think of that part of it. I was married when the next manic episode came and I was really interested in sex again, but that time all with my husband. Was he surprised!

"Finally, I drove eight hundred miles to see a friend who didn't even know I was coming. I arrived at 4 A.M. and woke her up and started talking and couldn't stop talking. After a while, she got the idea that something was wrong, and the next day she and another friend drove me back home. My folks met us and took me to the hospital. I don't remember too much about that except that I was singing and laughing and dancing in the ward."

This period of elation continued during hospitalization for another two months. Then, rather abruptly, it was followed by a very severe depression which lasted three months. Even after partial improvement, she was unable to return to work for an additional three months. The various cycles continued through most of her twenty-fifth year, then spontaneously went away. She subsequently married at twenty-eight, had two children without difficulty, worked on a reduced schedule and was quite happy with her life. In 1966, at the age of thirty-six, again apparently without clear cause, she became very depressed and made a serious suicide attempt by cutting the blood vessels in her neck. She barely survived this attempt on her life and when she regained consciousness, she felt very disappointed that she was still alive. She believed that she was a very sinful person and sat mutely for hours, staring straight ahead. Her posture was frozen except for the continual wringing of her hands. She usually made no response when approached or spoken to. At that time, a long series of electrical shock treatments was given. They helped but the tendency for depression remained to a greater or lesser degree over most of the succeeding year. She was not herself. While able to function in a superficial fashion, she derived little satisfaction or sense of continuity from her life.

During the succeeding four years from 1967 through 1971, there were two further episodes. One was a depressive period, the other a period of mania. Both were treated with electrical shock treatments, and in addition, following the period of depression, the newly developed antidepression medications were given for a period of one year. I first saw her in a good period in 1971. She was generally content with her life, devoted to her family and interested in her part-time job. She was concerned and guilty about the great financial burden which her illness imposed on the family and she was grateful to her husband. The history that she provided indicated that at least several members of her mother's and maternal grandfather's family had suffered nervous difficulties and that one uncle and one great-aunt from that side of the family had committed suicide. In 1971, she was placed on a new medication, lithium carbonate, and since that time she has been completely free of all symptoms of both depression and elation. That improvement has been sustained to the time of the writing of this book, a period of five years. Lithium carbonate appears to prevent both her manic and depressive episodes. Talking hadn't helped much. Neither did tranquilizers. Neither did family psychotherapy. The antidepression drugs gave an uncertain effect. Lithium seems to work!

Obviously, there are many kinds of depressions and a suicide attempt may signal many different meanings. In clinical practice, estimation of both the level of depression and the risk of suicide are among the most difficult problems. And severe depressions are often very refractory and recovery is slow in coming. But for family, friends and therapist, there is the reward that when it is finally over, one meets the most grateful and relieved person in the world.

186

CHAPTER 12

Alanda's Autobiography—
An Introduction to Schizophrenia

The pages that follow contain an autobiography written by Alanda Jenkins, a woman of thirty who had lived a haunted life filled with self-depreciation and torturing agitation for more than a decade. There were times when she was suicidal, confused and totally unreasonable. Many doctors had diagnosed her difficulty as schizophrenia. She was a sensitive person who was struggling desperately to maintain some semblance of order and dignity in her life. In many respects, she succeeded despite the intense level of her self-preoccupation and the bizarre nature of her symptoms. She was intelligent, sincere and touchingly grateful. In this woman's autobiography, the reader will sense a continuity between the insecure childhood days and the profoundly disturbed periods of her adult life. However, the relative importance and interrelationship of early life experience and various genetic, metabolic and neurochemical abnormalities in the development of unhappy, confused and disorganizing life-styles is only beginning to be understood. One more decade of research may solve many of the remaining questions. On reading Alanda's autobiography, the everyday joylessness, the absence of highs, the subdued sameness of everything in her life, are as striking as the descriptions of her periods of "decompensation." One's capacity to "turn on," get excited about and experience pleasure may be governed from earliest days by the same chemical systems within the brain which become grossly disordered in depression, mania and schizophrenia. There is currently intensive study of these variants of "normal" and "pathological."[1]

Preceding the autobiography are the admission notes of intern and nurses written on the hospital chart on the occasion of her evening arrival

187

at the psychiatric ward of the hospital. The date of admission was February 10, 1974.

Admission Note by Intern (February 10, 1974, 11:00 P.M.)

This thirty-year-old lady is admitted to the hospital with the chief complaint that "my whole life depends upon my hair. It either makes me or makes me not." According to the patient, the most important thing is how her hair feels and how it would feel to her hand. If her hair feels all right then it looks all right too. The patient is afraid to shampoo her hair. Any change or twist of her hair bothers her. If it gets limp or oily, the patient feels very frantic. She would like to fix it and never wash it, only comb it. She wishes it could always be the same. In the morning she always feels that her hair is worse, because there is a change in her hair from sleeping. She spends a great deal of the morning and the noon grooming and combing her hair. When she is not satisfied with her hair, the patient states, "I can't even sit and visit if my hair is not right. I have to make up some excuse and run to the bathroom and comb it. It's humiliating to leave someone sitting in my living room while I brush my hair like a lunatic." However, if she doesn't feel too bad, she forces herself to go out. There are good weeks and good days, but generally, the patient is upset because of her hair. Problems of less importance are: (1) complexion, (2) gaining weight—"I'm afraid to get fatter and fatter."

In the afternoons, the patient works as a beauty operator doing almost only hair work. She does not like her work but sometimes a hair case interests her. Sometimes with all these thoughts and feelings she gets confused and worn out. "Sometimes I feel I'm going to die. I would like to pick up the butcher knife and slash my wrists. The only thing that would help me is to be a man and then I would not have to worry about hair."

This patient seems to be very desperate and displays suicidal tendencies. Says she took RAT POISON! Her family doctor pumped her stomach and sent her here. There are no obvious hallucinations, no real delusions. The patient recognizes that her ideas about her hair are abnormal and sick. She appears neat, cooperative, friendly, somewhat depressed and pessimistic. She is very much handicapped by her ideas.

Medical History & Physical & Laboratory Examinations: Negative or noncontributory except 18 pound weight loss over two months' period.

Impression: Obsessive compulsive reaction with schizophrenic decompensation. End of Intern's note.

Nurse's Notes

February 10, 1974, 10:00 P.M. Patient admitted ambulatory to open unit unaccompanied. Ht. 5'6½", Wt. 100 pounds, Pupils equal. Although patient cried when she arrived on unit, she soon regained composure and was most cooperative. Alert and oriented. Assigned room 609. Dr. notified. Dr. talking with patient.

February 11, 1974, 6:00 A.M. Patient has had a good night. Slept well. Breakfast: One cup coffee, few bites toast, cereal.

8:00 A.M. Extremely neat—every hair in place. Commented how awful her hair looks in contrast to nurse's. Makes polite small talk only with encouragement. Says little else. Looks sleepy. On bed most of past two hours. Face down. Out of bed with encouragement. Reading. Little facial expression.

12:00 noon. Ate all but potato. States she likes the expensive things to eat.

2:00 P.M. Complains that medication makes her feel so drowsy. Approached nurse to request scissors. Seemed extremely tense. "I just have to cut a bit of my hair. Some is out of place and I can't stand it. Please—you may watch me, I'm not going to poke out my eyes, I just want to trim one spot on my head." Patient's hairdo very neat. Nurse unable to observe one hair out of place.

10:00 P.M. On bed all evening says, "Those pills make me drowsy."

February 12, 1974, 6:00 A.M. Slept fairly well.

8:00 A.M. Readily converses. When nurse entered room to chat, patient began to pat nurse's hair and feel it, wishing hers was like it. Topic changed by nurse and patient continually talked about glasses and food. Supposes she should wear glasses. Interested in

189

obtaining book about health foods and discussing a philosophy of food and life which her next door neighbor is very much a promoter of. Patient is afraid she is not feeding her child right, that he will not, therefore, grow up healthy. Apparently this philosophy attributes life's problems to faulty eating. Patient is not quite sure how she feels about this. Seems very open for suggestion. Enjoys to have someone listen to her.

ALANDA'S AUTOBIOGRAPHY—FEBRUARY 14, 1974

"I have tried to remember as far back into my childhood as I can. This is more difficult than I had thought.

"I was born on a farm, thirty years ago, the second of three daughters. Frieda is two years older than I and Anna two years younger. Therefore, I must have been two years old when my little sister was born, but this event I do not remember. To my knowledge, there were always three of us. But I do recall Anna as a little, blonde, curly-haired girl, not a baby, but probably in her second year. From then on, for three, four or even five years, life was about the same for me, as far as environment and relationships with other people were concerned.

"It is common to read stories in which the writer recalls the happy days of his childhood. Mine was not that way—not that my general living conditions were utterly miserable, but it was just a dreary, lonesome, unimportant, uninteresting, nil sort of stage that I was caught in. I do not remember really enjoying any activities, or laughing or having real fun.

"My mother and dad were honest, hard-working farm people—people who believed that children should be seen and not heard. They were kind enough and I respected and loved them—as I felt that was a child's duty.

"We were clothed and fed sufficiently, and the necessities, from their viewpoint, were sufficient. My mother made our big blousy bloomers from bleached feed sacks and I was always embarrassed about wearing them. But they were always clean, not too comfortable, cost little, and that way we were that much less expensive to them and some one day, the farm could be paid for.

"Frieda fussed, complained and grew angry at her home-sewed clothes, long underwear, and long stockings. In turn it made my mother angry and hurt and I felt sorry for my mother. I hated the clothes as much as Frieda, but I hated the wrangling and I didn't want to seem unappreciative, so I never complained—and there I received some praise—I never complained, and I found many times, no matter how unhappy I might be over a situation I did not complain because my mother appreciated me for 'being good and taking whatever I got.'

"Mom always tells of my being a 'good baby.' I would lie, even when awake, and cry very little. When I was older, she says she would put me on a chair and I never moved or spoke until she gave me permission. I will say I was proud of this, and I tried to live up to that reputation and do even better. From then on I guess my ambition was to do what mama wanted, and to be of as little trouble, expense and bother as possible. Then she would like me.

"I didn't care for school when I was little. I was afraid I couldn't do well enough. When Frieda was seven, she entered the second grade. I was five then and began first grade. But we were in the same class. At that time, in our country school, grades were combined—first and second, third and fourth, etc. The same subjects were taught both grades. Therefore, one year would be much easier than the other. I distinctly remember doing, or trying to do, long-division problems when I was in the third grade and I didn't know the multiplication table. I came home with pretty meager grades compared to Frieda's. I was in the eighth grade when for the first time I did not have to compete with Frieda. I enjoyed school a bit more that year.

"I knew I could never be another Frieda. Everything was easy for her, and everything she did, she did so well. I felt and knew people 'took to her naturally.' One aunt was very obvious about it. I especially took notice of the difference in gifts we received from her. I must have enjoyed feeling sorry for myself, because I'd rather have died than mention it, but my heart actually ached when I saw her preference.

"On the other hand was my cute, chubby baby sister, Anna. She was the highlight for her cute, interesting baby ways. And funny as it seems, almost like a hilarious joke, was this awkward character, me, in the middle.

"We were known always as Frieda, Alanda and Anna, their three girls. I do not know why, but I felt ashamed that there were three of us. It was an odd number. How much more fitting it would be if there were just Frieda and I (no reflection on Anna). It seemed unbalanced and awkward to be three of us.

"I felt a misfit in our family. My hair was straight and hard to manage; people remarked, 'What happened here, the other girls have naturally curly hair.' Dad cut our hair at home, and he hated cutting mine, because of the way it grew at the back of my neck. I was sorry I was so much trouble. It seemed I made them unhappy and ashamed of me.

"Often I, and that was when I was very young, five, six, seven, eight or nine even, wished for illness or even death to make them stop and care for me a little, or make them sorry if I would die, and when I was nine, I had an appendectomy—my one greatest childhood experience. I received attention and praise for being so sick and complaining so little.

"My mother was always tired and cross, and I was sort of half afraid of her—in the way that I was tense until she spoke so I could tell what mood she was in. She was cross a lot of the time with my dad. He never scolded her or talked harshly to her but as I saw it, she felt unappreciated. She cried a lot and one of her expressions which haunted me was 'You kids and your dad take me for a slave, and a dumbbell, etc.' (which was not true) and then she'd say, 'Sometimes I wish I could dig a hole in the ground and crawl in it.' I actually visualized this, but really didn't think she would do it. I knew that her mother (my grandmother whom I never knew) was supposed to have grown tired and weary of life and lay down on the railroad track in front of a train and died that way. My mother was only nine then and she cared for her two younger sisters until she married my dad at the age of twenty-five and then she still took care of the younger sister. I was afraid she might do something like her mother and I surely didn't want to be the cause of her having any feelings that I did not love or appreciate her.

"Sometime, I suppose when I was five or even four, this thing of masturbation entered the picture. I discovered my body and the peculiar exciting or pleasant feeling I obtained from it. That part of my body, naturally, I had been led to believe was almost unmentionable, secretive, forbidden, unmoral and nasty. So when I began this bad, embarrassing habit, I felt very guilty and ashamed, and now I was not the good girl I should be. I suppose, even when I was five, it is hard to be sure, I realized

192

where baby animals and human babies came from. I can't remember not knowing. From observing the bulls and cows and other animals on the farm, I assumed their physical contact was the cause of the growth of a baby within the mother. I did not understand or even think of anything passing from the male into the female. I remember holding my two hands over my abdomen and I was sure it was growing larger. I was not a thin child and if anyone mentioned I was heavier than a year ago, etc., I was stricken with fear. I remember praying in my simple way, 'God please forgive me and don't let me have a baby.' When somehow I realized something passed from male to female during sexual intercourse which caused conception, I was amazed. I was almost carefree.

"When I began to menstruate when I was not yet twelve, I was again frightened, ashamed and horrified. I knew something of it, little ideas here and there, but it was worse and something greater than I had expected. My mother had told me nothing, but I was suspicious of her and of Frieda at certain times of the month. When I told her of myself, she gave me the necessary extra clothing, etc., and her only words were, 'You will have this every month, but if you don't, something will be wrong, and you tell me.' It had been a secret from me and I felt I must not let Anna know anything of it. I was in misery trying to go to the bathroom to dress and undress, out of sight of Anna. I tried to get her to ask Mom to let her visit an aunt for several days at that time. I nearly wore myself out keeping it secret. Later, that wore away. I suppose when Anna became near that age too.

"Basically, this was my life until I started high school. High school wasn't what I had hoped for. I wished I was a town girl with nice clothes. I was ashamed we were not 'church people' and were definitely not the 'social' type. My clothes weren't right and my hair and my figure were all wrong. There was something about even the homeliest girls that I envied. They all had something, a good figure, clothes, nice hair. I sat in many classes and looked at and studied the girl's hair ahead of me. I felt I didn't have, and therefore, probably actually did not have, one ounce of personality.

"In my junior year I was voted homecoming queen and in the senior year I was voted 'most popular girl.' I did not accept this as 'honest'— to me it was an accident. I felt I knew how it happened both times.

193

Everyone, the girls that is, were jealous of the popular and pretty girls who were candidates and very apt to win so they voted for me, so their pretty friends would not receive the honor.

"I knew my mother was happy when I started my beauty culture career by working as an apprentice and taking a correspondence course. I was earning money and saving it and that was mom's 'cup of tea.' But I wasn't proud of it or pleased with it.

"Here I was, in this dumpy little town, kids going to college—the kids that really were somebody or wanted to be somebody; but I was afraid to go ahead and take a big step into something I was not sure I could accomplish.

"I began going with Carl four years after I graduated from high school. I was twenty-one and he was twenty-five, really a man. I didn't trust him in the first years of our marriage. When he was late from work, I was sure he was with another girl. I sneaked down dark alleys and watched and waited, but never saw anything.

"Carl always liked my long hair, but soon after we were married, I thought I should have it cut—I don't know why—and with it cut, I also lost the endearing term 'Fluffy' that he had called me. I had my hair cut, I disliked it and myself. Carl didn't like it, of course, and the one good feature I had finally obtained, I had now ruined of my own accord. I was heartbroken to the point of crying hysterically and had to quit my job.

"Then came the first 'nervous breakdown.' From then on, year in and year out, my hair haunted me. I would get along fair for a couple months and then I couldn't bear it. I recall the misery it caused. If I was not satisfied with my hair, I was 'no good' for anything. I was unsure of myself in every way. I made no definite plans if I could help it, for I never knew what state of mind I might be in. I envied my friends who casually combed through their hair, or nonchalantly stepped into a shop for a haircut. To me, setting or cutting my hair was a major act. I knew something was wrong in this idea—something peculiar. It is my hair, yes—but why can't I do what I can with it and then relax? What funny thing within me lets my hair rule my whole life?

"I had had shock treatments and although everyone marveled how wonderfully they helped me, I did not credit it to the treatment. The treatments frightened me to such an extent I was able to overlook every-

194

thing, including my hair, to get loose from that horrible 'asylum' I was locked in.

"My life was one horrible mess from one time to another. Carl and I quarreled and actually despised each other at times. I was unhappy, discontented and unsure of myself in every way possible.

"When I had the second nervous breakdown, as they called it, I thought I would surely lose my mind forever. To me it was six months of sheer torture, more or less before and after, but those months I wanted and prayed for death. More shock treatments, hospitalized, etc., etc., and then a third breakdown, and then a fourth.

"For hours and hours I stood in the bathroom combing my hair and crying until I was actually exhausted. I would tear myself away and try to scrub the kitchen floor then sit down amongst it all—crying and crying. My friends would drop in, and how embarrassed I was, caught in such a state. They would tell me I just had to 'snap out of it.'

"I begged my mother and dad to help me. It was like being lost. I could see them, but they couldn't see me or reach me. I was afraid—I tried to get dad to talk to me. He told me he could be the same way if he let himself be—in other words, 'You are a weakling who cannot face minor disappointments.' For a long time we saw little of each other. I was not angry, but I realized they could not help me, and I made them feel bad when they saw me in such spirits. So rather than burden them, I felt I was doing them a favor by remaining out of their sight.

"Carl became weary and angry with me very soon, which is understandable, and yet it would have been so comforting if he would have only told me we'd do something, or that he loved me and would help me. But most of the time he was quite harsh and belittled me for not 'wising up and thinking of someone else besides myself.' He would call Frieda and she often came after me and I would spend the day with her. I was off Carl's hands then. Finally, as good as she was to me, I learned that it also made her unhappy to see me that way, and she even told me she'd rather not come at all to see me. Then she could think, in her mind, that I was probably feeling better and she could go about her happy home without sad thoughts of me.

"On the day I came in here, I had eaten rat poison which did not work. Dr. Berson decided I should see a different doctor and he sent me here."

CHAPTER 13

Schizophrenic Living

INTRODUCTION

Under sufficient pressure, human beings have thought, said and done *everything* that is mentally or physically conceivable. And, no matter how unseemly or bizarre, any deed that one person can perform, any other can comprehend. We share, each person, a potential for understanding not only the refined and cultivated acts of others but also those that are eccentric, uniquely individual or even "uncivilized." It is the average man's inescapable intimacy with the very things his society labels as deviant which causes him to shout "bizarre," "sick," "incomprehensible" and "not me!"

A sustaining awareness of this tendency to deny parts of one's own self well serves students of the history of schizophrenic living. That history is a centuries-old pattern of rejection, gross neglect or persecution. It is borne to us by more than legend. Only a few decades ago, tens and tens of thousands of schizophrenics were warehoused and forgotten in remote dungeons euphemistically called "mental hospitals." Indeed, pessimism about these many individuals was so pervasive that the very nature of schizophrenic living itself was confused and falsely equated with living in a dreadful custodial hospital under the most grotesque circumstances. The social and medical consequences that were the direct result of being maintained in a mental hospital were often greater than the impairment from the initial symptoms. So total was the neglect in many of these institutions that deterioration of the patients during the first half of the present century was the ordinary, almost the inevitable, course. In such hospitals there were often two or three thousand patients with no more than three or four doctors. Often there were no nurses at all. Like

196

many contemporary prisons, the mental hospital of twenty-five years ago was a closed-off, restricted island, often a savage place, a setting feared and thus shunned. It was only when reclaimed by the society, when "those hospitals" and "their patients" became "our hospitals" and "our people," that many who lived in such institutions were able and willing to abandon schizophrenic living patterns. Thousands and thousands who were thought incurable were restored to the family and to the society! Schweitzer wrote of a reverence for life itself as a matter beyond logic and reason, and in a way, those who had been abandoned in chronic mental hospitals were, according to logic and reason, hopeless. From the perspective of that period, it took some sort of unique commitment to "life for everybody who was alive" to be interested in those hospitalized people. But ultimately, that "hope beyond reason" paid off and a great deal has been accomplished with individuals thought beyond hope.

WHAT IS SCHIZOPHRENIC LIVING?

Despite three millennia of individual, family and public concern and ten decades of scientific research, a precise explanation of the nature and cause of these astonishing human events is not yet possible. Theories abound. But no one can say with certainty what schizophrenic living is and why it occurs.

There are many varieties of schizophrenic living. Some who are called schizophrenic are like beaten and dazed fighters; they live their lives aimlessly, staggering without direction in a defenseless state as if awaiting a final blow. Their thinking seems dulled, obtunded. They are extremely withdrawn and unable to function outside a hospital. Such individuals often call forth a feeling of pity and compassion. They are clearly sick. There are others, however, who are much more threatening, whose strange thinking and odd behavior severely challenge the ideas, values and shared traditions of the "normal" members of the society. Of such individuals, called "paranoid" or "schizophrenic," Talcott Parsons, the sociologist, wrote, "They are the iconoclasts of our time." This idea as elaborated by psychiatrist Jules Masserman was earlier quoted but bears repetition: almost everyone is made more comfortable by faith in the validity of one or more deeply held beliefs.[1] Many hold to the existence of a transcending God. A second group have faith in the inherent

197

worthwhileness of the work of man and see purpose in his persistence in developing this planet and ultimately some other star satellite. For others, a belief in the essential truth of brotherhood, love and sexuality, a trust in loyalty, fidelity and the communion between fellow beings is the treasured basis for life. Many who are called schizophrenic refuse to believe in and act in accordance with such assumptions. By repudiating the style of life which others lead, schizophrenic individuals may be very threatening. Verification of the power of such a threat is evident if you consider the idea of living with someone who believes neither in a transcending spirit nor in the value of any work, nor who could ever appreciate how good it is to be together.

The question of how best to describe and define the schizophrenic way of living is one that has long been debated but remains unresolved. How much is sickness, a "disease of the brain"? How much is a deviant way of life deliberately chosen because of repeated defeat and unhappiness during the years of life shared with others? How much is a period of sickness followed by a determined choice never to return to the former, painful, vulnerable "normal" way of living?

Schizophrenic living is the ultimate "maladaptive life-style," one that is adopted in the face of overwhelming stress from among the psychological, biological and social circumstances in the life of the individual. The magnitude of this maladaptation is great indeed; the results of schizophrenic living can be death through suicide, starvation, maniacal frenzy or self-mutilation. It is the "last-ditch stand" of a person who is desperately trying to maintain some semblance of life with self-respect in the face of overwhelming defeat.

Descriptively, schizophrenic living is characterized by a changed manner of thinking and feeling and by a giving up of a shared life with others. That shared life is replaced by a solitary way of living dominated by preoccupation with the sensations, feelings and ideas experienced in the moment. The schizophrenic life frequently is a moment-by-moment life, a *now* life with little or no concern for maintaining the standards implied by past history and no apparent wish to actualize future possibilities. Instead, the sensations of the moment assume total importance. Passing sounds are listened to with such intense preoccupation that they acquire a significance and complexity beyond that of merely passing sounds. One's face in the mirror on close and prolonged scrutiny is revealed to possess new or previously unnoticed shapes, shades or areas of creasing. One's eyes are particularly capturing with their blends of red, white, green, blue, black and with a small round pupil in the middle which changes shape with shifts of light and at times with shifts of mood. Or, a simple word, repeated and repeated, discloses unsuspected sounds and meanings, some harmonic and friendly, some disturbingly cacophonous. Meanwhile, all else in the world is unnoticed. Such highly personalized preoccupation inevitably diminishes the individual's ability to understand or to be understood by others. There is, finally, a deterioration of the capacity to work, to think and to relate to any other person.

Schizophrenic living when well established dominates every sphere of thinking and behaving. The way in which this occurs was first described by a Swiss psychiatrist, Eugen Bleuler, in the early 1900s, and his descriptions require little modification a half-century later.[2] He pointed out that, above all, schizophrenic living is made up of a variety of extreme defensive stances assumed in an effort to avoid further hurt. One such stance is in the form of an actual fleeing or hiding, secluding oneself under a bed, for example. Another retreat is achieved by sitting with one's head buried in one's hands, knees drawn up before the covered face.* Or, the retreat and withdrawal may occur through a fracturing of the various mental processes. This form of retreat and withdrawal is accomplished by a blunting or inappropriateness of feeling, a discontinuity or irrelevancy of thought and ultimately a withdrawal of all concern from the reality formerly shared with others. While it is possible to describe separately each of these parts of schizophrenic living, they come together in a unified way in the form of an extremely guarded style of living in which a control of experiencing serves to prevent further loss of self-respect.

The disorder of feeling characteristic of schizophrenic living may be of several varieties. There may be an overall blunting of personality, a flatness, an experiencing of other people as if from afar, a dazed indifference to any and every aspect of life. Or, the defensive patterning may take the form of a misapplication and inappropriateness of feeling. The individual's emotions differ from those ordinarily felt in a like situation.

---

*This posture, this bundling up, is reminiscent of the resting position of the unborn fetus while still in utero. Whether it represents a "regression to a fetal period of life" or is simply a very practical way of retreating can be debated. The latter explanation seems the less complicated.

Instead, an opposite feeling or an apparently incongruous feeling of amusement, fear or puzzlement prevails. Tears accompany a trivial event and laughter marks a tragedy. The "usefulness" of such a splitting of feeling from life events was described by a twenty-five-year-old male engineering student, himself recovered from a period of grandiose, delusional preoccupation with the thought that he was Jesus Christ. He had been hospitalized for three months.

Case Study 1: *Schizophrenic Living as the Last Effort*

"It isn't easy to describe what I went through. After you have been hurt and hurt and hurt, humiliated, made to feel hopeless and it keeps going on, you finally come apart. That coming apart is the most terrifying thing in the world. The doctors called it an acute schizophrenic break. I was sure I was dying. But after a while, something happened and I just stopped feeling the terror. The horror went away. Something turned off the switch. Afterwards, either I didn't feel very much about anything or else what I felt had nothing to do with what others were saying or doing. Whatever came into my head was the way that I felt. For example, even if everybody else was crying, if I didn't feel sad, then it's not sad! You discover feeling is strictly up to you. It's optional. You don't have to feel any of the things that used to hurt you. That's one of the reasons that I am so shaky these days. Now that I'm better, I'm vulnerable again."

The "usefulness" of this separation of feeling from life situation may be demonstrated in the following imagined dialogue:

Accuser: "You are a bad, bad person."

Thoughts of schizophrenic person: "Perhaps he has been hired by the government to protect me and everything he says is to confuse the enemy so that they will not know he is my friend. I will smile at him. It will be a signal."

Accuser: "Your job is over. You have been fired. You will have no money to support yourself. Your family will need to go on relief. You are a failure."

Thoughts of schizophrenic person: "I can barely understand the words that he says. Something about money. But I don't have my wallet with me and I can't help him."

Accuser: "I want to help you. I am a doctor. I want to restore you to your former functioning self. You are sick."
Thoughts of schizophrenic person: "He is so serious. Is he really a doctor? He looks as if he might cry. But I feel like laughing."

A second characteristic of schizophrenic living is the loss or abandonment of the system of logical thought. Here again, avoidance of further hurt appears to be a predominating matter. There are a number of different ways in which the thinking characteristic of schizophrenic persons differs from normal thought processes. Schizophrenic thought may be utterly concrete and specific so that the symbolic or abstract meanings which are so much a part of ordinary language and conversation may be lost. Or, something of the reverse may be the case. Thinking may be so totally vague, irrelevant, disconnected or loosely symbolic as to defy understanding. In either case, the disordering of thought serves as a potent defense against the experience of a pyramiding of unpleasant realities. Certain of the characteristics of this way of thinking and communicating may be illustrated in the following examples:

Doctor: "I'm going to ask you the meaning of two proverbs. People sometimes use these statements as a way of describing either an individual or a situation. I want you to tell me what they mean. The first is 'A rolling stone gathers no moss.' "
Patient (a twenty-year-old college student): "Friction will rub off the moss as the stone rolls along the ground."
Doctor: "I'm going to give you a different proverb to explain. What does it mean when people say, 'A bird in the hand is worth two in the bush'?"
Patient: "A bird that will sit in your hand would cost more. A friendly bird is better than two birds you don't know about. It's like a dog. Well, that's not a good example because of hunting dogs which go out in the bush to kill birds. But some of those dogs are also expensive. By the way, if you should get lost in the woods when you're hunting, the moss is always on the north side of the trees and rocks. Once when I was a boy, I killed a bird with a stone."

The replacement of ordinary thinking by this kind of disordered intellectual process precludes the building up of ideas that hurt, maim or degrade. It is, however, an extraordinarily costly defense.

The third major characteristic of schizophrenic living is called autism, "auto-ism." Autism is the ultimate withdrawal into self, the final turning away from a world shared with other people. The individual preoccupies himself with a private realm in which nothing matters except his own bodily sensations or the thoughts being experienced in the moment. The itching of a finger, a word remembered from a childhood rhyme, the configuration of clouds in the sky, any or all of these matters completely absorb all consciousness and over a period of days, weeks, months or years transcend in importance anything and everything else.

Case Study 2: *The Man Who Looked Only at His Hands*

Arthur Robinson, age twenty-nine, had lived in a mental hospital for five years. In the hospital, he spent almost all of his time looking fixedly at his hands, turning them over, moving the fingers slowly back and forth, examining the tortuous blue veins and counting the many creases on the back of each hand. If not required to engage in some other activity, he would spend all day in this manner. He responded to specific requests to go to bed, get up, come to meals and so forth, but when he was left to himself he turned to the examination of his hands. He never spoke unless first spoken to. In this manner he lived his life, day after day, year after year.

Because I was his ward doctor, one day it fell to me to tell him the sad news that his mother had suddenly passed away. She was the only relative who visited or wrote to him. She came to see him from her home seventy miles distant once each week. She wrote letters to him that were never answered. She was a cheerful person, attentive and solicitous to Arthur when she visited. Although I had known her only a few months, I had liked her and felt a personal sadness on hearing the news. Arthur was, as usual, standing by his bed and examining his hands. They were held close to his eyes. He seemed to be counting something. I went over to him and said, "Arthur, I am afraid that I have very bad news for you. I am sad that I must be the one to tell you that your mother was found dead this

202

morning. She apparently had a heart attack. I am very sorry. We will help you go to the funeral if you wish." As I spoke, Arthur slowly dropped one of his hands toward his side, and simultaneously a single tear rolled down his cheek. Then quietly, almost inaudibly, he said, "No, no thank you. I will stay here." And, even as he spoke, the hand that had fallen began very slowly to rise. He was soon, within a moment, examining both hands as before.

Such are the characteristics underlying the myriad symptoms that are associated with schizophrenic living:

> I won't be hurt anymore.
> I feel nothing or if I feel, my feelings have no relation to what is happening.
> I can't be hurt anymore because my thoughts are disorganized and nothing adds up.
> I can't be hurt anymore because my life has been removed from the world of others.

There are many different kinds of beginnings and endings of periods of schizophrenic living. Most characteristically, at some point between late adolescence and early adult life, following a cycle of mounting stress, disappointment and failure, there occurs a period of enormous upheaval. The magnitude of this upheaval and the events that follow are astonishing when viewed by an outsider and catastrophic for the individual in whose life they occur. Variously labeled a "psychotic break," "acute schizophrenia" or "severe nervous breakdown," the experience is not easily compared with any other. It is, above all, an overwhelming, terrifying, uncanny series of experiences, an extremity of possible human happenings. With a mounting crescendo, the individual feels he is torn apart from his very world, that he is being betrayed by his own mind. He experiences his imminent annihilation as being at hand. Some respond to these events by a restless pacing leading to a shouting, maniacal state. For others, the mounting terror is signaled by the furtive and suspicious sleepless eyes of a man or woman grown sullen, expectant and silent. In either instance, whether in shouting agitation or reconciled despair, these moments in time are desperate and frightening, akin to waiting at the bottom of an elevator shaft with the elevator car falling rapidly from above and doom but a moment away. But in acute schizophrenia, the moments of terror continue for hours, days and even weeks. Individuals who live through this kind of "acute break" may devote much of the remainder of their lives to avoiding its repetition. This is equally true whether the individual recovers and is restored to his ordinary life or if he falls into a chronic pattern of schizophrenic living. One of the main purposes of the symptoms of chronic schizophrenic living is that they serve to protect against the repetition of another acute break!

One patient whom I have remembered quite vividly for the last two decades had been hospitalized for several years when I first met him. He spent much of his time secluding himself, often hiding in a bathroom. When as his new doctor I attempted to make contact with him, he began to spend time under the bed. When I joined him there, he struck me. When I returned under the bed the next day, the patient tried desperately to strangle me, saying, "Get away from here! You are not my friend. No friend would want me to go through again what I went through before I came to this hospital. Let me alone or I'll kill you. I'll never leave here."

An ominous event that may follow the first days of an acute break is the development of angry and resentful suspiciousness of other people. The transition is often quite remarkable. After several days of extreme agitation and fearfulness, a strange calm may fall over the individual, a sudden "clarification" having come with the belief that the responsibility for his travail rests not with him but with others. The pioneer American psychiatrist Harry Stack Sullivan described the process as follows:

> This is an ominous development in that the schizophrenic's state is taking on a paranoid coloring. If the suffering of the patient is markedly diminished thereby, we shall observe the evolution of a paranoid schizo-phrenic state. These conditions are of relatively much less favorable out-come. They tend to permanent distortions of the interpersonal relations. . . . A paranoid systematization is, therefore, markedly beneficial to the peace of mind of the person chiefly concerned, and its achievement in the course of a schizophrenic disorder is so great an improvement in security that it is seldom relinquished. . . . It is for this reason that the paranoid development in a schizophrenic state has to be regarded as a bad omen.[3]

Typically, the events that come before an acute break and the subse-quent development of schizophrenic living patterns occur gradually over a period of weeks or months. However, this is not always the case. On occasion, such reactions occur almost precipitously in individuals who are placed in situations of overwhelming stress. Battle-front breakdowns, prison camp decompensations, the long ordeals of sailors abandoned at sea or travelers lost in the desert, are examples of stressful situations so overwhelming that acute schizophrenic decompensation may occur in individuals without a prior history of emotional difficulty. In such circumstances, the relationship between the immediate death threat and the development of a schizophrenic defense against the experience of death may be seen. Once such a break with reality has occurred, however, it does not always correct itself when the immediate threat is removed.

Case Study 3: *A Man Whose Illness Began in a Hurricane*

Fred Means, age twenty-eight, was an officer on a naval vessel which was caught during a severe tropical hurricane in the South China Seas. The storm was so severe that several other boats of comparable size capsized that night. During the height of the storm, he left his duty post and went to bed in his cabin. The next afternoon, he was taken to the ship's doctor who found him to be confused. He was returned to a hospital in the United States where within a few months he tried twice to hang himself. And, on a brief visit from the hospital to his home, he tried to kill himself with a rifle. Despite intensive therapy including medications and electrical shock therapy, he remained preoccupied with bizarre ideas about homosexual practices, the control of human behavior by radar and the possibility that he was finding human bones in the food that he was being served. He tied these three areas together in his thinking into a vague and disconnected "plot." He remained aloof, distant and suspicious. He refused to see family members and walked away from them if they came to the hospital. Several times he struck hospital attendants, accusing them of planning his murder. He requested a release from the hospital and when this had been denied demanded an interview with the hospital director.

Doctor: "I can't let you go home, Fred. I think you'd try to kill yourself."

Fred: "I won't pay any attention to my voices. Even if they tell me to kill myself, I won't do it."

Doctor: "I have to believe your voices, Fred. You've tried to commit suicide three times now."

Fred: "Suicide is a possibility for any man."

Doctor: "For you, Fred."

Fred: "For *any* man."

Doctor: "For *you,* Fred."

Fred: "What if you were in the top story of a tall building and the building was burning down and the flames were coming closer and closer to you and you had a pistol with a bullet in it. What would you do in the moment you realized there was no way out?"

Doctor: "I'd never live to see that moment, Fred."

Fred: "Then you've never been in a hurricane in the South China Seas!"

As in this example, there are many times when it is tempting to conclude that "this episode of schizophrenic decompensation would never have come to pass except for event X." This is particularly the case when there is some sudden, shattering threat to survival or when a well-established dependency pattern is disrupted by personal illness, displacement or death of a significant other individual. On reading the case study that follows, one cannot help but wonder, "Would Joan ever have become so emotionally disabled if her husband had not been called away?" Or, "At what point might his return have interrupted the extending pattern of decompensation?" Another unsettled question about schizophrenic living pertains to the factors influencing a rapid return to previous patterns of thinking and behaving and those that produce chronic patterns of schizophrenic living. Until the causes of schizophrenic living are more precisely understood, one can have one's prejudices but without a feeling of absolute certainty. Frequently, an acute schizophrenic episode occurring as a response to a severe precipitating stress in a previously well-functioning person will rapidly terminate and there will be a return of normal personality patterns in a matter of days, weeks or one or two months. Conversely, a gradually developing schizophrenic decompensation in a marginally functioning person is more likely to be followed by a long interval of schizophrenic living. However, even these broad generalizations would probably have been of little use in predicting the pattern of decompensation that occurred in the life of this twenty-nine-year-old wife and mother.

206

Case Study 4: *Step-by-Step Decompensation into Schizophrenia*

Joan was one of identical twins born in a well-established South Dakota family. She was to all outward appearances the more passive of the two girls in personality structure, but she adjusted well within the family unit, school and community until she left home and went to college. At that time, Joan went west to a California university and her sister went to college in the East.

Within a few days after arriving at the university, Joan became extremely homesick, cried a great deal and experienced the first gross anxiety of her life. She called her parents a number of times during the first week of school. She also sought medical help at the school infirmary because she feared she was having a heart attack. However, she weathered this crisis and, ten days after arriving on the campus, she met Bob. Within two weeks she had become his steady date. Theirs was an idyllic four-year campus romance. All other friends, teachers, learning experiences and other factors were subsidiary to this relationship. Joan looked up to Bob and he was grateful for her admiration. They ate most of their meals together, took many classes in common and were, in a sense, not only sweethearts and lovers but best friends. Joan was very happy during her years at college. Indeed, she thrived.

They were married one week after graduation and moved to a suburban community in Pennsylvania. Two children were born during the first four years of their married life. They remained devoted to each other, yet each was successful in his or her respective areas of community activity and family life. Joan was active in the church, was the prime organizer of a cooperative nursery school and her health and spirits were good during those years.

However, after eight years of married life, in 1950, unexpectedly, Bob was called to active duty as a pilot during the Korean War. Joan was very shaken and during the weeks before his departure she cried a great deal, experienced much anxiety, but finally pulled herself together and bravely bid her husband farewell. Within a few days after his departure, however, Joan began to experience extreme anxiety and tearfulness. In an effort to retain her self-control, she composed a schedule of proposed work projects for herself. These included a four-month schedule of refinishing furniture in the home to be followed by a four-month project of sewing clothing for the children and new curtains for their room. Ultimately, she outlined a four-month project of sewing new clothing for herself in anticipation of her husband's return. She threw herself tirelessly into the furniture-sanding project, using all her spare time and working late into the evenings.

Two months after Bob's departure, she became concerned about heart palpitations and entered the local hospital for a three-day period of tests and examinations. The results of the hospital examinations were "essentially negative," and she was placed on mild sedatives. Her apprehension continued, however, and she began to supplement the sedatives with alcohol. She was particularly agitated during the late evening hours, and her sleeping patterns were disrupted by early morning awakening, bad dreams and preoccupation with night noises in the house.

Four months after her husband's departure, she took her children back to the family home in South Dakota and remained there for two months. She settled down somewhat, though not completely. She then returned to her own home in Pennsylvania with the children despite the objections of her parents who were very concerned about her restlessness. After her return to Pennsylvania there was a steady increase in the level of her agitation. She made a number of contacts with her physician and on two occasions made late evening calls to the police department because she felt the house was being invaded. She drank a good deal, ate sparingly and sustained a progressive loss of weight. She completely abandoned her work projects. By the seventh month after her husband's departure, Joan's condition had deteriorated alarmingly. She cried a great deal, was extremely anxious, felt certain that she would die of a heart attack before her husband returned and at times would sit mutely for hours, giving little attention to her home or children. The physician called her mother, who came to help Joan. Seven and a half months after Bob's departure, efforts were undertaken by the family physician through the American Red Cross to return Bob to his family. Joan handled this new development in a peculiar way. There was a sudden demonstration of an outward calm. She insisted on completing dental work before her husband's return, explaining to her mother, "I want to be perfect when he comes back." The family dentist told her that five teeth needed filling and was startled when she insisted that he remove these teeth. He declined her urgent request, and Joan began a search of the community to find a dentist who would remove all of the "decayed and rotten teeth." She was ultimately successful.

Immediately afterward, she became frantically agitated, alternately fearful and elated, grandiose and delusional. She stated that she was the Virgin Mary awaiting the return of God. She was floridly psychotic and actively suicidal when her husband returned.

Within an eight-month period of time in her life, Joan had been a "normal" wife and mother, an anxious and edgy person, obsessively preoccupied, phobic, somatically fixated, dependent on alcohol, suicidally depressed and finally delusional. She was, to all appearances, normal, neurotic and psychotic within a relatively short interval.

Joan required two years of almost continuous hospitalization* and she continued to receive outpatient psychotherapeutic help for several additional years after her release from the hospital and full return to her husband and children. Her recovery, ultimately, was almost a total one. However, there were certain changes in her attitudes and manner. She was somewhat less dependent on her husband than before her hospitalization, though no less devoted. She was a considerably less enthusiastic and vivacious person than she had been before. She was more cautious and restrained. Joan described this change in these words: "Maybe it's that I'm more grown-up than I was, not so silly and dependent on Bob. I used to get so excited when we'd start out to do something that he'd say it was cheap to get me drunk. I could get high without drinking a drop. I'm not so much that way anymore. I hold back a lot. I'm quieter, much more careful, maybe a bit moody." Bob felt "a little something has been taken away from Joan by that dreadful period."

---

*In all probability, her hospitalization would be considerably shortened today. That hospitalization began in 1952.

Schizophrenic living is a topic not easily summarized, particularly since so much is unknown about its precise nature and its cause or, more likely, its many causes. In patients who suffer acute schizophrenic decompensation in the face of some overwhelming personal disaster, it might seem unnecessary to theorize about some hereditary or bio-chemical predisposition. One can consider the stress and, placing him-self in the position of the patient, decide, "This could have happened to me. The stress to which he was subjected was just too much." Such understanding may or may not be sufficient. Many people live through enormous stress without falling into schizophrenic patterns. Why? In other patients, the onset may be so insidious as to make explanation of what is transpiring less convincing. When these patterns develop in early childhood, the outlook for reversing them and thereby allowing normal childhood development is rather bleak. Quite often, "childhood schizophrenia," even when treated from preschool days to adolescence in the most comprehensive residential treatment setting, resists modifi-cation. Literally before one's very eyes, despite years of effort, a with-drawing child grows into an eccentric and withdrawn adolescent, one bereft of real emotional involvement with any other person. It is diffi-cult to be a therapist in that situation, working year after year without success, without postulating the probable presence of some serious bio-logical deficit which alters the neurochemical processes within the cen-tral nervous system. What is certainly clear after many years of work with such children is that love alone is insufficient to restore or create their vitality, warmth and interest in life.

Other characteristics of mode of onset of some acute schizophrenic episodes also point to the possibility of biological abnormalities. Some episodes follow closely upon a serious physical illness such as pneumo-nia, pancreatitis or hepatitis or occur in the days immediately following a formidable surgical procedure. Another onset circumstance which points to possible disorders of metabolism or endocrine factors is the occurrence of schizophrenic episodes in association with pregnancy. One cannot put aside or ignore the psychological stress and the social risks associated with pregnancy. A number of women have experienced several episodes of schizophrenic living during the latter months of pregnancy or during the months immediately after the birth, but at other times in their lives they are symptom-free. Even one woman's experience can be

210

very persuasive that the hormonal changes associated with pregnancy were a cause of schizophrenic decompensation.

Case Study 5: *Schizophrenic Decompensation During Three Pregnancies*

Mrs. Edward Albertini, age thirty-four, sought a therapeutic abortion of an unwanted seven-week pregnancy because she had suffered three acute schizophrenic episodes in association with earlier pregnancies. She had five children ranging in age from three to thirteen. She had severe emotional difficulties with the second, fourth and fifth pregnancies and as a result each time had been hospitalized in a psychiatric ward. She had received electrical convulsive therapy (shock) during hospitalization after the fifth pregnancy. The period of incapacity after the fifth pregnancy began four weeks after delivery and continued for four months. Mrs. Albertini and her family stated that after recovering from each of the three prior episodes she was symptom-free and functioned well until late in a succeeding pregnancy, when difficulties began again. She was fully convinced, as were her husband and the family doctor, that the "nervous breakdowns" were caused by the hormonal changes associated with the end of pregnancy. She stated that she had no other problems and her husband agreed. The abortion was performed on the recommendation of two psychiatrists who felt, but of course couldn't prove, that continuation of the pregnancy posed a high risk of precipitating another acute schizophrenic break.

Many of the world's most distinguished scientists have worked much of their lives on the schizophrenia problem. Over the years, there have been repeated flurries of publications naming first one organ, then another, then one subtle biochemical system in the brain, then another, as responsible for the personality changes seen in schizophrenic living. Early in this century it was discovered that a form of bacteria, the spirochete, was the agent causing syphilis, one of whose late manifestations was the severe mental abnormality called general paresis. For many years, almost 10 percent of all admissions to psychiatric hospitals were of paretic patients whose symptoms of paresis mimicked schizophrenic living and other forms of serious mental difficulties. The discovery of one specific cause for mental derangement and its frequently successful treatment with antibiotics gave hope that it would be possible to find comparable explanation and cure in all instances of profound personality change.[4] With the passage of time, however, it has become clear that there is no bacterial or viral explanation for schizophrenic living. Neither is there any evident anatomical damage in the brain. Instead, the search for more subtle physiological and neurochemical factors has been underway for several decades. This search continues in hundreds of laboratories around the world. It is achieving a momentum with one and then another scientific discovery finding its place in an increasingly probable theoretical system. This theory includes and relates a "multiple gene" genetic transmission of predisposition to schizophrenic living patterns, an explanation of the effects of stress in precipitating or prolonging such patterns and a correlation of change in mood and behavior with predictable alterations in the preponderance of various brain amines. These substances, particularly the indoleamine serotonin and the catecholamines, dopamine and norepinephrine, are involved in the transmission of nerve impulse.[5] Another area of active study is the several-decade search for some abnormal chemical substance that might be produced by a disturbance in ordinary body metabolism. This line of investigation began in earnest after the discovery in the early 1950s that certain hallucinogenic chemical substances that produced episodes of delirious behavior resembling acute schizophrenic periods closely resembled in structure the normally occurring substances key to nervous system function. Enthusiasm for this area of investigation waxes and wanes as one laboratory after another reports, then refutes, results of an affirmative nature. Still, twenty years later, there is no convincing evidence that such abnormal chemical substances are produced and/or that they are the cause of schizophrenic living patterns.

It has always been evident that mental illnesses develop in certain families with much greater regularity than could be explained by chance. This has led to various theories emphasizing either genetic predisposition, early rearing patterns, the effects of social stress and so on. In recent years, carefully controlled studies are providing what appear to be definitive, highly reliable answers to questions about the "inheritance of schizophrenia." Doctors David Rosenthal and Seymour Kety took advantage of extraordinarily detailed childhood adoption and mental hospital record-keeping systems in Denmark, which go back several decades, related the two and demonstrated strong evidence in support of a genetic influence in the occurrence of schizophrenic symptoms in successive generations (even among parents and children who were separated from and unknown to each other).[6] Other studies have followed up and refined techniques applied in the research concerning mentally ill twins undertaken in the 1930s by Dr. Franz Kallman of the New York State Psychiatric Institute. He studied "concordance rates" for schizophrenia in identical and fraternal twins. That is, he was trying to establish how often it happened that, if one twin showed the symptoms of schizophrenia, the second twin would also show the same symptoms. He reported concordance rates for schizophrenia in 86 percent of identical twins (who share more or less identical genetic inheritence) and 16 percent for fraternal twins (who are, genetically speaking, siblings born at the same time).[7] Contemporary studies generally support Kallman's work, though with considerably lower concordance rates (35 to 50 percent for identical twins, 5 to 15 percent for fraternal twins). Simultaneously, other findings also make it clear that rearing patterns do have at least some effect on individuals with strong genetic endowment for schizophrenia and an appreciable effect on persons without such a background.[8] "Either-or" thinking with regard to psychological, sociological and biological factors as causative of schizophrenic living patterns usually will lead one astray. But at the same time *there is absolutely no question that many tenderly reared, deeply loved, skillfully nurtured individuals have developed schizophrenic living patterns because of what must be primarily genetically determined factors.*

Equally, despite research in many areas pointing to an association between the incidence of schizophrenic living patterns and the presence of various genetic, metabolic, social class, family relationship patterns and so on, it is not yet possible to offer a definitive or convincing explanation as to why this person, right here and right now, manifests symptoms characteristic of schizophrenic living or why another person does not!

If one could remake the world, it would be as well next time to leave out a genetically determined predisposition for severe mental illness. It just isn't fair. Perhaps that's one of the reasons so many mental health professionals, including some physician-psychiatrists, prefer to ignore, downplay or refute the relevance of "biological factors." They fear the consequences upon the patient's motivation for self-help if part of what is wrong cannot be overcome by work, talk, understanding and hope. But, in the long run, any approach that denies what is real cannot help the intended beneficiary. Anyway, people already know and with help can accept the words "Well, from what you've told me, there does seem to be a tendency for mood swings to run in the family, very strongly in some, a lot less in others. We'll work to make yours a lot less."

People who have strong family histories of serious mental illness (depressions, mania, schizophrenic living, perhaps chronic alcoholism, parental or sibling suicides), those who have sustained an acute episode themselves and/or people who care about someone else often come for advice. What have they to look to in the future? Should they marry, have children, move away from home? Move closer? What does one reply to the young woman who suffers severe anxiety and depression who asks if she has the same trouble that led to her father's suicide? What do the various statistics mean in terms of the most important yes and no matters in a person's life?

Obviously these are among the most complex and difficult questions. Sometimes there are no clearly correct answers. Certainly there are no casual, off-the-cuff replies that are appropriate. More than the doctor's personal philosophies are involved. Nor are the answers solely in psychiatry, medicine, science and statistical probability. The "eugenics" of the nazis made that all too clear. To be helpful, you must know the people and their feelings, you must know all the facts available. A reverence for the quality of life, the Golden Rule and an appreciation of the magnitude of the moment of the discussion are also essential. That discussion can be very important in a good and inspiring way in the lives of the individuals involved and their doctor.

The facts that must be considered relevant in advising an individual about the meaning of mental illness in the family are numerous and arise from many areas of medicine. There is no easy summary. There are some few, fortunately uncommon, degenerative central nervous system diseases, genetically determined, largely unmodifiable by contemporary therapeutics. For certain birth defect problems, the increasing age of the potential parents increases the risk to the baby. Some kinds of mental deficiency can be prevented by earliest diagnosis and dietary treatment. There is an increasing body of evidence that suggests some level of genetic predisposition in many of the more profound mental illnesses including schizophrenic living and severe depression. There is even stronger evidence of genetic predisposition (and high concordance) with manic-depressive illnesses. There is an increasing amount of information that would point to a high incidence of chronic alcoholism in some families where depressive or manic illnesses are present in other family members. Statistically, it seems clear that a history of schizophrenic living patterns in one parent increases to a limited degree the probability of similar patterns in offspring and that a history of such illness in both parents greatly increases the risk in their offspring. The precise nature of the history of schizophrenic living episodes is also important and there are some data that suggest that a single episode in a parent's history may have little or no genetic implications for offspring.

Often, though by no means always, I am able to tell the people who have come for advice that—if the problem was mine—I would not be influenced against marriage, having children and living with the expectation of a successful life. I offer that or other advice only to people I have come to know, after a careful review of all information about them and their family history and after reviewing what is known about the condition or conditions in question. I tell the truth about what I know.

With regard to schizophrenic living patterns, I can say that there has been a general improvement both in terms of rapid recovery from an acute episode and a brighter prospect for the control of the more disabling and disruptive manifestations of chronic schizophrenic living and that the prospects for still further improvement in outlook are strong in this very difficult area.

Neurotic and Psychotic Patterns of Living

After having chopped off the arms that reached out to me; after having boarded up all the windows and doors; after having filled all the pits with poisoned water; after having built my house on a rock of No inaccessible to flattery and fears; after having cut out my tongue and after having eaten it; after having hurled handfuls of silence and monosyllables of scorn at my lovers; after having forgotten my name and the name of my birthplace and the name of my race; after having judged myself and having sentenced myself to perpetual hope and perpetual loneliness, I heard against the stones of my gourd of syllogisms the moist attack, tender, insistent, of spring. (From *Eagle or Sun?* by Octavio Paz)[9]

Part 5

CONCLUSION

CHAPTER 14

Helping

The greatest gift is that which helps another person to become excited about his or her own life—to enjoy it, to be open to it, to be intrigued by its possibilities. The "helping" of a mental health professional is, at its best, that kind of gift. The ability to share in the excitement and pleasure as another person becomes enthusiastic about his own life is the essential personal quality of the effective therapist. Importantly, this wish to share is not to be confused with a need to "tell others how to live," "give people the benefit of my superior wisdom" or "teach people discipline (or the reverse)." There is an important difference between appreciating and enjoying another person and the wish to govern and control. The nature of that difference is suggested in Theodore Reik's description of his last visit with Sigmund Freud:

> I flew from Amsterdam to Vienna to say good-by to Freud. We both knew we would not see each other again. After we shook hands, I stood at the door and could not say a word. My lips were pressed together so hard that they were unable to part. He must have sensed what I felt; he put his arm on my shoulder and said, "I've always liked you." (He had never before said anything of this kind.) As I bowed my head wordlessly, he said in a low but firm voice, as if to comfort me: "People need not be glued together when they belong together."[1]

The therapist is privileged to look in, to offer help and for a brief interval to play a significant role in the life of the patient. But then there comes the moment when therapy is over and the patient continues in his search for meaning and satisfaction in other places. Doctor and patient continue on separate paths. No one can foretell what awaits either of them. When it is over, how will it seem? If changes occur, how lasting are

219

they likely to be? Do people ever get over their fears and anxieties in any final way?

Of course, there is no insurance against the exigencies, realities and disappointments of life. Neither psychotherapy, drug therapy nor any other form of treatment offers entry to a new existence. Into the life of the happiest man ample reasons for despair can come. Even the most successful person may see himself as a colossal failure if he is unlucky enough to meet all of his critics on the same day! Psychotherapy does not ensure that a man's wife will love him or that an unfaithful husband will come home to stay. It is not a metamorphosis into a new life that transpires. Even the patient who seems most "changed" after a successful therapeutic experience can still (with joy) report, "I am still me!"

There remains much to be learned and put into practice. The nature and causes of schizophrenia are not known and a single definitive therapy is lacking; the management of depression is very difficult and at times the patient must endure long weeks of suffering before relief is provided; psychotherapy, family therapy, group therapy, behavior therapy, separately or in sequence, sometimes fail to offer the help hoped for by therapist and patient alike. Perhaps, above all, no psychiatric remedies can undo the damaging effects of social deprivation, neglect or persecution, particularly when they continue even as efforts to administer therapy are underway. Nor is prolonged psychological treatment the best remedy for those who feel isolated because of divorce, the departure of children or the obsolescence of their earlier social or work skills. For such problems, the return to life activities, trying again and/or coming back in a new direction are the better approaches. Nevertheless, there are many who need help from mental health professionals who do not receive it now. When the existing knowledge and skill is made more fully accessible to all, many others will also be helped.

In the Introduction to this book I shared a carefully guarded professional secret, one that bears repetition. Specifically, it is not possible to know with certainty which, if any, of the many potential therapies will be most helpful.[2] There are some patients who respond ONLY to a sufficient dosage of one of the tranquilizers or antidepressant medications. All the talk in the world, no matter how sincere or convincing, will fail to provide relief of symptoms. For such persons, neither individual, marital-couple nor group psychotherapeutic approaches will be useful; nor will switching from a psychoanalytic to an existential or to a client-centered frame of reference make any difference. The tender talk of loved ones, the straight talk of close friends and the inspiring messages of minister, counselor and teacher are influential only in the moment they are spoken. There is no potency in the words. Talk without a listener is only noise. Medications and medications alone (and only the appropriate one and in sufficient dosage continued for a long enough interval) provide relief! Nothing else works!

Yet there are other persons who will respond ONLY to some form of relationship psychotherapy, that is, to the opportunity to learn about themselves, to reveal long-felt worries and fears and to review their hopes and plans for the future. For such individuals the administration of drugs provides no help. Worse, there may be a clouding of consciousness, a preoccupation with side effects and a blunting of motivation for self-help approaches as a result of inappropriate or ineffective drug use.

There are still others whose social needs are so overwhelming that the ONLY intervention with meaning will be that which offers voice to the voiceless, courage to the fearful, resources to the destitute and knowledge of their own potential strength to those who know only their weakness. Group psychotherapy for the hungry, like choral singing by alcoholics in skid row missions, may serve primarily the needs of the purveyors of such services. The same applies to those who advise all women, "Go home and adjust."

There are many others among the group called mentally ill who will respond ONLY to a therapeutic program that combines the effective use of a specific medication, the effective application of a psychotherapeutic relationship and specific intervention that modifies one or another of the social and economic problems handicapping their lives. A lesser approach inevitably fails.

And so it goes—patient after patient. Each is different. Each requires an individual approach. While an experienced therapist can make educated guesses which are often correct, they are only guesses and they may well be incorrect. *No matter how wise, how experienced, how careful the clinician may be, it is simply not possible to circumvent or gainsay a therapeutic trial.* The importance for the patient to be working with a clinician who can make available the *full* armamentarium of treatment techniques and perspectives can hardly be overstated. Having begun a specific kind of treatment program, the clinician should be prepared to modify that original plan unless the patient's response is a rapid and fully satisfactory one. Sometimes, therapists have allowed themselves a substantial block of the patient's time before abandoning a particular form of therapy because they felt that difficulties which had been developing for many years would not disappear overnight. But, sometimes they do! At this time in this field, prolonged therapy uninterrupted by experiment with alternative therapeutic programs seems clearly unjustified. For this reason, consultation between professional colleagues has acquired an important place in the practice of most mental health professionals. So many therapeutic advances have been achieved during the last decade that no single person can become expert in every area. That a therapist happens to be expert in techniques which are not effective with a given individual should not be an affront! The incompatibility should be recognized and corrected early in the course of treatment! Such recognition is easier if the therapist is not the kind of person who traps himself in a charismatic posture which makes it necessary to continue doggedly whatever regime is initiated.

THE USE OF PSYCHIATRIC DRUGS

For the average person, taking drugs of any sort is a rather questionable thing to do. From earliest childhood, people have learned that drugs can be habit forming and the image of the drug addict or of the individual grown dependent upon sleeping capsules is a very negative one. As with the person who becomes dependent on alcohol, people tend to look down on the user of prescription medications. There is a general sense that "one should be able to do it by himself and not have to depend upon a crutch." Prescription of drugs has been viewed by many mental health professionals as a step to be avoided, one in opposition to the "self-help" philosophy which is held in high regard. For psychotherapy-minded doctors and patients alike, drug prescribing and drug taking conjure up a cacophony of sounds that include crutch, weakling, addict, dependent, dry-mouth, skin reaction, hooked, suicide, narcotics, drinker, unpsychological, slurred speech and so on. One reason for the contemporary prejudice against use of drugs is that only in recent years have effective tranquilizers and antidepressants been developed. Large doses of alcohol, barbiturates, bromides and other drugs blunted the symptoms but

222

finished off the day in the process. It was in the early 1950s that the major antipsychotic drugs, the phenothiazines, came into use and it was not until the 1960s that there was finally sufficient evidence to back up the claim, "They really work." Specific antidepression agents were introduced into clinical practice in the latter 1950s. Before their development there had been no effective chemical remedy for the sleep disturbance, early morning awakening and desperate agitation characteristic of depression. The barbiturates given as sleeping pills gave little respite when prescribed in normal amounts and such sleeping agents in large doses left the patient blunted and dazed the next day. Many patients, despairing, used their sleeping pills as suicide agents.

Two decades later, one fact outweighs all other suppositions, prejudices, "common sense" advice and other "logical" ideas on the subject: in many situations and to a remarkable degree, *the new drugs work!*[3]

There is no clear dividing line between the many kinds of medications. However, it is possible to consider them in four general categories. The first are the mild sedatives, mild tranquilizers, muscle relaxers and sleep-producing agents. They include alcohol (ethanol), Librium (chlordiazepoxide), Valium (diazepam), Equanil (meprobamate), the barbiturates, bromides, paraldehyde and chloral hydrate. Their various therapeutic uses are as muscle relaxants, mild antianxiety agents and hypnotics. They are generally ineffective in the treatment of severe anxiety and they are almost totally ineffective in the treatment of severe depression. As with most drugs, these mild agents in sufficient dosage or used over a prolonged period of time can have serious detrimental effects. They should not be casually prescribed or self-regulated.

The second category is made up of agents that provide major tranquilization and have specific antipsychotic properties. They are used primarily in treating the very severe anxiety, excitement and disordered thinking associated with schizophrenic living. They are potent agents that produce their own problems, but their use is one of the main factors in diminishing the morbidity of schizophrenic living. It usually takes an experienced clinician to decide on their use, to persuade hard-to-convince patients to cooperate, to set and regulate the dosage and to try to prevent and/or manage side effects. It is very important work since there are now data that show that many seriously sick patients are more than twice as likely to suffer relapse and require return to the hospital if they remove themselves from major tranquilizers.[4] Unfortunately, many such patients aren't very reliable when it comes to taking their medications and there are times when it is better if someone else assumes that responsibility.

> Because Leonard required three periods of hospitalization within six months, his doctor attempted to "hold off" relapses into schizophrenic living patterns by prescribing a daily oral dose of a major phenothiazine tranquilizer, Thorazine (chlorpromazine). However, Leonard, age twenty-one, responded to stressful moments in his life by giving up responsibility, withdrawing into himself and stopping all medications. There are several phenothiazine medications that can be given in a single injection form that remain effective for two weeks. The doctor finally decided to switch to the injections. Leonard was furious and threatened to withdraw from treatment. His explanation was simple: "I don't ever want to be in a position where I can't go crazy if I need to." Leonard's family helped in the persuasion and he ultimately conceded. On a regular regime of injections, rather than now-and-again pill taking, he had been free of disabling symptoms for more than three years at the time of this writing.

The third category of medications is made up of the antidepression drugs. They have been in common use for only ten years. Their target symptom is severe depression and they are often extremely effective. Some of the drugs, the tricyclic antidepressants, closely resemble in chemical structure one of the major tranquilizer groups, the phenothiazines. The most commonly used of the tricyclic group are Tofranil (imipramine) and Elavil (amitriptyline). A second group, the monoamine oxidase inhibitors, are less frequently prescribed because of their relatively potent side effects, particularly in raising blood pressure. In general, the antidepressants are remarkable drugs, effective in a majority of instances in which, only a few years ago, prolonged hospitalization and electrical shock therapy were required. Further, they are not only useful in reversing existing depressive states but often can be used to head off a recurring episode.

There are, however, significant problems associated with their use. Most troubling is that an interval as long as two or three weeks may pass before relief is provided. Their delayed effectiveness poses great problems for both patients and therapists. For example, Elavil (amitriptyline) is a very effective antidepressant. At times, as few as three twenty-five-

224

milligram tablets daily will provide dramatic relief within three or four days. On the other hand, there are many patients who respond well to the drug but only if it is given in large amounts, ten or twelve tablets daily, and continued for an interval of three or four weeks! Consider the level of trust that must exist between doctor and patient in order for a desperately depressed and discouraged individual to complete this course of treatment. The patient is told initially to take three tablets a day. Then, over succeeding weeks, he is urged to take four, then six, then eight, then ten and possibly twelve tablets. And relief comes only at the end of three or four long, tormented weeks. Sustaining hope for that interval is very difficult for all participants. The importance of the patient's spouse as therapeutic ally during this period needs no further explanation.

The new drugs, major tranquilizers and antidepressants, are among the most remarkable scientific achievements of our era. I remember all too vividly what it was like to practice psychiatry without them. For a period of three thousand years people had written of the anguish of the depressive states. For the sufferers, all over the world, there was no greater torture. Now, for the first time in history, and only in these last two decades, a group of chemical agents have been synthesized which provide relief. These new drugs accomplish what no amount of talking, no amount of prayer, no amount of other medication, no amount of alcohol, no amount of love and no amount of self-exhortation could provide. It is unfortunate that there is usually a "lag time" between the development of a major scientific breakthrough and its general availability. There are still many psychiatrists and general physicians who underuse or ineffectively use the new medications.

In addition to the major three groups—that is, the sedatives and muscle relaxants, the major tranquilizers and the antidepressants—a compound used earlier and recently rediscovered as effective in controlling mania is lithium carbonate. Where all else had failed, and in one of my patients all else had failed for twenty-five years, this newest therapeutic agent effects rapid termination of the periods of elation, excitability, hyperactivity and poor judgment which are part of the "manic phase" of a manic-depressive illness. It is also useful in preventing recurrences of mania, and there is some evidence now that the use of lithium carbonate may prevent many of the depressive episodes as well. Further, if one studies families and near-relatives of individuals suffering manic-depressive illnesses, there is likely to be a greater than expected number of family members who provide histories of anxiety, alcoholism and/or aggressive behavior patterns.[5] Some recent reports suggest that lithium carbonate controls these latter symptoms in those relatives, implying that a specific genetic abnormality might result in differing clinical pictures in the same family. It also makes clear how important a comprehensive family history is in the assessment and management of many clinical problems.

Without question, there are many patients who will not benefit from the use of drugs. However, for any individual to be deprived of an adequate trial of at least several of the newer medications in the face of continuing anxiety, depression, mania or disordered thinking is a serious mistake in clinical judgment. No psychiatrist, psychologist, social worker, psychiatric nurse or religious counselor deserves the title "professional" unless he or she can, personally or through ready referral, make available medications for any patient who fails to respond to other forms of therapy. Period. Exclamation point!

THE DECONDITIONING THERAPIES

"Behavior therapy," a contemporary extension and application of principles outlined by Pavlov, has come into increasing use during the last decade. As a form of treatment, it usually employs relaxation and psychological desensitization to accomplish the suppression of anxiety and phobic reactions. If the body is relaxed, it is almost impossible to be anxious. Persons who have a localized fear such as a flying phobia, fear of a specific disease, fear of an animal, fear of public speaking, fear of a closed place and so on may respond best to this form of treatment. For the truck driver who becomes afraid of tunnels and bridges, the businessman who fears airplane travel or the minister who fears that he will faint while delivering a sermon, these symptoms result in severe incapacity.

In one of the many deconditioning procedures developed by Dr. Joseph Wolpe, a South African psychiatrist now working in Philadelphia, the therapist begins by teaching the patient a variety of techniques for achieving body (muscle) relaxation. After the patient has some experience in being able to achieve a relaxed state, he or she is then asked to think specifically about the feared situation. When the fear reaction begins, the patient is instructed to reinstitute relaxation efforts immediately. With repeated practice, the feared situation loses its ominous and tension-producing characteristics. Ultimately, the individual is desensitized and deconditioned to his own fear and is able to confront without fear that which he could not even think about before.[6] One young woman described the process as follows:

> Bob had to fly a great deal and since I wanted to go with him, I had to get over my terrible fear. And I did. There were four actual therapy sessions, plus a fair amount of home practice and two not-so-comfortable short airplane rides. But now, about 90 percent of the fear and discomfort is gone and I'm still getting better.
>
> I learned how to close my eyes and relax every muscle: first the toes, the ankles, calves, knees and right on up. At the same time, I would imagine that Bob and I were in our boat and that the water on the lake was just a little choppy. And there I'd be, eyes closed, very relaxed and happy, enjoying the mild bumps of the water and quite comfortable as the boat turned starboard. But, after a while, I was really on a 747 jet. I have the comfort of knowing that if I get uneasy on the plane, I can close my eyes, relax and return to the lake. The last trip I took, the fifth since I had the treatment, I didn't get back on the boat once.

This is only one of many varieties of this kind of therapy. One technique, called "flooding," combines chemically induced relaxation with very intense exposure to the frightening object or circumstance. This allows a psychological-physiological "unlearning" of the fear reaction. Other behavioral techniques emphasize the process of symptom substitution. If an individual suffers a particular fear, he can be taught to perform some alternate action or to think repetitively some alternate thought in any moment when the original fear comes to consciousness. Symptom counting is a similar approach, serving as a substituting act. Through counting, a kind of diluting process of the feared subject takes place. That moment of life that was formerly undiluted fear and pain becomes, instead, cluttered with numbers, comparisons, list making and a process of substitution. Other therapists use a contract in which the patient agrees actually to perform the feared behavior a certain number of times in the interval between therapy sessions. Generally, the process of making the feared matter very specific and then doing it and overdoing it usually serves to "extinguish" its potency. For instance, several of my patients have been willing to take their worst personality characteristic and to put it to words in a three-paragraph speech. Then, I asked them to recite that speech over and over for ten minutes, two or three times a day, continuing the practice for three or four weeks.

These kinds of approaches for dealing concretely with a specific fear or unwanted behavior don't sound particularly elevating in terms of a deepening of psychological or spiritual values. To an outsider they seem mechanical. For participants there is an obvious risk of feeling demeaned in any process of doing "precisely what one is told to do." The reader may wonder, "What is an existential psychiatrist doing teaching Bob's wife how to pretend to be relaxing on the lake while actually flying at thirty-five thousand feet?" And even more questionably, "Isn't it clearly demeaning to encourage someone to prepare and read a little speech that says, 'I must always be sure to defend myself at all times. If anyone seems to be offering criticism, I must set them straight immediately. I am a very good person with a very good heart. Many other people aren't as well motivated as I am. One of my jobs in life is to defend myself and point out to others that they have plenty of faults.'?"

I find that the overwhelming majority of people do a good job in sorting out what is designed to be helpful and what is primarily demeaning. For me, there is nothing contradictory about prescribing drugs or practicing anxiety-relieving exercises as part of an existential approach in psychiatry. What is important is an appreciation of the parity of the participants. We all share a time-limited life. We live in a biological world that greatly influences experiencing. And each of us has social needs that cause us to prefer some discoveries in life over others. The new drugs and the various behavioral approaches are often very helpful in freeing up people's energy and enthusiasm. So be it!

PRAYER AND RELIGIOUS PRACTICE

The power and meaning of prayerful acts in the lives of the great majority of the people in the world need no documentation or analysis here. In moments when life is least hopeful and equally in moments of ultimate exultation, millions of people find relief and exhilaration in acts of religious devotion. Attempts to analyze or dismiss the importance of particular customs or rituals pale in the shadow of the magnitude of religious meaning in people's lives today and throughout human history. Nor can one overlook the unambivalent freedom to make a commitment for service to others that is possible for many of those with strong religious convictions. Of course, the depth and goodness of any belief is limited by the intentions and humanity of the person who interprets the faith. And there are many who focus on the simple ritual and thus evade the profound questions that would serve to inspire awe and humility. But such perspectives are perversions and have little to do with the primary religious purpose: to keep the question of human meaning (and an answer as well) in the front part of people's consciousness. In this regard, both the religious and irreligious existential thinkers agree on the important question.

In earlier years, there was often a spirit of antipathy between many clergymen and the various mental health professionals. Fortunately (for the patients and parishioners), most of that has disappeared. Clinicians are less likely of late to analyze (attack) the spiritual values of their patients. Simultaneously, religious thought has turned increasingly to the nature of the biological, psychological and social realities that largely determine the life experiencing of people. Sometimes in clinical practice I have occasion to feel particularly sorry for an individual who feels guilty because his prayers and faith were not sufficient to control his depression or anxiety. But in the totality of things that is a small matter. For most people, their religious beliefs, along with their loving relationships, are clear bonuses in their lives and assets for therapeutic exploitation when things go wrong.

Whether as a part of religious experiencing or as an attempt to gain a deeper awareness of and ability to be "in touch with" self, the process of meditation appears to encompass important antianxiety elements. Obviously, meditation, like learned techniques for relaxation, provides the individual with a way of interrupting sequences of anxious moments. Trained meditation probably offers more. Many people have described their meditation experiences as offering significant enhancement of the quality, stability, depth and sense of appreciation they have for their own lives. Recent research reports would tend to back them up. Formal meditation training apparently has therapeutic effects beyond the obvious inspirational and contemplative dimensions. One of my colleagues at the University of British Columbia, Dr. Juhn A. Wada, a distinguished neurophysiologist, has been studying the possibility that procedures that focus consciousness internally may activate and integrate "silent" parts of the brain. This work, which depends upon highly refined electrical study of brain function, is particularly exciting since it touches on the great hope of all speculation and research: we may discover that the mind (and heart) of mankind is deeper than we knew.[7]

THE MANY PSYCHOTHERAPIES

Eliza Doolittle challenged Professor Henry Higgins to stop talking and to come across with something real:

> "Words, words, words!
> First from him, now from you.
> Is that all you blighters can do?"[8]

It is now eight decades since the first of Freud's theories were made known to his astonished contemporaries. Hundreds and thousands of books, tens of thousands of articles and literally millions of hours of discussion have been devoted to the application of the major Freudian ideas that behavior makes sense and that people can change the way they feel. These days, the psychiatrist, psychotherapist and mental health consultant are to be found not only in private offices, clinics and hospitals, but also in prisons, primary and secondary schools, colleges, homes for unwed mothers, factories, government agencies, city planning departments, religious seminaries, police departments, advertising agencies and on the bench with professional football teams. In contemporary North American culture, personal hang-ups are viewed as amenable to change and the widest variety of counselors, therapists and group leaders offer their services to those who seek to be different from the way they are.

By now the subject has lost most of its glamour. On radio talk shows, people talk about other things. But every year, millions of people build up their courage, make an appointment and somewhat self-consciously establish themselves as the patient of Dr. X. Even if the drama seems a bit dated on television or in the theater, for the participants in the real-life consultation the event is as moving and full of risk as ever.

After all these years, what is the status of talking as therapy? If the goal of life is to learn about, discover and enjoy it, how much of that can happen while sitting around talking?

Thinking over the several decades of my own experience, certain matters stand forth. Those undertakings that featured the patient as student-in-trouble and starred the therapist as impresario of life-living have been duds. Those patients who succeeded in trapping a therapist into a "let's pretend" role of teacher of the how-to-feel and how-to-live protected their lives from the risk of change through therapy. Learning to live as the therapist advises is like deciding to do something spontaneously two times daily. No one has figured out how to remember not to remember but to do it anyway. To a certain extent, the same problem arose in the process of trying to teach therapists how to make the correct responses. Such instruction went the way of the European academies of art: the more the students copied their teachers, who were copying Rembrandt, the worse the paintings became. I think that this is mostly because psychotherapy (and psychiatry) is not separable from the life of the times. It does not stand apart. Instead, it is part of the concentric ripples on the waves which make up the tide. The hopes and aspirations of the day, the prejudices that are in ascendance, the economic-political-social realities of the people, are not simply matters of relevance. They are the arena in which the person discovers or evades, declares or denies, who he is. The point of focus in the therapy is not the fantasy stirred up in the therapist; it's what happens and doesn't happen in the life of the person called patient. For a therapist, the task is to allow what the patient is saying to live on for a while without dissection, without categorization and without refutation. Then, after one has listened to, dwelled in, the words and life of the patient, suddenly the therapist discovers, "There is much I haven't heard. Is it unnoticed, unspoken, hidden, disguised?"

My own work as a psychotherapist has always been limited (or was it graced?) by my failure to find a highly specialized approach in psychiatry that could regularly encompass the wide variety of problems that are unfolded in a psychiatrist's office. My own early training, a personal psychoanalysis and the extraordinary scope of Freudian theory has greatly influenced at least one aspect of my work. Specifically, the indelible imprint of one's early years and their influence on what a person is willing and able to learn about life is a matter whose importance is reinforced both by my work with patients and by what I have learned

231

about myself. The courses we follow in our lives and the conflicts we spend a lifetime trying to solve come often from the do, the don't and the do-don't of early years. In particular, a good many people spend decades and decades worrying about who is the most loved.

Case Study 1: *The Sixty-three-Year-Old Kid Sister of Shirley Temple the Second*

Mrs. Angie Rogers became my patient during the first year that I went into practice. She was sixty-three years old at the time, a rather forceful person, challenging and sometimes very challenging. I saw her at the request of her family physician who was puzzled, disappointed and frustrated because a full year of various therapies had failed to get her up from bed and back to work. She had severe stomach pains and occasional dizzy spells. She was outraged when I first went to see her because I was a psychiatrist and she was practically apoplectic when I asked her to talk about her childhood, her relationship with her mother and father and her feelings about her only sibling, another sister. That sister she called "Shirley Temple the Second." It was still going on! I saw her twice in the hospital and listened to her angry complaints about everybody, everything and me in particular. Then she got up from bed, forgot about her pains and declared herself my patient "and don't try and get out of it."

There were many reasons for her dissatisfaction. She'd been unhappy as a youngster, felt that she was clearly "number two" behind her sister, and most of her subsequent relationships seemed to reinforce her doubts about herself. Undoubtedly, her techniques for making and holding friends contributed to the unchanging nature of her life. She had evolved a fairly predictable ritual of meeting someone, liking them, assaulting them and then offering to make friends. Then, after the friendship was established, every once in a while she had to test things. She was often disappointed and she didn't have very many friends. Her first husband had divorced her and her second was a quiet drinker who, "when we were first married, wanted to make love once a month. Now, he wants to talk once a month."

232

Helping

Mrs. Rogers came to see me once a week for what was to be a fifty-minute hour. Three-quarters of the time she was angry at me about something I said, didn't say, was afraid to say or had supposedly said the week before. One-quarter of the time she talked about her hopes, her tender feelings toward her husband, her sometime concern about the health of Shirley Temple the Second and her relief that I hadn't thrown her out of the office.

We'd been working together for five or six months and things seemed to be going fairly well. She went back to work. She also reported some progress with her husband: "It's better. Now he lets me make love with him once a month and talks with me once a month." Her relationship with me seemed to settle down a bit. I began to think about suggesting that her appointments with me could be less frequent. Perhaps she read my mind. Suddenly, I faced the angriest, most unreasonable, most aggrieved and self-righteous person in the world.

I had sensed that something was going on the week before. She was a bit aloof and serious. There was an unfriendly calm about her. At the end of that hour I said, "Well, I'll see you next week," and she replied with some emphasis, "Yes, you will indeed." The next week she was even more remote, mysterious and unfriendly. One and a half hours after she left my office, while I was talking with a young medical student, a woman, she burst in unannounced, holding a paper with two columns of figures. It was her record of the total minutes I had spent with other patients (average fifty-six) and the scant forty-seven minutes spent with her! She was outraged, deadly serious and frankly vengeful. All the rest of the world disappeared from her consciousness. She was totally involved in the hurt and betrayal. She even dealt scornfully with the medical student whom she had misidentified as another of my patients. Her parting words to me were, "I quit this farce!" and to the astonished student who was there she said, "If you want him that much, I'll give him to you."

The next several weeks were made more interesting by a series of angry letters with a carbon to the dean of the medical school where I worked and a number of telephone requests for the name of the young woman student. Mrs. Rogers wanted to "finish the story" that she felt needed to be told. She also decided to see another psychiatrist, but then became angry with him because he wanted to be a "neutral judge." A month later she was back as my patient. She insisted nothing much had happened. There was nothing in particular to learn from that episode. It related to nothing else in her life history. She had a right to be suspicious of me. She might be slightly too preoccupied with such matters but that was perfectly understandable and justified because of her earlier experiences. And, "If that's all you want to talk about, then there's no point in my coming back. That's over. Stop referring to it. I'm no criminal." We worked together another three months. Mrs. Rogers was a little "spent" and I was a bit gun-shy.

I am afraid that I had a clearer sense than did Mrs. Rogers as to how this particular style of drama, occurring with inexorable regularity throughout her life, had restricted substantially what she could learn from among the possibilities of life.

Freud thought of these kinds of events as a "repetition compulsion," an attempt to detoxify certain painful life experiences by repeating them over and over, asserting control over life by making the defeat occur again. This is a kind of perverse victory through defeat. It can come to feel good to feel miserable, particularly if you yourself write the script, orchestrate the music and manipulate the dialogue. Freud cast the drama in terms of instincts, repressions, unconscious motivation and compromise solutions between social realities and personal desires.[9]

An existential approach to the patient just described takes a different tack. The therapist keeps asking, "Why can't I be me and you be you? Why do I have to play out some tired drama with a grubby outcome assured for all?" And more to the center, the therapist points out, "In a life that must someday end, you insist on squandering your opportunities to learn and do something new and different." In dialogue form, the confrontation might go something like this:

> Therapist: "I am not the mother, father, aunt, uncle or teacher who spent all his or her time selecting Shirley Temple the Second over you."
> Mrs. Rogers: "You look like them."
> Therapist: "Look again; it's only me."

Mrs. Rogers: "I can't tell the difference."
Therapist: "Stop covering your eyes with your hands."
Mrs. Rogers: "Okay, but can I keep my fingers in my ears?"
Therapist: "No! You need your hands free to reach out."

In an existential approach in psychotherapy, one assumes that it is not so much the pull from the past that holds people back as it is the fear of the future. But what is it in the future that one fears? From an existential point of view, that which is most dreadful is our human fate, our anxiety about that fate and our guilt, and we are willing to do almost anything to avoid living the life of the being who knows his days are numbered.

One of the major changes in psychotherapy practice in recent years has been the extension of participation beyond two persons to include a wide variety of others. There are therapists who treat individuals and their mates. Others work with couples and their children or couples and their parents. Some prefer to work with three-generation family groups. Some therapists include the patient and the group with whom he lives or works. In a university setting, this could include ten other members of a rooming house. In skid row, the other participants might be the tenants of a small hotel in which the patient creates a nightly disturbance. Obviously, in this kind of effort, the "sickness" of any single individual rarely remains the exclusive focus of the discussion. Instead, the nature of "our life together" and the reciprocal effects that people are having upon each other becomes the concern of all. Including the wife as a coparticipant in the therapeutic work often reveals that she too is discouraged and depressed and that the marriage which they share lacks the hope and warmth for which both privately yearn. After a few shared sessions, it sometimes happens that the unhappiness of the parents seems to make problems for the children and it appears wise to include them in the therapeutic process. When it goes well, what started out as the treatment of one person who bore the label of "mentally ill" becomes instead a series of explorations, reevaluations and reordering of purposes which enriches the life of an entire group. It very often happens that the one who is designated as the patient is instead, or as well, the "symptom carrier" for the group, the one who cries "ouch" for a couple, a family

235

or a society that is aching.[10] Fanon, Halleck and Myrdal have said it better than I am able.

Because people are so accustomed to thinking about psychotherapy as a two-person process, they question how open and candid it is possible to be in the presence of a mate, children, parents, fellow workers or others. On first consideration, the average individual is likely to be quite wary. "I'm not an exhibitionist!" might summarize the usual response. However, someone, who had himself experienced a couple, family or group therapy program could well reply:

> I felt that way too at first. But actually, it worked the other way for me. The other patients in the group inspired me and they were as helpful as the therapist. I started out thinking, "Oh God, I can't say anything in here. I don't even know if I can trust these people not to blackmail me." And then, some other member of the group cautiously speaks up, "I hope I can trust you all because I've decided to tell you honestly why I've come. It isn't easy. . . ."
>
> With the passage of time, you come to feel very close to the other members of the group. You get past competitiveness and you want the other guy to succeed. You've helped each other. You've learned a lot about yourself because someone else took a chance and spoke about things that have been bothering you. And finally, one day, you decide it's time to risk it. You decide: *Today I'm going to get something for myself!* And you do!

Beyond the extension of participants in the therapeutic group, there has also been a change away from the earlier emphasis on retrieving memories in order to find causes in early life experience for later attitudes. Contemporary therapies are much more likely to focus on the *here* and *now* in search for the answer as to why an individual is not able to enjoy and adequately participate in his life. His or her way of dealing with the here and now of the therapy hour (right here! right now!) becomes a point of focus. An emphasis on the here and now may be indicated by the following brief vignette:

> A marital therapy meeting with husband, wife and therapist. This is the twelfth appointment. Gene is twenty-nine and Sue is twenty-seven. They have been married for four years and came for treatment after Sue had consulted an attorney to start divorce proceedings. Both Sue and Gene were frequent complainers about the other's indifference.

Doctor: "Gene, I'd like you to stop now in what you are saying and turn your chair so that you are directly facing Sue. Say it to her. You've been talking about her without looking at her. And you don't have a chance to see the emotion which she is feeling while you speak."

Sue: "It won't do any good. He never——"

Doctor (interrupting Sue): "Wait, Sue, please say it to Gene, and look at him when you say it. I've noticed that both of you talk without seeming ever to talk directly to each other."

Sue (looks at Gene, starts crying): "Oh Gene, please help me."

Gene (pushing back his own tears and speaking to the doctor): "This is the first time Sue has ever asked me to help her."

Doctor (standing up, going over and turning Gene's chair so that he now directly faces Sue): "Gene, tell it to Sue."

Over a period of many weeks, individuals in a psychotherapeutic group are likely to become quite open and direct with each other. The give and take, though painful at times, gives participants an opportunity to learn for the first time that it is possible to become angry, to speak one's mind, to express a foolish idea or a tender one and return without shame and fear to the next meeting. Simultaneously, when therapy is successful, there are often changes in the individual's attitude to other people. They may be less concerned with pleasing anonymous others and more particular about what happens with those closest in their lives. That concern sometimes takes the form of a lessened possessiveness and at the same time a greater reverence and respect. Above all, there is usually a fuller appreciation of the existentiality of others. The joys of experiencing and choosing for oneself are desired for one's fellows. This is the matter of love.

There are by now a good many kinds of psychotherapies. For each variety, there are advocates and converts. Indeed, every "school of psychotherapy" has within it several prized individuals who as patients of "the other kinds of therapists" gained little or nothing. Then, at last, coming into the fold, they discovered the people and the kind of therapy that "really works." Such total conversions notwithstanding, there is no single therapy that is uniformly successful.

There are important existential dimensions in many therapies, even those that bear other labels. Perhaps any approach is existential which is undertaken in a spirit of parity between therapist and patient and which does not obscure the fact that in the future, therapist and patient will be continuing their life searches for meaning and satisfaction individually. The therapist and the patient, it is hoped, will each be enriched and made more curious about life by virtue of their contact with each other.

Certainly, existential psychotherapy cannot be conducted according to a script. Success, if it comes, may be a consequence more of the spirit in which the therapy is conducted than of the techniques employed.

Existential therapists often quote a Hasidic legend which tells of Zusha the rabbi who lay dying. He called his family and students together and told them, "When I meet my creator, he will not say, 'Zusha, why were you not as Moses?' He will say, 'Zusha, why were you not as Zusha?' "[11]

LOOKING AHEAD: QUALITY CONTROL

It is quite likely that the near future will provide an evaluational system that will objectively discover and discreetly inform both the psychiatric clinician and patient as to "how are we doing?" This is necessary since, as has been indicated earlier, it is never possible to know with certainty in advance whether a given form of therapy will be effective. Several medical specialties have the beginnings of a system for the retrieval of information built into their practice, particularly when the patient is hospitalized. Most general hospitals have "patient care committees" which survey the progress of the various doctors' patients, the responses to medicine, the length of time required for recovery and the incidence of infections. Surgical practice, in particular, has been made much more dependable and precise by the presence in almost all hospitals of surgical pathologists who report back on the examination of all tissue removed during surgical procedures.

In psychiatry, however, and in the other mental health professions, no effective system beyond his own experience allows the clinician to know early that he is on the wrong track and that some other therapeutic method should be considered. We lack a "tissue committee"* and a "surgical pathologist" for psychiatry and the other mental health professions.

*This was suggested originally by Dr. Martin Loeb, formerly the dean of the School of Social Work at the University of Wisconsin, Madison.

One possible answer to this problem is the use of a consultant in the therapeutic hour between clinician and patient, who shares with both his or her assessment of the treatment program. Such consultation is considerably less intrusive than it may sound. It is rare for a patient of mine to go longer than a month without some other clinician being asked to consult, either as my cotherapist or in an individual meeting with the patient. So many patients require weeks and months and sometimes longer to recover that one becomes accustomed to symptoms. The very intimacy of the relationship between therapist and patient can make it difficult to gauge progress objectively.

An additional reason for outside evaluation of treatment progress is that therapists working with slowly improving patients often have difficulty in retaining as the therapeutic goal 100 percent recovery or, better yet, "The patient not only gets well, he gets weller." Seeing a little progress, the clinician and patient may be tempted to stay with a therapeutic program that has some, though limited, effectiveness. A small amount of progress makes it difficult to consider a new approach. The outside consultant can often bring useful perspectives to the participants. Therapeutic relationships that are structured to allow and welcome such "intrusion" will in the long run be most conducive to maximum success.

The use of a computerized evaluation system offers another possible approach to treatment review. This kind of evaluational system would not require the presence within the consulting room of any third party. It might work something like this: The clinician and the patient would each fill out an initial brief description form which would be coded and made part of a computerized record. For the clinician, the filling out of forms might be a three- or four-minute task. For the patient, completing a problem list of forty items might be adequate. Fewer than five minutes would suffice to finish the paper work. The privacy of the patient would be maintained by a code number, but not necessarily the privacy of the doctor. The computer center (serving many hundreds of clinics, hospitals and individual therapists) would regularly report back to the clinician and patient. At the end of one month of treatment, a second set of reports would be submitted to the computer with the patient stating simply that he is much better, a little better, about the same or worse. The doctor would record from a treatment checklist the treatment system employed. The computer, after comparing the experience of this doctor and patient with that of hundreds or thousands of others from its data pool, might reply in a friendly but realistic manner something like this:

> At the end of one month on a regime of once-weekly interviews, with two family visits and the use of mild tranquilizers, the patient notes only a limited sense of improvement. The computer's experience indicates that continuing this form of therapy over the succeeding four weeks will lead to improvement in only approximately 15 percent of cases. The computer's further experience indicates that, at this point, the clinician and patient may wish to consider the addition of. . . .

The technology is presently available. What is much less certain is whether its introduction in the name of quality control would introduce a depersonalizing element that would do more harm than good.

I think not. The coming of outside evaluation into mental health care will produce many changes. But the wish to help, engendered by the words "Please do what you can for me," is a force so powerful that even the awe-inspiring computer can likely be harnessed in its service.

Epilogue

My profession has changed a great deal in the last two decades or more—and so have I. I began my career as a psychiatrist by trying to understand and to categorize what was wrong with people. "Advocacy" for my patient, for his or her hopes, needs, endeavors, then seemed beyond the scope of my responsibility. I feared that "advocating" interfered with understanding. I didn't understand at first that where humans and their aspirations are involved, one cannot really understand except from the stance of advocate. A lesson, mercifully early in my career, served to highlight the problem. I had been working closely with a young woman who had become quite depressed after the death of her parents. Shortly afterwards, her husband left her and she made a serious suicide attempt. With therapy, she improved rapidly and decided to return to graduate school and resume the education she had interrupted seven years earlier. With permission, she wrote my name on the medical treatment portion of her application and asked that when solicited, I write a letter indicating my sense of her readiness, her competence, her potential. A few weeks later, a formal request came from the college admissions office along with a letter asserting that an "objective, candid" appraisal was in the interest of the applicant. My letter was impartial, balanced, fair, to patient and school. They turned her down. My patient, wiser and more human than I, abandoned the therapy and explained, "Good-bye! My life is too short to share intimately with people who can be 'objective' about me."

I find that most of the people I have come to know well are happiest if, in their personal lives, they have one or more persons with whom to share their intimate hopes, fears and love. Money is also a very key matter and I find that asking people about their debts may be as revealing as asking about their sexual relationships. Very, very few people are ungrateful for efforts to help them, yet almost everybody is terrified of being made the fool. I find almost everybody quite as decent as I and as yet have failed to find a concept so complex or a listener so dense as to negate the necessity for 100 percent honesty on my part. Adlai Stevenson, in losing the American presidential elections in 1952 and 1956, advised, "Speak up, not down, to the [North] American people." The results of the balloting notwithstanding, I find his advice altogether correct.

NOTES

APPENDIX

INDEX

NOTES

PART 1

Prologue

1. Carl A. Whitaker, Graduating Address, University of British Columbia Psychiatrists, June 6, 1975.
2. Karl A. Menninger, quoted in Samuel Silverman, *New Ways to Predict Illness* (New York: Stein and Day, 1973).
3. C. G. Jung, *Modern Man in Search of a Soul*, W. S. Dill and Cary F. Baynes, trans. (New York: Harcourt, Brace and Company, 1933).

Chapter 1

1. N. N. Wagner and E. S. Tan, *Psychological Problems and Treatment in Malaysia* (Kuala Lumpur: University of Malaya Press, 1971).
2. M. Buber, *I and Thou*, 2d ed. (New York: Charles Scribner's Sons, 1958).
3. C. R. Rogers, *The Therapeutic Relationship and Its Impact* (Madison: University of Wisconsin Press, 1962).
4. R. Stuart, *Trick or Treatment: How and When Psychotherapy Fails* (Champaign, Ill.: Research Press, 1970).
5. C. A. Whitaker and E. Olsen, "The Staff Team and the Family Square Off," in *New Hospital Psychiatry*, G. M. Abroms and N. S. Greenfield, eds. (New York: Academic Press, 1971).
6. E. Becker, *The Denial of Death* (New York: The Free Press, 1973).
7. J.-P. Sartre, *Nausea* (New York: New Directions Publishing Co., 1964).
8. M. Heidegger, *Being and Time* (New York: Harper and Row, 1962), pp. 163–167.
9. R. G. Martin, *The Woman He Loved* (New York: Simon and Schuster, 1974).
10. M. H. Miller, "Beginning at the Beginning in Psychotherapy: An Existential Point of View," *Can. Psychiatric Assoc. J.* 18 (December 1973):459–465.

Notes

Chapter 2

1. P. Tillich, *Dynamics of Faith* (New York: Harper and Row, 1957).
2. M. Buber, *I and Thou.*
3. R. Rodgers, *The King and I,* a musical play; music by Richard Rodgers, book and lyrics by Oscar Hammerstein II (New York: Williamson Music Inc., 1951).
4. M. Heidegger, *Being and Time.*
5. R. Hovey, "Unmanifest Destiny," in *Masterpieces of Religious Verse,* Morrison James Dalton, ed. (New York: Harper and Row, 1948).
6. Lao Tzu, "The Secret," in *Shadow and Substance* (New York: Seabury Press, 1974).
7. R. M. Pirsig, *Zen and the Art of Motorcycle Maintenance* (New York: Bantam Books, 1974).
8. H. Hesse, *Siddhartha,* Hilda Rosner, trans. (New York: New Directions, 1974).

PART 2

1. M. H. Miller, F. K. Yeh et al., "The Cross Cultural Student," *Bull. Menninger Clin.* 35 (1971):128–131; M. H. Klein, A. A. Alexander et al., "Far Eastern Students in a Big University," *Bull. Atomic Scientists* 27 (1971):10.
2. J. M. Thornburn, quoted in S. K. Langer, *Philosophy in a New Key* (New York: New American Library, 1961), p. ix.

Chapter 3

1. S. Jackson, *The Lottery; or, The Adventures of James Harris* (New York: Farrar, Straus, 1949).

Chapter 4

1. J. H. Masserman, "Faith and Delusion in Psychotherapy: The Ur-Defenses of Man," *Am. J. Psychiatry* 110 (1953):324–333.
2. J. D. Salinger, *Catcher in the Rye* (Boston: Little, Brown & Co., 1951).
3. J. H. Kellogg, *Plain Facts for Old and Young* (Burlington, Iowa: I. R. Segner and Co., 1891).

Chapter 5

1. B. Dylan, "A Man's Not Busy Living, Busy Dying," in "It's Alright Ma (I'm Only Bleeding)," *Bob Dylan Song Book* (New York: Witmark, 1965).

2. G. M. Abroms, J. R. Marshall and M. H. Miller, "The Doctor, the Dying Patient, and the Bereaved," *Ann. Intern. Med.* 70 (1969):615–620.

3. J. G. Kepecs, J. Chosey and D. Graham, "Description of a Jointly Managed Medical Ward at the University Hospitals," University of Wisconsin, Madison, Wisconsin, Departments of Medicine and Psychiatry. Personal communication.

PART 3

Chapter 6

1. B. Brecht, *Threepenny Opera,* English translation by Desmond Vesey; lyrics by Eric Bentley (New York: Grove, 1964).

2. R. D. Laing, *Knots* (New York: Pantheon, 1970).

3. R. D. Laing, *The Divided Self* (London: Tavistock Publications, 1960).

4. H. Arendt, *Human Condition* (Chicago: University of Chicago Press, 1969).

Chapter 7

1. WHO Expert Committee on Addiction Producing Drugs, "First Report" *Wld. Hlth. Org. Tech. Rep. Ser.* 273 (1964).

2. *Henderson and Gillespie Textbook of Psychiatry,* 10th ed., rev. by Ivor R. C. Batchelor (London: Oxford University Press, 1969).

3. C. Castaneda, *The Teachings of Don Juan* (New York: Simon and Schuster, 1968); *A Separate Reality* (New York: Simon and Schuster, 1971); *Journey to Ixtlan* (New York: Simon and Schuster, 1972).

4. T. P. K. Lin, "Mental Health in the Peoples' Republic of China," The Adolf Meyer Lecture, American Psychiatric Association Meeting, Honolulu, Hawaii, May 1973.

Chapter 8

1. A. Wheelis, *Quest for Identity* (New York: Norton, 1958).

2. A. M. Marcus, *Nothing Is My Number* (Toronto: General Publishing Co. Ltd., 1971).

3. M. Boss, *The Meaning and Content of Sexual Perversions,* Liese Lewis Abell, trans. (New York: Grune & Stratton, 1949).

4. T. Capote, *In Cold Blood* (New York: Random House, 1966).

5. C. L. Kline and C. L. Kline, "The Dyslexic Child, the Parents and the Schools: A Study in Mutual Futility and Hostility: Analysis of 700 Cases," American

Orthopsychiatric Association Annual Meeting, New York, May 1973. Abstracted in *Am. J. Orthopsychiatry* 43 (March 1973).

6. R. R. Fieve, "The Lithium Clinic," *Am. J. Psychiatry* 132 (October 1975):10.
7. C. H. Mark and F. R. Ervin, *Violence and the Brain* (New York: Harper and Row, 1970).
8. A. Frank, *Anne Frank: The Diary of a Young Girl* (New York: Doubleday, 1967).
9. S. L. Halleck, *Psychiatry and the Dilemmas of Crime* (New York: Harper and Row, 1967).

PART 4

Chapter 9

1. J.-P. Sartre, *Being and Nothingness*, Hazel E. Barnes, trans. (New York: Philosophical Library, 1965), p. 626.

Chapter 11

1. M. H. Miller, "Continuing Incapacity Despite 'Medical Recovery,' " *J.A.M.A.* 176 (April 22, 1961):205–207.
2. H. S. Akiskal et al., "Overview of Recent Research in Depression," *Arch. Gen. Psychiatry* 32, no. 3 (March 1975), pp. 285–305; H. Lehmann, "Epidemiology of Depressive Disorder," In *Depression in the 1970s*, R. R. Fieve, ed. (Princeton, N.J.: Excerpta Medica, 1971).
3. H. M. Bogard, "Follow-Up of Suicidal Patients Seen in Emergency Work Consultation," *Am. J. Psychiatry* 126 (1970): 1017–1020.
4. B. Shopsin et al., "The Current Status of Lithium in Psychiatry," *Am. J. Med. Sci.* 268, no. 6 (December 1974), pp. 306–323.

Chapter 13

1. J. H. Masserman, "Faith and Delusion in Psychotherapy: The Ur-Defenses of Man."
2. M. Bleuler, "Schizophrenia: Review of the Work of Professor Eugene Bleuler," *Arch. Neurol. Psychiat.* 26 (1931):611–627.
3. H. S. Sullivan, *Clinical Studies in Psychiatry*, H. S. Perry, M. L. Gawall and M. Gibbon, eds. (New York: Norton, 1956).
4. W. L. Bruetsch, *Penicillin in Neurosyphilis* (New York: Grune and Stratton, 1949).
5. S. S. Kety, "From Rationalization to Reason," *Am. J. Psychiatry* 131, no. 9 (September 1974), pp. 957–963; J. G. Funderson, J. H. Autry and L. R.

Mosher, "Special Report: Schizophrenia 1974," *Schizophrenia Bull.,* no. 9 (Summer 1974).

6. S. S. Kety, D. Rosenthal, P. H. Wender et al., "Mental Illness in the Biological and Adoptive Families of Adopted Individuals Who Have Become Schizophrenic," in *Genetic Research in Psychiatry,* R. R. Fieve, H. Brill and D. Rosenthal, eds. (Baltimore: Johns Hopkins University Press, 1975).

7. F. J. Kallman, *Heredity in Health and Mental Disorder* (New York: Norton, 1953).

8. D. Rosenthal, "The Genetics of Schizophrenia," in *American Handbook of Psychiatry,* vol. 3, S. Areti, ed., pp. 588–600.

9. Octavio Paz, *Eagle or Sun?,* Eliot Weinberger, trans.

PART 5

Chapter 14

1. T. Reik, *Search Within: The Inner Experiences of a Psychoanalyst* (New York: Funk and Wagnalls, 1968).

2. M. H. Miller, J. E. Miles and M. H. Klein, "Quality Control in Psychiatric Treatment: 100% Well in Three Weeks or the Doctor Says 'Why,' " *Can. Psychiatr. Assoc. J.* 20 (June 1975):267–272.

3. *Psychopharmacology Bull.,* prepared by Psychopharmacology Research Branch, National Institute of Mental Health.

4. F. J. Ayd, "The Depot Fluphenazines: A Reappraisal After 10 Years' Clinical Experience," *Am. J. Psychiatry* 132, no. 5 (May 1975), pp. 491–500.

5. G. Winokur, "The Iowa 500: Heterogeneity and Course in Manic-Depressive Illness (Bipolar)," *Comp. Psychiatry* 16, no. 2 (March-April 1975):125–131.

6. J. Wolpe, *The Practice of Behavior Therapy* (New York: Pergamon Press, 1969).

7. J. Wada and A. E. Hamm, "Electrographic Glimpse of Meditative State: Chronological Observations of Cerebral Evoked Response," *E.E.G. Clin. Neurophys.* 37 (1974):201.

8. A. J. Lerner, *My Fair Lady* (New York: Coward-McCann, 1956).

9. S. Freud, *Collected Papers,* vol. 2 (London: Hogarth Press, 1949).

10. F. Fanon, *Wretched of the Earth,* Constance Farrington, trans. (New York: Grove, 1963); S. L. Halleck, *The Politics of Therapy* (New York: Science House, 1971); G. Myrdal, *The Challenge of World Poverty* (New York: Pantheon Books, 1970).

11. M. Buber, *Tales of the Hasidim,* vol. 1 (New York: Shocken Books, Inc., 1947).

APPENDIX

STATE MENTAL HEALTH PROGRAM DIRECTORS

State	Title, Agency	Address
Alabama	Commissioner Department of Mental Health	502 Washington Ave. Montgomery, Alabama 36104
Alaska	Director Division of Mental Health Department of Health and Social Services	Pouch H-04-B Juneau, Alaska 99811
Arizona	Assistant Director Division of Behavioral Services Department of Health Services	2500 E. Van Buren St. Phoenix, Arizona 85008
Arkansas	Commissioner Mental Health Services Department of Social and Rehabilitative Services	4313 W. Markham St. Little Rock, Arkansas 72201
California	Health Treatment Systems Department of Health	744 P Street, Rm. 742 Sacramento, California 95814
Colorado	Chief Division of Mental Health Department of Institutions	4150 S. Lowell Blvd. Denver, Colorado 80236
Connecticut	Commissioner Department of Mental Health	90 Washington St. Hartford, Connecticut 06115

Appendix

State	Title, Agency	Address
Delaware	Division of Mental Health Department of Health and Social Services	New Castle, Delaware 19720
District of Columbia	Administrator Mental Health Administration Department of Human Resources	1875 Connecticut Ave., N.W. Room 824 Washington, D.C. 20009
Florida	Division of Mental Health Department of Health and Rehabilitative Services	1323 Winewood Blvd. Tallahassee, Florida 32301
Georgia	Director Division of Mental Health Department of Human Resources	47 Trinity Ave., S.W. Room 530 Atlanta, Georgia 30334
Guam	Director Community Mental Health Center	Guam Memorial Hospital P.O. Box AX Agena, Guam 96910
Hawaii	Director Department of Health	P.O. Box 3378 Honolulu, Hawaii 96801
Idaho	Acting Administrator Division of Community Rehabilitation Department of Health and Welfare	Len B. Jordan Building Room 327, Statehouse Mail Boise, Idaho 83720
Illinois	Director Department of Mental Health and Developmental Disabilities	160 N. LaSalle St. Chicago, Illinois 60601
Indiana	Commissioner Department of Mental Health	5 Indiana Square Indianapolis, Indiana 46204

Appendix

State	Title, Agency	Address
Iowa	Division of Mental Health Resources Department of Social Services	Lucas State Office Building Des Moines, Iowa 50319
Kansas	Division of Mental Health and Retardation Services Department of Social and Rehabilitative Services	State Office Building Topeka, Kansas 66612
Kentucky	Commissioner Bureau for Health Services Department of Human Resources	P.O. Box 678 Frankfort, Kentucky 40601
Louisiana	Director Division of Mental Health Health and Social Rehabilitative Services Administration	P.O. Box 44215 Baton Rouge, Louisiana 70804
Maine	Director Bureau of Mental Health Department of Mental Health and Corrections	State Office Building Room 411 Augusta, Maine 04330
Maryland	Commissioner of Mental Hygiene Department of Health and Mental Hygiene	State Office Building 301 W. Preston St. Baltimore, Maryland 21201
Massachusetts	Commissioner Department of Mental Health Executive Office of Human Services	190 Portland St. Boston, Massachusetts 02114
Michigan	Acting Director Department of Mental Health	Lewis-Cass Building 320 Walnut St. Lansing, Michigan 48926

State	Title, Agency	Address
Minnesota	Assistant Commissioner Bureau of Comprehensive Programs Department of Public Welfare	Centennial Office Building St. Paul, Minnesota 55155
Mississippi	Executive Director Department of Mental Health	607 Robert E. Lee Office Building Jackson, Mississippi 39201
Missouri	Director Department of Mental Health	P.O. Box 687 2002 Missouri Blvd. Jefferson City, Missouri 65101
Montana	Bureau of Mental Health Division of Community Based Services Department of Institutions	1539 Eleventh Ave. Helena, Montana 59601
Nebraska	Director Department of Public Institutions	P.O. Box 94728 State Capitol Lincoln, Nebraska 68509

Nevada	Division Administrator
	Division of Mental Hygiene
	  and Mental Retardation
	Department of Human
	  Resources
		4600 Kietzke Lane
		Suite 108
		Reno, Nevada 89502

New Hampshire	Acting Director
	Division of Mental Health
	Department of Health and
	  Welfare
		105 Pleasant St.
		Concord, New Hampshire
		  03301

New Jersey	Director
	Division of Mental Health and
	  Hospitals
	Department of Institutions and
	  Agencies
		P.O. Box 1237
		Trenton, New Jersey 08625

254

Appendix

State	Title, Agency	Address
New Mexico	Secretary Department of Hospitals and Institutions	Lamy Building 425 Old Santa Fe Trail Santa Fe, New Mexico 87501
New York	Commissioner Department of Mental Hygiene	44 Holland Ave. Albany, New York 12229
North Carolina	Commissioner Division of Mental Health Services Department of Human Resources	325 N. Salisbury St. Raleigh, North Carolina 27611
North Dakota	Director Division of Mental Health and Retardation State Department of Health	State Capitol Bismarck, North Dakota 58501
Ohio	Director Department of Mental Health and Mental Retardation	2929 Kenny Rd. Room A-204 Columbus, Ohio 43221
Oklahoma	Director Department of Mental Health	P.O. Box 53277 Capitol Station 408-A Walnut Oklahoma City, Oklahoma 73105
Oregon	Administrator Mental Health Division Department of Human Resources	2570 Center St., N.E. Salem, Oregon 97310
Pennsylvania	Acting Deputy Secretary for Mental Health and Medical Services Department of Public Welfare	308 Health and Welfare Building Harrisburg, Pennsylvania 17120
Puerto Rico	Assistant Secretary for Mental Health	G.P.O. Box 61 San Juan, Puerto Rico 00936

Appendix

State	Title, Agency	Address
Rhode Island	Director Department of Mental Health, Retardation and Hospitals	600 New London Ave. Cranston, Rhode Island 02920
South Carolina	Commissioner Department of Mental Health	P.O. Box 485 Columbia, South Carolina 29202
South Dakota	Director Division of Mental Health and Mental Retardation Department of Social Services	200 W. Pleasant Dr. Pierre, South Dakota 57501
Tennessee	Commissioner Department of Mental Health	300 Cordell Hull Building Nashville, Tennessee 37319
Texas	Commissioner Department of Mental Health and Mental Retardation	Box 12668 Capitol Station Austin, Texas 78711
Utah	Director Division of Mental Health Department of Social Services	544 S. 300 East Salt Lake City, Utah 84111
Vermont	Commissioner Department of Mental Health Agency of Human Services	120 Date St. Montpelier, Vermont 05602
Virginia	Commissioner Department of Mental Health and Mental Retardation Office of Human Services	P.O. Box 1797 Richmond, Virginia 23214
Virgin Islands	Director Mental Health Services Department of Health	St. Thomas, Virgin Islands
Washington	Chief Office of Mental Health Department of Social and Health Services	P.O. Box 1788 Olympia, Washington 98504

256

Appendix

State	Title, Agency	Address
West Virginia	Director Department of Mental Health	State Capitol 1800 Washington St. Charleston, West Virginia 25305
Wisconsin	Administrator Division of Mental Hygiene Department of Health and Social Services	1 West Wilson St. Madison, Wisconsin 53702
Wyoming	Director (State MH Authority) Mental Health and Mental Retardation Services Division of Health and Medical Services Department of Health and Social Services	State Office Building Cheyenne, Wyoming 82001

ORGANIZATIONS AND AGENCIES OF INTEREST
TO PSYCHIATRISTS

American Association of Psychiatric Services for Children
  1701 18th St., N.W.
  Washington, D.C. 20009

American Geriatrics Society
  10 Columbus Circle
  New York, New York 10019

American Hospital Association
  840 North Lake Shore Dr.
  Chicago, Illinois 60611

American Medical Association
  535 N. Dearborn St.
  Chicago, Illinois 60610

American Medical Society on Alcoholism, Inc.
  2 Park Ave., Suite 1720
  New York, New York 10016

American Psychiatric Association
  1700 18th St., N.W.
  Washington, D.C. 20009

American Psychological Association
  1200 17th St., N.W.
  Washington, D.C. 20036

Association for Research in Nervous and Mental Disease
  722 W. 168th St.
  New York, New York 10032

British Medical Association
  Tavistock Square
  London W.C.1
  England

Canadian Association for the Mentally Retarded
  Kinsmen NIMR Building
  4700 Keele St.
  Downsview, Ontario M3J 1P3
  Canada

Canadian Medical Association
  1867 Alta Vista Dr., P.O. Box 8650
  Ottawa, Ontario K1G 0G8
  Canada

Canadian Mental Health Association
  2160 Yonge St.
  Toronto, Ontario, M4S 2Z3
  Canada

Canadian Psychiatric Association
Association des Psychiatres du Canada
  225 Lisgar St., Suite 103
  Ottawa, Ontario K2P 0C6
  Canada

International Association for Social Psychiatry
  8 S. Michigan Ave.
  Chicago, Illinois 60603

International Committee against Mental Illness
  18 E. 67th St.
  New York, New York 10021

Mexican Psychiatric Association
  Av. Insurgentes Sur 1748
  Desp. 503, Mexico 20, D.F.
  Mexico

National Association for Mental Health, Inc.
1800 N. Kent St.
Arlington, Virginia 22209

National Association for Mental Health (Great Britain)
22 Harley St.
London W1N 2ED
England

National Association of Private Psychiatric Hospitals
One Farragut Square So., Suite 201
Washington, D.C. 20006

National Association of State Mental Health Program Directors
1001 3rd St., S.W., Suite 115
Washington, D.C. 20024

National Committee against Mental Illness
1101 17th St., N.W.
Washington, D.C. 20036

National Council on Alcoholism
2 Park Ave.
New York, New York 10016

National Medical Association
2109 E St., N.W.
Washington, D.C. 20037

National Rehabilitation Association
1522 K St., N.W.
Washington, D.C. 20005

Psychiatric Outpatient Centers of America
P.O. Box 1048
Oil City, Pennsylvania 16301

Veterans Administration
Mental Health and Behavioral Sciences Service
810 Vermont Avenue, N.W.
Washington, D.C. 20420

World Federation for Mental Health
2255 Wesbrook Crescent
University of British Columbia
Vancouver, British Columbia V6T 1W5
Canada

World Psychiatric Association
Maudsley Hospital
Denmark Hill
London S.E.5
England

CANADIAN ORGANIZATIONS

Alberta   Director of Mental Health
                           Administration Building
                           Edmonton, Alberta

Appendix

British Columbia	Associate Deputy Minister of Mental Health Programmes Parliament Buildings Victoria, British Columbia
Manitoba	Assistant Deputy Minister Mental Health Services Legislative Buildings Winnipeg, Manitoba B3C 0V8
New Brunswick	Director of Mental Health Services Fredericton, New Brunswick
Newfoundland	Director of Mental Health Services Government Services Building St. John's, Newfoundland
Nova Scotia	Administrator Mental Health Services Box 488 Halifax, Nova Scotia
Ontario	Ontario Mental Health Foundation 45 St. Clair Street, W. Toronto 7, Ontario
Prince Edward Island	Director of Mental Health Box 3000 Charlottetown, Prince Edward Island
Quebec	Department of Social Affairs Mental Health Programme 1075 Ste. Foy Quebec G1A 1B9 Quebec
Saskatchewan	Director Psychiatric Services Branch Provincial Health Building Regina, Saskatchewan

INDEX

Acute schizophrenia, 203, 204, 205
Acute schizophrenic decompensation, 210
Acute love, 26
Adolescents, of 1950s through 1970s, 78–79
Adults and youth
    eastern (Asian) pattern, 63–66
    relationship between, 62–72
    western pattern, 66–70
Alcohol, 123–28, 223
Alcoholism, 123–24
Amitriptyline. *See* Elavil
Amphetamines, 129, 131
Antidepression agents, 223
Antidepression drugs, 224
Antisocial personality, 114
Anxiety, 47
Appearing foolish, 28
Arendt, Hannah, 116
Asia, childhood education in, 63–66
Asocial personalities, 114
Autism, 202
Aversion treatment, 142

Barbiturates, 131, 223
Becker, Ernest, 30–31
Behavior therapy, 226
Being and Time (Heidegger), 39
Belief, 74

Bleuler, Eugen, 199
Boss, Medard, 138
Brecht, Bertolt, 106
Buber, Martin, 25, 38

Camus, Albert, 32
Castaneda, Carlos, 32, 127–28
Charisma, 30–34
Childhood schizophrenia, 210
Children. *See* Youth
China, heroin addiction in, 130
Chlordiazepoxide. *See* Librium
Civilization, beginning of, 70–72
Compulsive living, 151–59
Conditioning, 142
Conformity, 39
Criminals, 139–43
Crisis intervention, 183

Death, 40
    denial of, 97–100
Decompensation, 156–57
Deconditioning, 142
Deconditioning therapies, 226–28
Delusions, 75
Denial of Death, The (Becker), 30–31
Depression, 54–55, 172–76
    drugs for, 177, 224–25
    hospitalization and, 177–78
    illness and, 174–75

management of severe, 176–78
older people and, 95, 97
suicidal gesture in young people
and, 178–83
suicide and, 175–76
Dexedrine, 131
Diazepam. *See* Valium
Discoveries, making, 116
Drug abuse, 127–32
Drug addiction, 128, 129–30
Drugs
antipsychotic, 223
criminal behavior and, 142
depression and, 177
mental health and, 220–21
reasons for use of, 131–32
use of psychiatric, 222–26
Dylan, Bob, 91

Education, western pattern of, 66
Elavil, 224–25
Elderly. *See* Older persons
Emotional disorder, 151
Empathic relationship, 34
Empathy, 34–36
Equanil, 223
Ethanol. *See* Alcohol
Evaluation, 238–40
Extended family, 75–76

Faith, 23
Faith healers, 23
Families, therapy and, 16–18
Flooding, 227
Folk healers, 23, 24

Generational stresses, 59–61
Genetics, schizophrenics and, 212–14
Grand hysteria, 166

Grandparents, role of, 73–74, 75
Group therapy, 236, 237
Guilt, 16
sex and, 79–80

Halleck, Seymour, 146
Healing, nature of, 23–24
Health, older people and, 94–97
Heidegger, Martin, 32, 35, 39
Helping, 219–40
Henderson and Gillespie Textbook of Psychiatry, 124
Heroin, 129
Heroin addicts, 129–30
Hesse, Hermann, 38, 44
Humiliation, avoidance of, 112
Hysterical living, 160–71

Illness
depression and, 174–75
serious, 97–100
Imipramine. *See* Tofranil
Indians, American, 37
Internal restraint, 135
Intoxication, 123

Jackson, Shirley, 69
Journey to Ixtlan (Castaneda), 128
Jung, Carl, 9

Kallman, Franz, 213
Kety, Seymour, 213
Kline, Carl, 141, 142

Laing, R. D., 32, 106, 116
Lao Tzu, 41
Lehman, Heinz, 15
Librium, 223
Lithium carbonate, 142, 225–26

Index

Lottery, The (Jackson), 69
Love, 25–30, 73–74
LSD, 128, 129, 131

Manic-depressive episodes, 184–86
  lithium carbonate and, 225–26
Marcus, Anthony, 137
Marijuana, 128
Marriage
  in Asia, 64
  relationship in, 28–29
Martin, Ralph, 35
Masserman, Jules, 74, 75, 197
Maturity, 41–45
Meaning and Content of the Sexual Perver-sions, The (Boss), 138
Meditation, 229
Menninger, Karl, 7
Mental illness
  defined, 47–56
  origins of, 45–47
Meprobamate. *See* Equanil
Mescaline, 128
Methadone, 130
Ministers, 83–86
Mistrust, 45
Moment-by-moment existence, 111
Muscle relaxers, 223

Nausea (Sartre), 32–33
Nothing Is My Number (Marcus), 137

Obsessive living, 151–59
Oedipal complex, 118
Older persons
  happiness as, 88–91
  health problems of, 94–97
  living as, 87–101
  unhappiness and, 91–94

Parsons, Talcott, 197
Passive-aggressive personalities, 114
Passivity, 115–22
Phenothiazines, 223
Pirsig, Robert, 43
Plain Facts for Old and Young, 79–80
Poverty, older people and, 91–94
Prayer, 228–30
Pregnancy, schizophrenia and, 210–11
Prevert, Jacques, 62
Prison
  life in, 133–47
  sex offenders and, 136, 137, 138
Prison code, 136
Psychiatric drugs, 222–26
Psychiatry and the Dilemmas of Crime (Hal-leck), 146
Psycopaths, 114
Psychotherapies, 220, 230–31
  prisoners and, 142–43

Quality, 43
Quest for Identity, The (Wheelis), 135

Rebellion, surrender and, 105–22
Regional Medical Centre, 143–46
Reik, Theodore, 219
Religious practice, 228–30
Repetition compulsion, 234
R.M.C. *See* Regional Medical Centre
Rogers, Carl, 26, 35
Rosenthal, David, 213
Roy, Chunilal, 143

Sartre, Jean-Paul, 32, 38, 152
Satisfaction-seeking, 46–47
Schizophrenia
  drugs for, 223–24
  genetics and, 212–14

introduction to, 187–95
pregnancy and, 211
Security-seeking, 46–47
Sedatives, 131, 223
Self-doubt, 47
Separate Reality, A (Castaneda), 127–28
Sex
  guilt and, 79
  older people and, 88–89
Sex offenders, 136, 137, 138
Sexuality, depression and, 173
Suicide, 26, 76, 81, 176–77
  depression and, 175–76
  young people and, 178–83
Sullivan, Harry Stack, 204
Symptom counting, 227

Teachings of Don Juan, The (Castaneda), 127
Television, 77–78
Tension, handling of, 110–11
Thorburn, J. M., 60
Tillich, Paul, 38
Tofranil, 224
Tranquilizers, 223
Treatment, psychiatric, 8–13
  changes during, 10, 11

relationship during, 11
unsuccessful, 12–13
Tricyclic antidepressants, 224
Trust, role of, 115

Unconditional love, 74

Valium, 223
Value, 42
Violence, weakness and, 105–22

Wada, Juhn A., 229
War, 65
Wheelis, Allan, 135
Whitaker, Carl, 7, 28, 98
Wolpe, Joseph, 226
Woman He Loved, The (Martin), 35
Women
  in Asia, role of, 64
  hysterical living and, 164

Youth
  Asian education of, 63–66
  criminal behavior and, 140–42
  of the 1950s, 1960s, 1970s, 77–78

Zen and the Art of Motorcycle Maintenance (Pirsig), 43

If the Patient Is You

MILTON H. MILLER, M.D.

"What is it like to be that person whose way of living is called schizophrenic, or neurotic, or perverse, or normal?" This enlightening book explores the nature of mental illness from the most important perspective—that of the person with the problem.

More than eight million Americans consult psychiatrists each year, and many others seek out other health professionals for help. Most psychology books advocate a specific therapeutic technique. But Dr. Milton Miller, a psychiatrist with over twenty-five years of clinical experience, feels that a single approach, however valuable and interesting, is not adequate. Using case histories from his own practice, Dr. Miller illustrates that the extraordinary diversity and complexity of mental illness require an "existential" approach—one that allows the therapist to experience life from the point of view of the patient and use a variety of techniques.

A profoundly optimistic book with valuable insights for both doctors and patients, IF THE PATIENT IS YOU (OR SOMEONE YOU LOVE) asserts that every human being can learn to live a richer and more meaningful life.